The Representation of Economics in Cinema

Santiago Sanchez-Pages

The Representation of Economics in Cinema

Scarcity, Greed and Utopia

Santiago Sanchez-Pages
Department of Political Economy
King's College London
London, UK

ISBN 978-3-030-80180-9   ISBN 978-3-030-80181-6 (eBook)
https://doi.org/10.1007/978-3-030-80181-6

© The Editor(s) (if applicable) and The Author(s), under exclusive license to Springer Nature Switzerland AG 2021
This work is subject to copyright. All rights are solely and exclusively licensed by the Publisher, whether the whole or part of the material is concerned, specifically the rights of translation, reprinting, reuse of illustrations, recitation, broadcasting, reproduction on microfilms or in any other physical way, and transmission or information storage and retrieval, electronic adaptation, computer software, or by similar or dissimilar methodology now known or hereafter developed.
The use of general descriptive names, registered names, trademarks, service marks, etc. in this publication does not imply, even in the absence of a specific statement, that such names are exempt from the relevant protective laws and regulations and therefore free for general use.
The publisher, the authors and the editors are safe to assume that the advice and information in this book are believed to be true and accurate at the date of publication. Neither the publisher nor the authors or the editors give a warranty, expressed or implied, with respect to the material contained herein or for any errors or omissions that may have been made. The publisher remains neutral with regard to jurisdictional claims in published maps and institutional affiliations.

This Palgrave Macmillan imprint is published by the registered company Springer Nature Switzerland AG
The registered company address is: Gewerbestrasse 11, 6330 Cham, Switzerland

To Maria and Pol

Acknowledgments

My name may be on the cover, but a book is always a collective work.

I am extremely thankful to Jordi Sánchez-Navarro for pushing me to write about cinema and economics three years ago. During this period, I have benefitted from many colleagues' suggestions and advice. Let me mention Carmen Beviá, Antonio Cabrales, Luis Corchón, Fabian Gouret, Pedro Rey-Biel, Mónica Serrano, and Marián Vidal-Fernández among others.

Some of the ideas in this book have come from my experience writing non-academic pieces for *Miradas de Cine* and the now-defunct *Canino* magazine. There I published my first texts on film, science fiction, and the Great Recession. I thank my editors at these online outlets, Diego Salgado and John Tones, for giving me that opportunity. Some of the film reviews in this book are based on a weekly newsletter on cinema and economics I published between 2018 and 2020. Let me thank its subscribers for their encouragement and attention.

I am also grateful to Ruth Jenner and Ruth Noble at Palgrave Macmillan for their interest and endorsement and for their understanding during the very trialing year 2020.

Special thanks to my friends and family, who have supported me along the way. Finally, I would like to thank Maria Cubel for her unwavering and loving support while writing this book.

Contents

1	**Introduction: Mr. Smith Goes to the Movies**	1
	References	8
2	**Scarcity, Conflicts, and Dystopia**	9
	The Dark Side of the Force	10
	Dystopian Inequalities	14
	"We Will Control the Horizontal. We Will Control the Vertical"	18
	Property Wars	20
	References	28
3	**Evil Is The Root Of All Money**	29
	The Life of Money	30
	"Greed Is Good"	32
	"I Don't Make Anything? I'm Making You Money"	36
	Scrooge's Arc	38
	Can't Buy Me Love	41
	The Devil Among Us	43
	The Secret Life of Money	46
	References	47
4	**Brokers, Bankers, and Boiler Rooms**	49
	A Tricksters' Game	50
	A Giant Casino	53
	Trades with Wolves	55

	Selling the Intangible	59
	The Good, The Bank, and The Needy	61
	Reference	69
5	**Evil, Inc.**	71
	Corporate Dramas	72
	Corporate Idiocracies	78
	Corporate Hell	82
	Corporate Buffoons	84
	Corporate Irresponsibility	88
	References	95
6	**Disruptors**	97
	Randian Innovators	98
	The New Economy	103
	Creative Destruction	108
	Innovators vs The World	115
	References	119
7	**The Path of Workers**	121
	White-Collar Blues	122
	Solidarity Forever	126
	Unions on the Screen	131
	Waiting for the Robots	139
	Freedom of Movement	146
	References	150
8	**Women at Work**	153
	Stay Home or Else	154
	Working-Class Girls	159
	Fairy Tales	162
	Corporate Comedies and Femme Fatales	166
	Confused, Discriminated, and Stressed	169
	Sex Trades	174
	References	180
9	**Crises**	181
	"I'll Be There Too"	182
	Understanding the Crisis	187
	Macroeconomics on the Screen	192
	Post-Crisis Landscapes	195

	References	199
10	**Conclusion: Post-Scarcity and Utopia**	201
	The Better Future Is in the Past	202
	Techno-Utopias	203
	Collective Utopias	206
	Post-Scarcity Economics	208
	The End?	212
	References	213

Film Index 215

About the Author

Santiago Sanchez-Pages is an economist and a writer. He holds a Ph.D. in economics from Universitat Autónoma de Barcelona.

He is an Associate Professor in economics at King's College London, where he teaches microeconomics and game theory. Before that, he taught undergraduate and postgraduate courses in economics at the University of Edinburgh and the University of Barcelona.

Santiago's research focuses on political economy, economic theory, and experimental economics. He has published over twenty scientific articles in leading international journals. He also writes popular pieces on economics for the Spanish blog *Nada es Gratis*.

He has written on film and popular culture for online outlets in Spain and has published several science-fiction short stories in anthologies.

CHAPTER 1

Introduction: Mr. Smith Goes to the Movies

The great English economist Alfred Marshall once wrote that economics "examines that part of individual and social action which is most closely connected with the attainment and with the use of the material requisites of well-being".[1] A boring definition, perhaps, but one which nevertheless highlights the pervasiveness of economics in our lives. It is an inescapable reality. We are part of the economy, whether we like it or not. It is not by chance the word "economics" comes from the Greek word "oikonomia", which means the management of a home and its finances.

Every day we consume goods and services that other people have produced for us and work (or try) to produce goods and services that other people will use. We save and invest (if we can). We devote time to cook for our relatives and help our friends. We think of ways of stretching our budget. We ponder whether it is a good idea to ask for a loan, get married, have children, go to our favorite pub, or stay home studying; whether to accept a tedious but secure occupation or take the risk and keep searching for our dream job.

In the news and social media, we see that some countries develop and grow, whereas others become poorer or more unequal. We hear news about teams of scientists making incredible breakthroughs that hi-tech companies later convert into mind-blowing new products. We see how

[1] *Principles of Economics* (1920), p. 1. London: MacMillan.

© The Author(s), under exclusive license to Springer Nature
Switzerland AG 2021
S. Sanchez-Pages, *The Representation of Economics in Cinema*,
https://doi.org/10.1007/978-3-030-80181-6_1

natural resources are extracted from the earth, transported to the four corners of the world, and transformed into energy and goods. We also see the pollution and environmental degradation that these processes bring. We feel the constant humming of the stock markets, going up and down, of banks endlessly lending and investing money, and firms hiring and firing employees, trying to find better ways to reallocate their human and capital resources.

Because economics is so pervasive in our lives, economics is everywhere in cinema too, in one way or another. It does not matter whether it is a film about a clan of Neanderthals, or a film set in a galaxy far, far away. Already one of the first films in history, *La Sortie de l'Usine Lumière à Lyon* (1895) portrayed a group of laborers coming out of the Lumière factory at the end of their working day. In D.W. Griffith's *A Corner in Wheat* (1909), a financier cornered the wheat market to control its price and make millions.

Filmmakers create new worlds in which people and institutions become real before our eyes; parallel, symbolic worlds that contain enough elements from our reality to become credible and plausible. That is precisely what good economic models do; they focus on an agent (a firm, a voter, a consumer) and try to understand what motivates them and how they will respond to changes in their environment. Like economic agents, characters in films do not have full information about the consequences of their actions and rules of the game constrain them; laws, institutions, and social norms deem which behaviors are acceptable and which ones are not. Like economists, screenwriters are concerned with the effect of changes in technology and markets on individuals and societies. Like economic models, films tell stylized stories that nevertheless contain exciting seeds of reality. Many films seek to shape our attitudes and emotions to change the future. Similarly, economic thinking allows us to understand better why some events have happened and why others have not, and helps us build policies that can shape the future for the better.

To date, the relationship between economics and cinema has been chiefly explored under the premise that films are full of economic ideas and concepts. Cinema can indeed help us see the relevance of economic principles in our daily choices. As a result, there are many exciting academic and popular pieces on how economics can be effectively taught using cinema.[2] Several websites contain lists of films with economic content or collect clips where specific economic concepts are well represented.[3] Most books and articles published on the intersection between economics and cinema share this approach, which I will call henceforth the "economics in film" approach.

However, the relationship between economics and film is bidirectional. For starters, the economic climate directly affects cinema's content and topics. On the other hand, the influence of cinema on public opinion is considerable, many orders of magnitude larger than that of economics as a discipline. Thomas Piketty's *Capital in the Twenty-First Century* (2013), arguably the best-selling economics book of all time, sold 2.5 million copies worldwide. In contrast, *The Big Short* (2015), a medium-budget film about the 2008 financial crisis, sold 8.2 million tickets in the United States alone.[4] Films actors and actresses are often catalysts for campaigns with far-reaching economic implications; that was the case with *Blood Diamond* (2006) and *Dark Waters* (2019). Cinema plays a vital role in shaping people's views on many economic issues and the policy proposals professional economists put forward. For example, many films dealing with businesses, finance, or unemployment show a very dismissive attitude toward markets and economics as a discipline, to the point that the term "neoliberal" has become a negative, albeit empty signifier in film criticism. Another example of the influence of cinema can be found in a very recent article by Espósito et al. (2021), who show that films change people's preferences and decisions. These authors reconstruct at the monthly level the staggered screening of D.W. Griffith's classic *The Birth of a Nation* (1915), which popularized the Lost Cause narrative, a revisionist account of the American Civil War that sought reconciliation between North and South by blaming the conflict on African Americans. The results of this study show that the film induced an increase in patriotism, measured by recruiting rates for the army during World War I, and a strengthening of segregation against African Americans in the labor market.

---

[2] See Leet and Houser (2003), Bookman and Bookman (2009), Mateer et al. (2016) and Acchiardo and Vachris (2018) among others.

[3] See http://dirkmateer.com/media/Film+Clips or https://econ.video/category/source-of-clips/movie/.

[4] https://www.the-numbers.com/market/.

However, a frequent response of economists to the representation of their trade in film is to dismiss filmmakers' ability to contribute to the advancement and dissemination of economics. Their standard argument is that directors and screenwriters do not know much about the discipline or are biased against it. It would seem then that the interest of cinema for economists is confined to teaching or outreach activities based on those films that "can conveniently illustrate truths economists already know".[5] But economics is a social reality made up of people who make decisions based on emotions, ideas, and narratives (Shiller, 2019); film can help us understand them. It is a mistake to think that there is very little that movies can teach us about economics that we economists did not already know. Films articulate the economic anxieties and opinions specific to each generation of filmmakers and audiences. The fact that cinema has displayed a primarily negative view of economics since its inception in 1895 is not just proof of filmmakers' ignorance or intellectual laziness; it tells us something meaningful about the discipline and its prescriptions. We economists would do well to learn more about what directors and screenwriters have to say about the economy, economics, and its tenets.

It is possible to characterize a type of films which, with some abuse of the English language, I will call "economic films" throughout this book. They form an extensive filmography in which economic life is at the center of the plot and is its dominant element. In these films, the economy is the stage on which the characters move, and the action unfolds. These are fictions in which work, speculation, fraud, and ambition play an essential role, or in which the state of the economy is a fundamental element of the narrative, even if only as a "budget constraint" on the choices of the characters. Through their characters and stories, economic films explore the consequences of economic policies and phenomena.

Besides, filmmakers can provide us with valuable lessons that we are still unaware of. Cinema offers revealing forays into seemingly irrational preferences, preferences that defy traditional principles of economic behavior, such as a taste for surprise and unpredictability or the destructive or self-destructive behaviors that characterize the protagonists of *American Beauty* (1999) or *The Wolf of Wall Street* (2013).

The present book explores this less often tread pathway between economics and cinema. It focuses on how cinema has represented

---

[5] Morson and Schapiro (2017), p. 17.

economics and the economy by studying the dramatic and stylistic elements that films have used to that end. Each chapter focuses on one economic topic and the films relevant to it. The book is aimed at a general audience and presupposes no knowledge of economic principles; I will be providing all the necessary concepts along the way. The analyses of the more than 100 films discussed at some length in this book come from my own viewings and a wide variety of sources, from film studies to economics. I have watched all films mentioned; even those only alluded in passing. I have chosen to focus mainly on English language films since they are the most well-known and widely available. That said, I briefly discuss several non-English language films because economics and the economy have been the object of interest of filmmakers from all over the world. These films build a more global and historical picture of how cinema has represented economic phenomena.

The analyses in the following chapters will retain some elements of the "economics in film" approach to persuade the reader that economic concepts and economic thinking are pervasive and can be found in very diverse films, from *Goldfinger* (1964) to *Charlie and the Chocolate Factory* (2005). It will also allow me to discuss some popular misconceptions about the discipline that repeatedly transpire in film.

An excellent point to start exploring how economics has been portrayed on the silver screen is to clarify what economics is not (only) about. Film narratives about economics and the economy are inevitably construed upon several misunderstandings and misconceptions.

The use of the term "the economy" in our daily language refers typically to a country's economic prosperity or the state of its economy. But that is a relatively recent use of the word. But the term started to take off around the Great Depression in the 1930s (Karabell, 2014). At that time, the public was understandably worried about how the economy was going, whether it was about to improve, or whether joblessness and poverty would continue unabated. The economic debate started to be centered around a single magnitude that we now all recognize: The Gross Domestic Product (GDP). When the value of the goods and services in a specific year -that is, the GDP- goes up, we say that the economy goes well. If it goes down, we say the opposite. Economists are interested in the GDP because we believe (for the time being) that it is the best way to measure whether people find it easier or harder to satisfy those "material requisites of well-being" Alfred Marshall talked about.

But public debates about "economics as the economy" would be (even more) boring if they focused on a single figure. That is why we often hear about other magnitudes such as inflation—how much prices go up—interest rates—the price of money—unemployment rates, or the Dow Jones. Don't get me wrong. All these indicators are pretty important (the last one less so, to be honest). But their constant presence in the media obfuscates the actual scope of economics and, more worryingly, distorts how the public perceives it. Still, too few economists have the talent or the inclination to convey to the general public what economics is about, although this is changing rapidly. The present book is an effort in that direction.

Talking about inflation, the stock market, or the GDP has become the most popular way to talk about economics for an obvious reason: it is the simplest and most direct way. This popular way of understanding economics perpetuates the belief that the discipline is merely interested in predicting whether such or such macroeconomic magnitude will rise or fall next year or next month and by how much.

By extension, economists are most often seen as fortune-tellers looking at computer screens filled with numbers rather than crystal balls. Hence, the joke: "Economists have predicted nine out of the last five recessions".[6] The oddball protagonists of *Pi* (1999), *The Big Short*, or *A Beautiful Mind* (2001) helped maintain the belief that orthodox economics is just a branch of mathematics mainly applied to the study of the stock market. But economics is not a predictive science. Only a small fraction of economists is interested in forecasting. Still, that facet is socially perceived as what economists really do, and hence it is pervasive in economic films.

Similarly, there is a common misconception that economics is mostly about money, businesses, and financial markets. Most films with explicit economic content have focused on these areas, in a significant part because of their dramatic and visual appeal.

Cinema is full of wealthy and successful characters who are however miserable and lonely, who are despised by their neighbors and society. In fact, one of the main theses of economic films is that money does not bring happiness. We will survey these films in Chapter 2.

---

[6] There are not that many jokes about economists, but they are all very telling. For a taster, check out the shows by Yorum Bauman, comedian and self-proclaimed stand-up economist.

Cinema has had a keen interest in finance. Trading floors, with their frenzy of buyers and sellers gesticulating and shouting, exchanging abstract commodities, and making or losing millions in an instant, are very cinematographic. In Chapter 3, we will discuss films such as *Trading Places* (1983) or *Rogue Trader* (1999), where economics is seen as a scam or as a sophisticated form of gambling and the stock exchange is represented as a giant casino.

Chapters 4 and 5 deal with corporations, entrepreneurship, and innovation. Firms offer an attractive backdrop for dramas and thrillers fueled by clashes of ambitions and struggles for power. The evolution of the portrayal of corporations in cinema mimics the changes in their social perception; as powerful engines of the economy in corporate fictions of the 1950s such as *Executive Suite* (1954), and as shadowy entities only interested in profit at any price, human or environmental, in more recent films like *Michael Clayton* (2007). In contrast, movies like *The Social Network* (2010) or *Joy* (2015) highlight individual innovators' struggle and the positive disruption they bring to the economy. Their protagonists are complex characters, geniuses with very diverse motivations who, against all odds and difficulties, create a technical breakthrough that changes how people behave or firms operate.

The following chapters deal with the other side of the economy: labor. Film has been very interested in past and present labor conflicts. Narratives about trade unions like *Germinal* (1993) have portrayed their importance during the Industrial Revolution in improving workers' conditions. In contrast, others like *On the Waterfront* (1954) were concerned with union leaders' racketeering activities. Chapter 6 explores the historical trends in the portrayal of trade unions, and two of the topics workers around the world are most worried about: Massive immigration and job automation, already present in Charles Chaplin's classic *Modern Times* (1936).

There have been other sweeping changes in the world of work since cinema was invented. A crucial one has been the increasing participation of women in the labor market and the economy. The problems women encountered during this process and the upturning in gender roles that ensued were portrayed in films like *Norma Rae* (1978) or *9 to 5* (1980). We will review these in Chapter 7.

Chapter 8 will look at the economic representation of recent crises. Since the oil crises of the 1970s, economic insecurity has remained latent and widespread in the West. The 2008 financial crisis damaged the trust in economic institutions and future economic prosperity. Films like *Margin Call* (2011) tried to shed light on the events that led to that collapse, whereas *The Company Men* (2010) and *99 Homes* (2014) explored its human toll. In the concluding chapter, we will look beyond this grim panorama to examine how films have represented utopian futures and the role of economics in post-scarcity societies like the one depicted in the *Star Trek* film franchise.

But our starting point will be exactly the opposite: Scarcity.

References

Acchiardo, C.-J. R., & Vachris, M. A. (Eds.). (2018). *Dystopia and Economics: A guide to surviving everything from the apocalypse to zombies*. Routledge.

Bookman, M. Z., Bookman, A. S. (2009). *Economics in film and fiction*. Rowman & Littlefield Education.

Esposito, E., Rotesi, T., Saia, A., Thoenig, M. (2021). *Reconciliation narratives—The birth of a nation after the US Civil War* (Working paper). University of Lausanne.

Karabell, Z. (2014). *The leading indicators: A short history of the numbers*. Simon & Schuster.

Leet, D., & Houser, S. (2003). Economics goes to Hollywood: Using classic films and documentaries to create an undergraduate Economics course. *The Journal of Economic Education, 34*, 326–332.

Mateer, D. G., O'roark, B., Holder, K. (2016). The 10 greatest films for teaching Economics. *The American Economist, 61*, 204–216.

Morson, G. S., & Schapiro, M. (2017). *Cents and sensibility: What economics can learn from the humanities*. Princeton University Press.

Shiller, R. J. (2019). *Narrative Economics*. Princeton University Press.

CHAPTER 2

Scarcity, Conflicts, and Dystopia

In 1932, Lionel Robbins gave a definition of economics which eventually became more popular than Alfred Marshall's: "the science which studies human behavior as a relationship between ends and scarce means which have alternative uses".[1] The key word in Robbins' definition is scarcity. If we all had plenty of food, time, and energy, there would be no need for economics. But because limited resources constrain our wants and needs, we are forced to choose; we are constantly forced to think about what the best uses of our time, money, and physical energy are.

In cinema, as in life, scarcity shows up everywhere. In the decisions characters face, the time and financial constraints limiting their choices and influencing their relationship with other characters. Economic models and film fictions tell stories about imaginary characters who make decisions over a finite horizon, live finite lives, from youth to old age, constrained by limited amounts of time and money they allocate, considering the opportunity cost of the various options available. For that reason, there is no better place to start talking about film and economics than scarcity.

---

[1] *An Essay on the Nature and Significance of Economic Science* (1935), p. 16. London: MacMillan.

The Dark Side of the Force

The best place to start our journey is one type of extreme economy: The post-apocalypse. In the typical post-apocalyptic economies in cinema, scarcity is rife, and individuals face very stark choices between starvation and survival, between cooperation and conflict. Worlds ravaged by nuclear war or zombie plagues are an extreme version of our economies. In them, individuals still need to allocate their resources to satisfy their basic needs and meet their goals, but markets, formal institutions, and the rule of law are entirely gone.

Post-apocalyptic films work very well as a distorted mirror of our reality. A world devastated by war or disease is a very apt setting to depicting class conflict because scarcity could not be more urgent in a scenario where the powerful rise above the dispossessed by force. In post-apocalyptic films, money, markets, and even businesses may still exist, albeit in a very different form to the ones we know. Barter is the norm, as in the very aptly Bartertown, the community of survivors in *Mad Max Beyond Thunderdome* (1985). New forms of money emerge, based again on valuable and scarce goods. For instance, in *Waterworld* (1995), most land is covered by the seas after the polar ice caps have melted. The different clans that roam the oceans seek to find dry land, which is even more valuable than fresh water and is used as currency in commercial transactions.

The fundamental differences between the economies we live in and those in post-apocalyptic films are two. One is the absence of property rights and law. The second is extreme scarcity.

In the desolated worlds of *Mad Max 2* (1981) or *The Road* (2009), individuals and communities struggle for survival. There is no functioning economy that can provide them with essential goods, so they need to grab food and shelter from wherever they can, be it empty shopping malls or rival factions.

If the world remains relatively intact after the apocalypse as in *Five* (1951), *The Omega Man* (1971), or *A Quite Place* (2018), the survivors face the challenge of creating a new economy. They need to learn new tasks like hunting, building houses, or growing food. They have been forced to live in a world without much specialization. It seems a strange life to us, but, from a historical perspective, it is the life most humans have lived throughout history. This reversal to a more primitive economy in post-apocalyptic films like *Day of the Dead* (1985) highlights two ideas:

First, that the extreme specialization of our economies dispenses us from the need to acquire such basic knowledge; we delegate on others the task of building houses, growing food, and even cooking it for us. The second idea—this one much more explicitly stated—is that most of the jobs and tasks we learn to do in our world would be utterly useless in case of a major collapse.[2] Post-apocalyptic films also underscore a trope common in many economic films; namely, the only valuable activities produce essential, tangible commodities. Major West (Christopher Eccleston) understands this quickly in *28 Days Later* (2002). He keeps a zombie prisoner to learn about the enemy. The fact that the captive is just a rabid beast "is telling me he'll never bake bread, farm crops, raise livestock. He's telling me he's futureless".

But even if the characters in these films learn to use the resources at their disposal, they still need to fight off the aggressions from others.

In regular economies, individuals, organizations, and communities try to be happier and become more prosperous and profitable by producing goods and services that they then trade. These activities have most often the positive by-product of enhancing aggregate wealth. But there is another way of attaining those objectives: appropriate what others have produced. This is what iconoclast economist Jack Hirshleifer called, using a very cinematographic reference, "The dark side of the force of self-interest" (Hirshleifer, 1994). This is a type of economic activity that leads to a conflict over who gets what and, unlike trade, cannot improve everybody's welfare. In our economic reality, these economic activities are illegal. Those who steal the property of others are considered thieves and prosecuted. Others may be more cunning and swindle other people's money with all kinds of scams, but they are considered criminals alike. Firms that violate environmental standards and deliberately poison the air and the soil killing their workers and potential customers to increase their profits also face punishment (a separate matter is if they do as much as they should). Our societies' relative prosperity and the presence of legally enforced property rights limit the scope of appropriation efforts, of the "dark side of the force". As Steven Pinker has argued,

---

[2] The novel *World War Z* (2006) by Max Brooks is very explicit about this; surviving corporate executives and stockbrokers need to go through retraining to adapt to the post-zombie apocalypse economy. This cheeky inversion of the retraining programs for unemployed manual workers was absent in the 2013 film version.

interpersonal violence, whose primary source is competition over scarce resources, is today at an all-time low since records exist.[3]

But in post-apocalyptic societies where there is barely anything to eat and almost all forms of government and judicial systems have collapsed, the dark side of the force of self-interest is rampant. The characters of dystopian and post-apocalyptic films must spend a great deal of their time and energy protecting their lives from marauders, zombies, or aliens and fencing off the attacks from those who want to steal their property. They are even forced to steal when hunger calls. Other, more proper, economic activities like education and investment become subsidiary to the need for protection. There is investment in capital goods, yes, but in the form of fortresses and walls. There is education, but mainly in the form of combat training. There is very little time left for other types of innovations and transactions. Insecurity and a constant uncertainty about the future discourage any productive investment. As a result, there are almost no innovations and technological advances in post-apocalyptic societies. Technologies from before the apocalypse are recycled; one exception is Bartertown power system based on the methane gas extracted from pig feces. There are no incentives to innovate in these worlds since any resulting benefit or surplus production is likely to be appropriated by raiders or tyrannical leaders. As a result, most post-apocalyptic economies are subsistence economies.

Post-apocalyptic films also portray hypercompetitive societies punctuated by communities that put their differences aside and cooperate. They illustrate recent theories showing that cooperation and conflict go hand in hand in human societies (Choi & Bowles, 2007). With the possible exceptions of Vic in *A Boy and His Dog* (1975) and the protagonist of *The Book of Eli* (2010), characters in post-apocalyptic films soon realize that their chances of survival are very slim if they stay all alone. Smaller groups organize themselves by combining their defensive efforts and working together to obtain essential resources such as shelter, weapons, and food. There is some degree of specialization in these small communities. Some defend them, others produce goods, and others provide leadership, depending on their comparative advantage in each of these tasks. The result is a pale reflection of the hyperspecialized pre-apocalypse society. The bands of marauders who populate the wastelands of *Mad*

---

[3] *The Better Angels of Our Nature: Why Violence Has Declined* (2011). New York: Viking Books.

Max 2 and the pirates who infest the oceans of *Waterworld* cooperate among themselves to appropriate what others have produced. Tribes and clans fight with each other to control valuable resources while remaining (relatively) peaceful inside.

The more complex communities of survivors can organize themselves in very different ways. The *Mad Max* franchise offers us several compelling examples. The Vuvalini, the matriarchal female warriors of *Mad Max: Fury Road* (2015), take decisions cooperatively and display high social capital levels. Aunty Entity (Tina Turner), the ruler of Bartertown, is a tyrant, but the outpost hosts a relatively thriving trading economy. In contrast, Immortan Joe governs the Citadel with an iron fist. The warlord and his closest acolytes live amidst lavish luxury: abundant food, ancient knowledge, and a harem of mistresses. They occupy the top of an impressive rock tower resting on a reservoir of water. Below him live the mechanics, the doctors, and the soldiers who maintain order. Below them are the slaves, whose physical exertion provides energy for the citadel and its Great Lift. At the lowest rung, we find the wretched of the earth, the sick, the malnourished, the homeless, kept at bay with the promise of the water that Immortan Joe administers in dribs and drabs. His extractive regime exploits humans to increase production: women produce babies and mothers' milk and prisoners to provide regular blood transfusions to his War Boys. The Citadel's economic prosperity relies on domination by force and the blind faith of his followers in Immortan Joe.

The economic system imagined by George Miller and his co-writers Brendan McCarthy and Nico Lathouris for *Mad Max: Fury Road* is characterized by three monopolies, each of them equally hierarchical and governed through dictatorial rule. Each of them controls a key resource for the survivors: Immortan Joe owns the water, which grants him a quasi-divine authority over the inhabitants of the wasteland. The syphilitic People Eater controls Gastown, whereas the Bullet Farmer controls the production and supply of ammunition. These three outposts have followed David Hume's theory of trade. Each of them has specialized in the production of the good they have a competitive advantage in and exchange among themselves for water, "guzzoline", bullets, and mother's milk. In turn, they all need these commodities to assert their control over their monopolies and keep any competitors at bay.

Dystopian Inequalities

Post-apocalyptic films are a subgenre of dystopian fiction. Films in this tradition are set in societies with great injustices and dysfunctional governments (when they exist). These are highly unequal societies where the population is subjugated either by a police state, the rule of evil corporations, or an oppressive elite. It is not surprising that economic insecurity, inequality, and the impending climate crisis had spawned a surge in dystopian films in recent years.

The financial crisis of 2008 and the recent coronavirus pandemic have accentuated a process that started in developed countries in the early 1980s. The share of national income accruing to the 1% top of earners has increased substantially in the United States and the United Kingdom, less so in continental Europe (Atkinson et al., 2011). Real wages have remained stagnant for most US workers,[4] while executive pay has continued growing.[5] A new social class has emerged: the "working poor" or the "precariat". In the United Kingdom, most people in poverty belong to a household where someone is working.[6] Billions of taxpayer money were injected into the banking systems to save institutions deemed "too big to fail". Austerity and budget cuts affected health services and education; schools in Southern Europe did not have enough funds to pay for heating or toilet paper. Hundreds of thousands of people in the United States were evicted from their homes in the aftermath of the 2008 financial crisis, the most significant displacement of people since the Great Depression. Three out of ten British children live now in poverty,[7] and life expectancy in the United States fell in 2014 for the first time in decades.

---

[4] "For most U.S. workers, real wages have barely budged in decades", Pew Research Center. August 7, 2018. Last accessed March 30, 2021, https://www.pewresearch.org/fact-tank/2018/08/07/for-most-us-workers-real-wages-have-barely-budged-for-decades/.

[5] "CEO compensation surged 14% in 2019 to $21.3 million", Economic Policy Institute. August 14, 2020. Last accessed March 30, 2021, https://files.epi.org/pdf/204513.pdf.

[6] "UK Poverty 2019/20", Joseph Rowntree Foundation. February 7, 2020. Last accessed March 30, 2021, https://www.jrf.org.uk/report/uk-poverty-2019-20.

[7] "Households Below Average Income, Statistics on the number and percentage of people living in low income households for financial years 1994/95 to 2018/19", Department for Work and Pensions, March 26, 2020. Last accessed March 30, 2021, https://www.gov.uk/government/statistics/households-below-average-income-199495-to-201819.

The bleak trends summarized in the paragraph above expectedly led to a surge in dystopian fiction. Because science fiction is concerned with "the next five minutes", as British writer J. G. Ballard put it, the genre became interested in the narratives of economic insecurity, unfair inequalities, and class (and generational) conflict that emerged from the now widespread social unrest.

This trend became first apparent in the surge of dystopian YA literature, which soon spilt over to films. A more unequal and environmentally degraded world has direct consequences for young people: Fewer jobs and fewer prosperity opportunities. Younger generations should work and study harder to achieve the same standard of living as their parents. Suzanne Collins' *The Hunger Games* trilogy (2008–2010) was the first to express this growing anxiety. The novels and their four-part film adaptations portrayed the United States as a dystopia where a ruthless and hedonistic elite has taken control of the country after an environmental disaster and a civil war. Once pacified, America is divided into various regions that have taken the lessons of classic international trade theory to the extreme; each has been forced to specialize in producing one type of goods, although labor cannot move across sectors. Districts trade with "The Capitol" in exchange for protection. Also, they must select a boy and a girl each year to compete in a gruesome series of trials to entertain the masses called the Hunger Games. There can only be one winner. These young contestants kill and tear each other apart to attain freedom and glory for their district—a not very subtle metaphor of the present labor market. The four films chronicle the trials and tribulations of Katniss Evergreen (Jennifer Lawrence), who goes from participant in the games to icon of the rebellion against the Capitol. But the rebels are no innocents either; the portrayal of their leader Alma Coin (Julianne Moore) is meant to summon the specter of populism.

The box-office success of the franchise fueled other dystopian novels and film adaptations with a similar premise. The *Divergent* trilogy (2011–2013) by Veronica Roth described a post-apocalyptic world where an apparently peaceful social order has emerged based on a strict division of the population into factions; 16-year-olds must select which faction they want to join, a choice that will define them for life. Those who fail to choose a faction or are deemed unsuitable are ostracized. *The Maze Runner* series (2014–2018), based on James Dashner's novels, is also set in a post-apocalyptic world where a group of young rebels fights against an all-powerful corporation that has experimented with them. Finally, *The*

Thinning (2016) plays with the idea of population control through a school aptitude test; those with the lowest scores are executed. All these films depict futures of rampant inequality where those at the top are essentially corrupt and in which the lives of young people are a permanent steeplechase.

Dystopian films have used the trope of immortality to depict the growing health inequalities between rich and poor (Bleich et al., 2012). The pioneer in doing so was Andrew Niccol's *In Time* (2011), a film so full of economic concepts that it could articulate an entire course on economic principles. *In Time* is set in a futuristic society where it is possible to stop aging after 25, when a fatal countdown begins. People are granted a year of life at this point and die when the digital readout on their forearm reaches zero. The scarcity of time is thus made very clear. Time has become a currency. People are paid in hours or days by working and lose time when they buy something or pay a bill: A coffee costs four minutes, a bus ride 30 and a luxury car 59 years. It is also a society of rampant inequality, both in income and lifestyle. The rich are de facto immortal. They enjoy all kinds of technological advances and make extravagant displays of their wealth.

Meanwhile, the poor's existence is one of working tirelessly to stay alive and running from one place to another to avoid losing time. Travel between areas costs time too, ensuring total spatial segregation between classes. Inflation has dramatic repercussions because a generalized rise in prices means that ordinary people must literally sacrifice more of their lives to buy the goods they need. Prices are not determined by markets but by the wealthy, who raise them to keep the poor in check. The hero played by Justin Timberlake is mistakenly embroiled in a murder and teams up with a wealthy socialite (Amanda Seyfried) to re-establish social equality.

Other films have used immortality to represent economic inequality. In the forgettable *Self/less* (2015), a real estate tycoon used body exchange to dodge a terminal illness. In *Jupiter Ascending* (2015), Jupiter (Mila Kunis) is a modest cleaner who discovers that our planet belongs to an intergalactic empire whose royal class keeps itself eternally young by feeding off the life energy of those they consider inferior (that is, everyone). Jupiter seeks to regain control of her life, overthrow the empire, save humanity, and find love.

Immortality is indeed a powerful way of representing the growing health inequalities, which in England translate into a gap of 9.4 years in life expectancy between the least and the most deprived areas.[8] *Elysium* (2012) articulated this reality in the form of an unabashedly Manichean dystopia. It is not by chance that the film's release happened in parallel with the debate in the United States Congress over the so-called Obamacare plan for universal public healthcare. The film is set in 2154. While the poor live a miserable existence in a polluted, dusty, and crime-ridden urban sprawl, the rich live happily and healthily in Elysium, a space station orbiting the Earth. The colony hosts a plethora of green spaces, robot servants, and medical scanners that can cure even cancer. The mayor of Elysium is played by Jodie Foster, dressed as a Christine Lagarde's imitation, the controversial head of the International Monetary Fund. At the other extreme is the character played by Matt Damon, an inhabitant of Earth crippled by a work-related accident who intends to board Elysium to use one of its medical robots.

One common to all these fictions is the centrality in the plot of a conflict to restore equality. The scenes of angry apes tearing up San Francisco in *Dawn of the Planet of the Apes* (2011) coincided in time with the protests of the Occupy Wall Street movement, the Arab Spring, the London riots that turned into looting, and the student protests over rising university fees all over the United Kingdom. Even with his usual broad brush, Christopher Nolan could not avoid the temptation to include a popular uprising against the rich—portrayed as millionaires from the board game Monopoly—in *The Dark Knight Rises* (2012). Far more fascinating was the futuristic financial debacle in *Cosmopolis* (2012), David Cronenberg's adaptation of Don DeLillo's visionary novel. There, a vampiric Robert Pattinson plays a representative of the 1% who glides in his limousine through streets taken over by ragged, angry protesters wielding dead rats and placards reading "A specter haunts the world: the specter of capitalism".

---

[8] "What are health inequalities?", The King's Fund. February 18, 2020. Last accessed March 30, 2021, https://www.kingsfund.org.uk/publications/what-are-health-inequalities.

"WE WILL CONTROL THE HORIZONTAL. WE WILL CONTROL THE VERTICAL"

Elysium is not the only example of recent science fiction influenced by the economic crisis and increasing inequality to depict a divide between elites and impoverished masses through extreme spatial segregation. *Total Recall* (2012), the remake of Paul Verhoeven's classic based on a Philip K. Dick story, depicts a dystopian Earth where survivors from the last world war live on opposite sides of the globe under a system of apartheid. The ragtag rabble in the slums is confined to Australia and travels to the other side of the globe to work for starvation wages on the prosperous British Federal Union's assembly lines. A very thinly disguised update of Australia under British colonial rule. The romantic fantasy *Upside Down* (2012), starring Kirsten Dunst, took this idea to the extreme by having two unequal planets kept apart by the force of gravity. A super-powerful corporation manages the contact between these two social classes for its benefit.

Social stratification was also represented as a spatial hierarchy—in this case, vertical—in *High-Rise* (2015), the intricate and superb adaptation directed by Ben Wheatley of J. G. Ballard's 1975 novel. As the inhabitants of a towering, brutalist skyscraper descend into primitivism, class divisions sharpen between the wealthy who dwell on the upper floors and the humble below. There are inter-floor conflicts, invasions, looting, and a war of all against all that culminates in a catharsis of animal violence. In the film's sardonic coda, we hear a speech by Margaret Thatcher, which repositions the movie as an exploration of the genesis of the 1980s conservative revolution that would usher in the rise of income inequality in the developed world.

Another vertical dystopia is the brutalist tower-like prison of *The Platform* (2019), an allegory of class warfare, social stratification, and greed. Goreng (Iván Massagué) enters voluntarily into the Orwellianly named "Vertical Self-Management Centre" for six months to obtain an "accredited diploma", stop smoking, and read, finally, *Don Quixote*. What he founds inside is a gruesome regime composed of hundreds of cells stacked one over the other, connected only by a platform that descends every day with food. The problem is that the lower levels' inmates can only eat whatever those above them left. The cooks of the mysterious Administration which oversees the center prepare an extravagant banquet at level zero. By the time the platform reaches the lower levels, there is nothing left.

This vertical structure is a grotesque metaphor for capitalism. Its feeding system is a literal application of trickle-down economics, the central tenet of the supply-side economics championed by Ronald Reagan. This economic doctrine supports the idea that low taxation and light regulation are good for the economy because they stimulate entrepreneurs and investors, whose profits will then "trickle down" to the middle and working classes. *The Platform* seems to make an indictment of this system because greed is always there to ruin it. The food prepared at level zero is enough for everyone, but because those at the top levels gorge on it, those at the bottom are bound to starvation and cannibalism. Goreng and some other characters try to change the system peacefully and through violence. They try to convince others to eat just the portion they need, but no one listens because the prison structure leads inmates to believe that they are entitled to eat as much as they want and forget about others. Less literally, *The Platform* is also an allegory for the intergenerational conflict of interest underlying environmental conservation. Each generation receives the previous ones' resources and faces a dilemma between exhausting these resources further or handing them down to the next generation.

Oscar-winning director Bong Joon Ho transposed class conflict into a horizontal geometry in *Snowpiercer* (2013). Adapted from the French comic *Le Transperceneige* (1982), the story is set in a post-apocalyptic world plunged into an ice age after a geoengineering experiment failed to stop global warming. The few survivors live on a constantly moving train that travels around the world. The carriages are literally separated into the economy and first-class: The poor are crammed into the last cars while the wealthy occupy those closer to the locomotive where the demiurge responsible for the invention is said to dwell. This caste division is maintained through brutal coercion of the poor, strict population control, and indoctrination of the middle classes, who will even kill to keep their privileges.

The three tyrants who rule the world of *Mad Max: Fury Road* might share the resources they control, but they choose to administer their scarcity to their advantage. This is a common aspect of most of the dystopian fictions we have discussed so far: the dystopian social contract between the rich and poor is a scam, a lie, mimicking the increase on distrust on the government and the economic institutions of the EU after the eurozone crises of 2010 (Algan et al., 2017). In the interesting Swiss film *Cargo* (2009), the survivors from Earth's ecological collapse live in space stations. The authorities discipline them with the promise of a trip to an idyllic planet that does not actually exist. In *In Time*, the wealthy keep the plebe at bay by artificially raising the (literal) cost of living, and in *Elysium* they deny access to a healthcare system that could technically benefit the entire population. In *Snowpiercer*, an unpleasant truth lurks behind the protein bars the poor eat. In the *Ares* (2016), the 15 million unemployed in a futuristic and crisis-ravaged France have no option but to sell their bodies as cannon fodder in violent sports or as guinea pigs in clinical trials of new doping drugs produced by corporations.

But we can find the clearest (and least subtle) representation of the social anxiety toward excessive income inequality and the distrust of government in *The Purge* film series (2013–), set in the near-future United States where an elite has risen to power after an economic collapse that led to revolt and chaos. The so-called New Founding Fathers have instituted an annual purge, a night when murder is permitted. Officially, The Purge serves to release the population's libidinous energies through violence, allegedly helping to restore social harmony. This policy seems to be successful because there is law and order again, and unemployment and poverty rates have fallen to historic lows. Installment after installment in the series, we gradually discover that the real reason behind such resounding economic success is that the rich use The Purge to obliterate the poor because only those who have the means to buy enough protection for themselves remain alive.

Property Wars

Post-apocalyptic futures or fantastic dystopian societies are not the only way to represent extreme economies ridden by scarcity and insecure property rights. That was the everyday reality for millennia, and it still is for most people in many parts of the world. In the pre-historic adventure *Quest for Fire* (1982), clans of marauding early humans fight violently to possess a source of fire. Slaves captured after wars and raids were treated as objects and deprived of their labor, as depicted in Mel Gibson's *Apocalypto* (2006). In pre-modern times and today's developing countries with a weak state apparatus, rival individuals, tribes, gangs, or nations could and can expropriate others. Throughout history, property rights were often the result of such appropriation efforts rather than a voluntary commercial exchange. Resources and territories belonged to those who conquered them. Once force established these rights, property titles were bought and sold in markets peacefully and without coercion.

Pixar's *A Bug's Life* (1998) offers a miniature portrait of an economy that transitions from scarcity and insecurity to eventual prosperity. The ant colony at the center of the film starts as a typical primitive economy: an island in a dry riverbed, closed and autarchic, with no connection to the rest of the world; an agrarian subsistence economy in which the ants barely manage to survive on the fruits of their labor.

A band of grasshoppers appropriate the little surplus they manage to produce. They demand an "offering" in exchange for protection. The anthill's institutions—a benevolent monarchy—are unable to resist the invasion because both the queen and her subjects believe that the natural order of things is for the ants to produce and the grasshoppers to eat what they make. The anthill would thus seem a primitive economy subjected to extractive colonialism. The ants produce a surplus, that is, more food than what they consume, which another nation (the grasshoppers) that contributes nothing to production takes away from them. The threat of violence and their conquerors' ideology sustain this economic system and perpetuate the oppression the ants suffer, by disabling any collective action they can muster to change their predicament. As Hopper, the grasshopper leader, explains to Princess Atta, the natural order of things is "the sun feeds the plants, the ants harvest the food, and the grasshoppers eat it".

In this context, Flik stands out. He is a very ingenious ant who has invented a labor-saving machine that could significantly increase the colony's production. His innovation could allow the ants to abandon their labor-intensive and unproductive technology in favor of a capital-intensive and surplus-generating one. Just as the invention of the plough did for the Neolithic Revolution. But Princess Atta orders Flik to stop wasting time with his machine and collect grain like all the other ants. He explains to the princess and her foremen that his invention is a much more efficient production method and that it intends to save time: "We never have time to collect food for ourselves because we spend the whole summer harvesting for the offering". The colony is not a complete autarky. The need for superior technology arises from the grasshoppers exploiting the ants, which creates the need to increase production to ensure the colony's subsistence. As long as the grasshoppers remain unaware of that new technology, Flik's plan can work.

The problem is that Flik is also somewhat clumsy and inadvertently spoils the offering, causing the grasshoppers to raze the colony and demand double the tribute. In true *Seven Samurai* (1954) fashion, Flik volunteers to leave the island to recruit a group of insect warriors who can protect them from the threat. And so the hero embarks on a journey that takes him to the city of bugs, a modern economy and marketplace depicted as a tremendous hustle and bustle of skyscrapers, cars, people, and advertising. This society has well-defined property rights and offers unusual services for someone coming from a primitive economy, such as public transport. It also harbors inequality and poverty impossible to find in the anthill.

Unlike in Kurosawa's classic, Flik does not manage to hire a cast of brave samurai, but a troupe of critter performers and comedians recently dismissed from a circus and whom he believes to be fierce warriors after a tavern scuffle. Flik and his new friends are greeted as heroes when they return to Ant Island, and after a series of funny misunderstandings, they teach the ants that they can defeat the enemy if they cooperate and work together.

Flik understands that grasshoppers are as afraid of birds as ants are. He leads the insects to build a mechanical bird that will make the invaders flee when they come to claim their tribute. Each ant contributes their unique talents to produce a weapon to defeat their cruel exploiters jointly. For the first time, the ants have solved the collective action problem, also called the "free-rider problem", that underlies the provision of any public good, protecting the anthill in this case. But things get complicated when the attack is consummated, and Flik's plan goes down in flames. The ants must then compare the costs and benefits of stepping forward: risk death if they are not strong enough, and the rebellion fails or overthrow their oppressors if they join forces and their revolution triumphs. The rage they feel and what they have learned from Flik and his circus insects help them coordinate and change the established system. As Princess Atta says, "nature has an order: the ants harvest the food, the ants keep the food and the grasshoppers... leave".

But the genre that has best reflected the conflict over property, their negative economic consequences of the absence of strong institutions, and the need for collective action to overcome that problem is the western. There are many to choose from. Films such as *The Magnificent Seven* (1960) -based on *Seven Samurais*- and its 2016 remake show the insecurity of property rights that exists when the rule of law is weak. Such situations allow unscrupulous men to create local monopolies using force, as shown in *The Pale Rider* (1985), where the villain aims to obtain exclusive rights over a mining territory by all means necessary. Similarly, *Tombstone* (1993) dramatized the infamous gunfight at OK corral between Wyatt Earp and the Clantons, emphasizing the role of lawlessness in the carnage that ensued.

The vast open territories of the United States offered excellent possibilities for agriculture and ranching once the buffaloes and the Native Americans were almost completely wiped out. In the 1870s and 1880s, railways spread westward, facilitating cattle transport and the creation of a livestock market. At the same time, farmers, the vast majority of whom were immigrants, occupied the land, triggering a conflict between them. Although the pastures were of communal property, i.e., they had no defined owner, the ranchers fought to keep the farmers off "their" land, while the farmers fenced off streams and crops with barbed wire—which represented a true technological revolution (Hornbeck, 2010)—to prevent them from being overexploited. These atavistic conflicts between ranchers and farmers over the control of grazing land, often called "range wars", were portrayed with varying degrees of historical accuracy in films such as *Shane* (1953), *Chisum* (1970), *Heaven's Gate* (1980), and *Open Range* (2003).

But conflict also took place between the ranchers themselves. Free access to land was the generalized custom, but the lack of definition of property rights often led to the depletion of pastures and troughs. This phenomenon is called "the tragedy of the commons": the depletion of natural resources without a clear owner that results when users exploit it for their benefit without thinking of the rest. It is the same phenomenon underlying the sharing of food across levels in *The Platform*. The Tragedy of the Commons is the central conflict at the heart of classic westerns such as *The Big Country* (1958), *El Dorado* (1966), and *Man Without a Star* (1955), directed by the great King Vidor.

In *Man Without a Star*, Kirk Douglas plays Dempsey Rae, a wandering cowboy who arrives in Wyoming fleeing the barbed wire ranchers are erecting everywhere to claim the prairies as their own. He is intelligent, handsome, a good gunfighter, and a better cowboy, but he is becoming a relic of another time as economic progress drives him off the accessible prairies of yesteryear. Dempsey thus anticipates Douglas's character a few years later in the much more crepuscular *Lonely Are the Brave* (1962), the last cowboy to survive the avalanche of progress.

Dempsey meets young Jeff Jimson (William Campbell) on the train to Wyoming, whom he takes under his wing, a widespread trope in westerns. The two find employment in the biggest ranch in the county. There, Dempsey gives his impetuous pupil a crash course in manners and gun handling. But soon, the new owner arrives, Reed Bowman (Jeanne Crain), an ambitious, beautiful, and wealthy woman from the East who has very clear ideas, ideas that involve breaking the conventions among ranchers that prevent the overgrazing of pastures. Reed wants to double her herd of cattle and let them feed on the open range until they run out. Come winter, she will return to the East even richer and leave the problem to others. Reed is a female character very close to the femme fatale of film noir, unusually liberated for the time: she negotiates Dempsey's support for her project with sex as currency and without the slightest restraint (only those imposed by film censors).

Man Without a Star contains all the elements of the classic western - a saloon, gunfights, beautiful scenery, fistfights, the good-hearted prostitute–and one key innovation: for much of the film, it is not very clear who are the good guys and who are the bad guys. Although Reed is greedy, her rivals use barbed wire to fence off their meadows (to avoid the Tragedy of the Commons). This ignites Dempsey's hatred because, as we soon learn, he lost his brother to barbed wire. He also discovers that the seductive Reed has as few scruples as any other greedy rancher. She fires the most experienced cowboys on her ranch and hires a group of gunslingers to intimidate her rivals. In other words, she replaces productive workers with unproductive appropriators in preparation for the coming conflict. When Dempsey begins to question the morality of his loyalty to his boss, his world turns upside down, Reed abandons him, and Jeff betrays him.

One of *Man Without a Star*'s most attractive points is the transformation of Kirk Douglas's character. A man with a painful past who starts as a complete individualist, weary of anything that could curtail his freedom, and ends up defending the small landowners by helping them put up the barbed wire fences he had so abhorred as a symbol of oppression. This plot arc is typical in other screenplays by the great Borden Chase, notably in two westerns directed by Anthony Mann, *Bend the River* (1952) and *The Far Country* (1954). Dempsey's character undergoes a metamorphosis from *homo economicus* to *homo socialis*, from steppe wolf to caring benefactor concerned with his community's problems. We will come back to this character's arch in the next chapter because it is the template used in many economic films.

The Old West was not the only place and time where weak property rights led to overexploitation and conflict. When Europeans arrived on Easter Island in the eighteenth century, they found primitive tribes, a desolate landscape, and enormous stone statues, the moais. That a culture so backward and apparently unable to navigate or carve stone would have been responsible for such wonders seemed impossible. That fired the imagination of a few, among them a cheeky Swiss hotelier named Erich von Daniken for whom the moai could only have been the work of aliens. However, the archaeological evidence offered a more sensible, albeit equally fascinating account. The celebrated historian and geographer Jared Diamond recounted it in his famous book *Collapse: How Societies Choose to Fail or Succeed* (2005). Easter Island had been very fertile, but overexploitation of the forests and natural resources plunged the island into a period of scarcity, war, and anarchy, cannibalism even. That was the state of decadence and stagnation the Europeans found the island once natives called "the navel of the world".

Rapa Nui (1994), the name of Easter Island in the native language, portrays this process of economic decline quite well, albeit compressing its duration from centuries to mere months. The film was the second collaboration between Kevin Costner, who served as producer, and director Kevin Reynolds; the third one would be *Waterworld*. Both *Rapa Nui* and *Waterworld* show the importance of scarcity and share their concern for the environment.

Rapa Nui is an average adventure film with somewhat laughable dialogues and actors whose only merit seems to look good in loincloths. That said, the film explains very well the tragedy of the commons. The film's plot centers on the impossible love affair between Noro (Jason Scott Lee) and Ramana (Sandrine Holt), each belonging to one of the island's two clans, the long-eared and the short-eared. The former clan holds power while the latter carves the moais, which are supposed to bring back the gods from beyond the sea. The problem is that palm tree trunks are needed to transport the moais. The trees are cut down until there are none left, and the soil becomes poorer and poorer due to the resulting erosion. In one scene, we see a farmer who complains about how barren the land has become and who is then forcibly recruited to carry the statues. Noro's grandfather is the Birdman (Eru Potaka-Dewes), the island leader, a position that decided in a race among the young men of each tribe, a dazzling scene which, incidentally, is the best of the film. The Birdman's right arm is an ambitious shaman in charge of enforcing the religious code of conduct. These rules are designed in part to curb the overexploitation of the island's natural resources. In one scene, the shaman kills a fisherman for catching a kind of fish whose capture the gods forbid during certain months. The underlying reason for that rule is to allow the fish stock to regrow. As Noro's grandfather becomes obsessed with building more statues and food becomes scarcer, conflict arises between the clans over their livelihoods. Eventually, a coup d'état takes place, plunging the island into a spiral of violence and chaos. That is how Rapa Nui's inhabitants joined the Mayans and the Nazcas in the long list of human civilizations that caused their own downfall by abusing their environment.

But the lack of well-enforced property rights over natural resources has dire consequences even when they are durable. The "natural resource curse" is an empirical regularity that associates countries richer in natural resources with lower economic growth. Among the various explanations for this phenomenon, one that is particularly relevant in underdeveloped countries is that the discovery of oil or mineral deposits increases the risk of civil conflict. When institutions are weak, violence becomes a substitute for the state when defining property rights. That is why organizations specialized in violence, such as guerrillas and paramilitary groups, can emerge in these contexts. The income they earn by appropriating natural resources allows them to buy weapons and exert more influence. The resulting conflict perpetuates poverty in these countries. One of the best-known examples of the natural resource curse occurred in the early 2000s when the rising demand for mobile phones and the release of the Playstation 2 drove up the price of coltan, a mineral found mainly in the Democratic Republic of Congo and used in many electronic devices. The "coltan rush" did not make the country prosperous. It instead plunged it into a fierce civil conflict over the mineral's control. Farmers near the mining regions were driven off their land, villages were brutally attacked, women were raped, and thousands were displaced. A similar phenomenon had taken place in Sicily in the late nineteenth century when a global rise in the price of lemon zest—used by Western sailors to fence off scurvy— led to a conflict over lemon orchards in the island, which eventually gave birth to the Sicilian Mafia (Dimico et al., 2017).

Blood Diamond (2006) deals with one of the most famous examples of the natural resource curse, Sierra Leone's blood diamonds. These gems were mined during the country's long civil war, and the Revolutionary United Front (RUF) rebels used them to finance themselves. The main plotline follows Danny Archer (Leonard DiCaprio), a former Rhodesian mercenary with a murky past who, after being arrested while trying to smuggle diamonds, finds himself in prison with a fisherman named Solomon Vandy (Djimon Hounsou). A group of RUF rebels kidnapped Solomon and forced him to work as a slave in the diamond mines. There he discovers a huge specimen and manages to bury it, hoping to use it one day to get out of the country and save his family. But government forces attack the mining camp, and Solomon is arrested. Archer offers Solomon help to find his lost wife and children in exchange for the diamond. After escaping the besieged capital, the two men are aided by Maddy Bowen (Jennifer Connelly), a courageous American war journalist who wants to uncover the blood diamond trade promoted by the world's leading trader, Van de Kaap, a thinly veiled reference to the De Beers family. Things get even more complicated when Solomon learns that the rebels have kidnapped his son and turned him into a child soldier. Each with their own agenda, Danny, Solomon, and Maddy must help each other if they are to make their way in a country engulfed in a brutal war fueled by the illegal diamond trade.

Director Edward Zwick had no problem showing scenes of murder, riots, and mutilations to depict the reality of a country descending into a spiral of destruction and chaos. Nor does he hesitated to present the diamond trade as one of the leading causes of the conflict. The World Diamond Council, the association that brings together the world's top diamond traders, prepared a campaign to counter the bad publicity that the film's release brought them. As we will see in Chapter Four, many films have portrayed large corporations as evil entities always willing to shy away from their social responsibility to increase their profits. One distinctive feature of *Blood Diamond* is that the film focuses on De Beers, an actual cartel that, in addition to trafficking with blood diamonds, employed anti-competitive practices throughout the twentieth century to abuse its dominant position in the international diamond market.

First, De Beers tried to convince independent producers to join its distribution monopoly. When it failed, the company flooded the market with diamonds of similar quality to those of its competitors to drive down the price. That practice disciplined buyers who wanted to trade directly with the mines by never dealing with them again. Another of its tactics, very typical of monopolies and well explained in the film, was to reduce the world supply of diamonds to keep their price artificially high. Finally, there were times when De Beers bought diamonds to keep the price up;

indeed, the famous advertising slogan "a diamond is forever" was created by De Beers at a time when the industry was struggling.

In the early 2000s, producers' decision in Canada and Australia to distribute diamonds without De Beers and the development of synthetic diamonds forced the monopoly to change its strategy. To maintain its control over the world's supply, De Beers decided to buy the diamonds rebel armed groups in Sierra Leone, Liberia, and the Democratic Republic of Congo were selling to buy weapons. But growing consumer awareness reduced its sales. De Beers went from controlling 80% of the rough diamond market in 1980 to 35% in 2019.[9] *Blood Diamond* played a significant role in this change in public opinion—a good proof of film narratives' influence on economics.

References

Algan, Y., Guriev, Y., & Papaiaonno, E. (2017). The European trust crisis and the rise of populism. *Brookings Papers on Economic Activity*, forthcoming.

Atkinson, T., Piketty, T., & Saez, E. (2011). Top incomes in the long run of history. *Journal of Economic Literature, 49*(1), 3–71.

Bleich, S. N., Jarlenski, M. P., Bell, C. N., & Laveist, T. A. (2012). Health inequalities: Trends, progress, and policy. *Annual Review of Public Health, 33*, 7–40.

Choi, J.-K., & Bowles, S. (2007). The coevolution of parochial altruism and war. *Science, 318*(5850), 636–640.

Dimico, A., Isopi, A., & Olsson, O. (2017). Origins of the Sicilian Mafia: The market for lemons. *The Journal of Economic History, 77*(4), 1083–1115.

Hirshleifer. (1994). The dark side of the force. *Economic Inquiry, 32*, 1–10.

Hornbeck, R. (2010). Barbed wire: Property rights and agricultural development. *The Quarterly Journal of Economics, 125*, 767–810.

---

[9] "A Brief History of De Beers", Paul Zimnisky. March 20, 2019. Last accessed March 30, 2021, http://www.paulzimnisky.com/a-brief-history-of-de-beers.

CHAPTER 3

Evil Is The Root Of All Money

The first word that comes to most people's minds when they think about economics is "money". That word carries several connotations that describe well the bulk of cinema with explicit economic content. One connotation would be "boring" (many may have thought exactly that when coming across this book). Another is "attractive", which is why many films about economics have displayed their fascination with the opulence and luxury we tend to associate with the world of finance. A third idea often linked with money is a lack of ethics—greed, selfishness—another pervasive theme in economics films. We will come back to all of these in the following pages.

It may come as a surprise, but economics and economists have little interest in money as a study subject. Of course, economists know what money is: a mean of payment sufficiently widespread and accepted to allow goods and services to be exchanged easily. But the word "money" barely appeared in the one thousand articles published in the top five

---

I am borrowing this title from Kiyotaki and Moore's (2002) masterful play with Timothy 6:10.

economics academic journals between 2014 and 2017.[1] That said, given the strong popular association between economics and money, it is probably best if we discuss how cinema has represented money next.

The Life of Money

In the hilarious prologue to *The Laundromat* (2019), Jürgen Mossack (Gary Oldman) and Ramón Fonseca (Antonio Banderas), the senior partners in the law firm where the notorious Panama Papers were leaked from, go back to the Stone Age to tell us the story of money. It first emerged to solve the problem of the double coincidence of wants in primitive barter economies: If I want milk, but I have bananas, and you have cows, but you do not like bananas, there is no way we can barter unless a mean of exchange allows us to trade. That was the role of money, to solve the evil of friction in exchange. In the beginning, precious metals, or any other scarce object with value, served as money. For example, some economies in the Bronze Age used salt as currency because it was very difficult to extract; that is where the word "salary" comes from. Cigarettes were used as money in prisons and concentration camps, as depicted in *The Shawshank Redemption* (1994) and many other prison films.

When the economy became more complex, paper money began to be issued. That represented a giant leap because money went from being something with intrinsic value to something that had value only because a central authority backed it with a promise of convertibility into some precious metal, generally gold. That was how the international monetary system worked for much of the twentieth century. It was called the gold standard. Precisely the economic institution that the supervillain in *Goldfinger* (1964) tries to manipulate for profit.

Goldfinger is probably the most iconic film in the James Bond franchise, to a large extent thanks to the image of Shirley Eaton's naked body lying covered in gold paint. The film's plot is simple: MI6 sends James Bond (Sean Connery) to investigate the activities of a gold trader, Auric Goldfinger (Gert Fröbe), who is using fluctuations in the price of the precious metal to profit from smuggling.

Several Bond films across the years have featured supervillains whose machinations involve disrupting the economy in one way or another.

---

[1] Oriana Bandiera "What Economists Really Do", 2018 Royal Economic Society Annual Public Lecture. Last accessed March 30, 2021 https://youtu.be/1KEzLtbpEVg.

For example, in *Live and Let Die* (1973), *A View to a Kill* (1985), and *Quantum of Solace* (2008), Bond's antagonists sought to become monopolists in their respective markets (drugs, microchips, and water, respectively). Auric Goldfinger's plan is the best grounded on economics.

The blond villain plans to detonate what today we would call a "dirty bomb" at Fort Knox to make all US gold reserves radioactive and multiply the value of his reserves. A simple plan based on one of the most basic principles in economics: the law of demand. If a product's supply shrinks and its demand remains constant, the price will rise. As a result, the evil tycoon expects to increase his wealth tenfold.

Ian Fleming's original novel contains a fairly good exposition—absent from the film—of the mid-century international monetary system, better known as the Bretton Woods system. Under this system implemented in the aftermath of World War II, the central banks of the participating countries pegged the value of their currencies to the US dollar, which in turn was convertible into gold, initially at $35 per ounce. This ensured global economic stability. In exchange, countries had to keep their currencies within narrow fluctuation bands. Adjustments were usually made by purchasing the currency itself using gold from national reserves.

For private individuals, buying and storing large quantities of gold was illegal unless you had a license to use gold for industrial purposes. This is the case with Goldfinger, who has caught the UK authorities' eye because he seems to be taking advantage of another fundamental concept in economics: arbitrage. Arbitrage occurs when price differences make it possible to make a profit by buying a product where it is cheaper and reselling it where it is more expensive. Since gold could not flow easily across national borders and exchange rates could hardly rise or fall under the Bretton Woods system, the price of gold could vary widely from country to country. As Colonel Smithers explains to 007, Goldfinger uses his industrial permits to obtain gold in Britain and then sell it in other countries where the price of the metal was higher. In fact, the character was based on the real-life figure of Charles Engelhard, a wealthy gold mine owner in South Africa who, like the fictional Goldfinger, used gold art objects to avoid export controls (Karl, 2008). It is not by chance either that the film's release coincided with the efforts of British Prime Minister Harold Wilson to keep the trade deficit in check and avoid a devaluation of the sterling by using the country's gold reserves. Blaming the payments imbalances on the gold smugglers and promising that MI6 would intervene to stop their nefarious activities was a good propaganda stunt. Still, it did not help Wilson, who had no choice but to devalue the pound in 1967.

A side effect of Goldfinger's plan is the likely collapse of the Bretton Woods system. Without the gold with which the United States backed the value of the dollar, the currency would have depreciated precipitously, the system would have broken down, and the era of remarkable post-war stability and economic development known as "The Glorious Thirty" would have come to an end. This is, in effect, what happened in the real world a few years later. The Bretton Woods system officially disintegrated in 1971. Until then, nobody was particularly interested in converting dollars into gold. The trust in the international monetary system was healthy. But the United States had run up huge deficits during the 1960s due to spending on the Vietnam War and the "War on Poverty" championed by President Johnson. To finance both efforts, the Federal Reserve printed money in droves and began selling its gold reserves on a massive scale. The US currency lost value—inflation soared—because it was now in plentiful supply. Rumors arose that European central banks would convert their dollars into gold. Richard Nixon was then forced to abandon the dollar-gold peg. The era of floating exchange rates and free trade in gold that we live in today was born.

"Greed Is Good"

But money does not need to be convertible to be accepted as a medium of exchange. What is crucial is that it is widely used. For example, in eighteenth-century French Canada, legal tender was in short supply, and playing cards became a payment method in a purely decentralized way. This was purely fiat money (from the Latin *fides*, faith), like the money issued today by the Federal Reserve or the Bank of England, backed only by the value of their respective economies. We accept these banknotes because everyone else accepts them too.

Fiat money creates, however, a problem between the issuer and the holder, the central bank and us because we must have confidence in the future validity of that piece of paper. The instability triggered by the 2008 financial crisis eroded that implicit trust. That is why films like *The Contestant* (2007) argue that money is "fake", that it does not exist because it is "created" by banks. An alternative take is that money is fake because it can be counterfeited. Films like *The Counterfeiters* (2007) and several others used this attractive premise: it would seem that to become a multimillionaire or bring a whole economy to the brink of collapse, all you need is a bit of ingenuity and a printing press.

The last stage in the history of money that Mossack and Fonseca tell us in the prologue to *The Laundromat* is abstraction. Money does not even need to have a physical form anymore. It is no longer gold or paper with the face of someone famous on it. Money has become desubstantiated, intangible. The theme of the abstraction of money is a very recurrent one in economic films, as shown in this and the following chapter. On the one hand, the fact that money has become desubstantiated has created new forms of money such as bonds, collateralized debt, or financial instruments, allowing us to bring money from the future into the present. These immaterial and ghostly forms of money—we are told in films like *The Big Short*—flow following their own rules in our increasingly financialized economies.

On the other hand, the economy also dematerializes when money adopts those new and exotic forms. It is no longer based on the production of tangible objects but on disembodied capital flows. As Henry, the trickster tycoon James Garner played in *The Wheeler Dealers* (1963), said, "it is no longer the Morgans and the Rockefellers who are investing [...] It is the pension funds and the mutual funds". The greed, ambition, and corruption resulting from the decoupling between physical production and financial activity are at the heart of key economic films such as *Wall Street* (1987) and *Other People's Money* (1991).

But greed and unscrupulousness are only one side of the representation of money in cinema. It is true that the films we will be discussing next display some moral revulsion against those who deal with money. But directors and screenwriters have also felt attracted to luxury and opulence, as shown in films such as *L'Argent* (1928), *Rollover* (1981), or *The Secret of My Success* (1987). Gordon Gekko, the main villain of Oliver Stone's Wall Street, epitomized this ambivalence.

Stone turned Gekko into an icon and a spokesman of a very particular historical and economic context: The United States of the 1980s. Ronald Reagan's conservative revolution elevated the pursuit of profit and individualism to tenets of moral virtue. This doctrine is summed up in Gekko's famous dictum, "Greed is good". Gekko is a character repellent and fascinating in equal parts. He is not a one-dimensional villain like Goldfinger; he is the son of a blue-collar worker who became a finance shark to avoid ending up like his father, sick and poor. The relevance of his famous quote transcends the context in which *Wall Street* was released because it was conceived as a deliberate and distorted echo of one of the founding pillars of economics.

In 1776, Adam Smith, the father of economics, published his seminal work, *The Wealth of Nations*. In what is probably his most quoted phrase, Smith wrote that "It is not from the benevolence of the butcher, the brewer, or the baker that we expect our dinner, but from their regard to their self-interest". In other words, societies thrive thanks to the self-interested decisions of their members. Economics as a discipline assumes that people make decisions to maximize their happiness given their constraints. This model of human behavior is known as the *homo economicus*.

In *The Wealth of Nations* and the lesser-known *The Theory of Moral Sentiments* (1759), Adam Smith made clear that the pursuit of self-interest is not the same as selfishness. It may be in my interest to share my time and food with people I care about or help others improve their lives. Nor does economics claim that the pursuit of self-interest is the only human motivation, that people are lone wolves who live in a social vacuum. It is just a simplification that can help us understand how humans behave in the same way a map simplifies the world to helps us navigate it. Adam Smith's famous quote has often been misinterpreted. Some have used it as the definitive proof that economics is a morally bankrupt science and as a justification for totally unregulated capitalism by others.

Gordon Gekko's "greed is good" inspired hundreds, perhaps thousands of American kids to become stockbrokers. The irony of it is that Gekko's oft-quoted and oft-repeated monologues, which had such an influence on the careers of so many young people, were inspired by the words of investor Ivan Boesky, who would end up in prison for insider trading. Screenwriters Stanley Weiser and Oliver Stone used as source material the figures of several real speculators such as Boesky, David Levine, and Michael Milken, the father of the so-called junk bonds—securities with a high risk that in return pay a high-interest rate. He was sentenced to 10 years in prison for tax and stock fraud in 1990.

Wall Street tells the story of Bud Fox (Charlie Sheen), an ambitious stockbroker who has just graduated from New York University. Although he is not doing badly, Bud wants to make it to the top and spends his spare time courting successful speculators. He meets Gekko (Michael Douglas), a corporate rider with no scruples, a big investor who hops from company to company acquiring large stakes and using his voting rights to increase their shares' value. The problem is that his tactics often involve replacing the current management, the downsize of operations, massive layoffs, and the liquidation of the companies he gains control of.

Bud learns that Gekko is successful because he never takes risks. He operates using inside information, often obtained illegally. Bud manages to attract Gekko's attention because his father (Martin Sheen), who works for Blue Star Airlines, has told him that a still-secret court ruling will favor the company. Bud then signs a Faustian bargain with the shark: he will supply Gekko more inside information, and in return, Gekko will make him rich. The pact breaks down when Bud learns that his new boss plans to liquidate Blue Star and loot his employees' retirement fund.

The film is a reflection of the turning point in the financial sector that took place in the mid-1980s. Until then, ideas about stability, ethics, and the importance of personal relationships had prevailed. Bud's bosses try to impress upon him the belief that he must rise slowly and that the money he makes for his clients creates jobs and is invested in research and development. *Wall Street* shows the arrival of a different order, one of hostile takeovers, insider trading, telesales, investment banking, and complex financial products.

Stone contrasts Gekko and sharks like him with men like Bud Fox's father, working-class people who see hard physical work as the only source of real wealth and thus of moral value. For him, a job is not a real job if it is not honest and does not create something tangible. In his worldview, Bud is merely playing with money and being manipulated by Gekko, who in turn personifies greed, understood as an unethical quality. Gekko contrasts this worldview with his father's life, an industrial worker who played according to the rules and died in poverty. Bud oscillates between these two poles. Initially, he just wants money and status; he wants to become a member of elite clubs, eat in expensive restaurants, bid at art auctions, and own a luxury flat. This pulls him toward Gekko. In the third act, Bud tries to regain his moral integrity, which sends him back to his father. His journey emphasizes the importance of honesty and hard work instead of money, which represents a destructive and corruptive force.

But *Wall Street* is not entirely Manichean. Gekko is not the role model many saw in him, but he is not a full-blown villain either. Stone and Weiser's script and Michael Douglas's Oscar-winning performance make him a complex character. Gekko is a man of humble origins who rose to the top on his own and against the *establishment*. He appreciates art beyond its investment potential and sees Bud as a son he could raise in his image. The film also admits that the financial sector plays a vital role as a generator of wealth and a source of the credit that the real economy needs to function. The problem seems to be confined to just a few bad apples like Gekko.

"I Don't Make Anything? I'm Making You Money"

Wall Street presented hostile takeovers as a dramatic battleground between capitalists, managers, and workers. It also posed a fundamental dilemma. While companies cannot be left at the mercy of financial sharks like Gordon Gekko, who are only interested in the short term, the truth is that without shareholders' pressure, it is difficult to curb inefficient corporate management. Many of the corporations Gekko takes over are run by incompetent executives with bloated salaries and outdated ways of doing things that look like they were out of a Dilbert comic strip. These nuances were explored soon after by another film about firm takeovers, *Other People's Money*.

The arrival of the 1990s meant that the ways of making money associated with Reaganism—the exploitation of ordinary workers by greedy corporate riders—were no longer socially acceptable. It was also around this time when large corporations adopted legal countermeasures designed to thwart potential hostile takeovers. These included the so-called "poison pills", which preserved shareholders' rights in the event of a takeover, making it less attractive, and "golden parachutes", the large severance packages that board members received if dismissed. Corporate language is full of such metaphors.

Other People's Money reflects well those changes. Its plot deals with the takeover of New England Wire & Cable, a family-owned company, by financial shark Larry "The Liquidator" Garfield (Danny DeVito). New England Wire & Cable is a well-run company with no debt and genuinely cares for its employees. It is attractive to big investors interested in increasing their portfolios' value.

Garfield seems at first a cartoonish character. In his introductory monologue, he explains that money, along with dogs and doughnuts, are the only things in life that accept you unconditionally. He is not friendly or polite except with his computer—which he calls Carmen—who informs him every morning of the stock market prices. His antagonist is Jorgenson (Gregory Peck), the New England Wire & Cable factory manager, a patrician and honest Republican who believes in family values, hard work, and

America. Sparks fly at their first meeting. Garfield begins the conversation by saying that his company is worth more dead than alive, to which Jorgenson responds by calling him a little weasel. Jorgenson is the film's moral pole, but unlike Bud Fox's father in *Wall Street*, his position is not presented as superior. His refusal to compromise looks admirable at first, but as the film progresses, his recalcitrant integrity becomes a stubborn self-righteousness.

Garfield, who at one point describes the free enterprise system in Darwinian terms as the "survival of the fittest", is not entirely coldhearted either. He falls in love with Jorgenson's daughter Kate (Penelope Ann Miller), an attractive lawyer who chooses to defend her father's company from Garfield's takeover. The relationship between Kate and Garfield seems an update of the romance between a corporate raider (James Garner) and the daughter of an industrialist (Natalie Wood) in *Cash McCall* (1960).

The final confrontation between capitalists and humanists occurs at the shareholders' meeting where the company's fate is decided. As in *The Solid Gold Cadillac* (1956), corporate governance is represented as a citizens' assembly. Garfield and Jorgenson give dramatic speeches in front of an audience of shareholders who then vote on whether to keep the current board or replace it. Jorgenson, who embodies honesty and decency, mourns the imminent demise of his company, and describes Garfield as "the entrepreneur of post-industrial America who plays God with other people's money [...] He creates nothing, builds nothing", thus highlighting the idea that the economy is dematerializing and thus becoming corrupt. Jorgenson trusts the factory's survival on the government reinvesting in infrastructure sooner or later and appeals to investors' patience. He ends by saying that killing the company would be "murder in the name of maximizing shareholder value, putting dollar notes where conscience should be [...] A company is more than money. Here we build things, and we care about people". He receives a standing ovation.

It is then when *Other People's Money* shines by offering the capitalists' perspective. Garfield disagrees with traditional forms of business management, yes, but he defends the shareholders. "I didn't kill it. It was dead when I got here", Garfield says of the company. He invokes Schumpeter's principle of creative destruction: The relentless push of markets and innovation has rendered the sector obsolete "as the automobile put the horsewhip companies out of business". The result of that process is losses for specific groups of individuals, the factory workers in this case, but gains for society as a whole. The only alternatives are either the company's immediate liquidation or a painful agony until it becomes the last one standing in a tiny market. From their perspective, the shareholders should not worry about the workers. They bought shares to make money. And if they care about the real economy, the best thing they can do is sell their shares, invest elsewhere and create new jobs there.

Scrooge's Arc

Wall Street and *Other People's Money* exemplify very well the almost universal representation of capitalists in cinema as cold-hearted egotists. But these films are distinct from others in that by the end, their charismatic villains do not redeem. They do not change their mind. Garfield may be in love with Kate, but he still believes that money is the best thing in the world. Gekko goes to jail but remains unrepentant (at least until *Wall Street 2: Money Never Sleeps*, 2010, where Stone betrayed him).

Like the Grinch, these specimens of *homo economicus* are rather unpleasant beings: selfish, rational, and calculating. But like Dr. Seuss' character, the *homo economicus* is a figment of fiction. It is an appealing type of character because we are simultaneously fascinated by their amorality and their disdain for social conventions. But at the same time, we feel repelled by them because we understand that the networks of esteem and trust that make up society—what economists call social capital—would not exist if everybody were relentless egoists like them.

That is why there are so many films where a selfish and cruel character undergoes a transformation that leads him to understand that success and profit do not really matter in life; it is personal relationships. I will call this character arc the *Scrooge's arc* in honor of the protagonist of *A Christmas Carol* (1843). Charles Dickens created Scrooge precisely to caricature the self-interest maximizing human portrayed by Adam Smith. Scrooge goes from being a miser to become a generous benefactor after the three ghosts show him the suffering his behavior causes to others and the pettiness of his life goals.

The plot of *A Christmas Carol* is well known so I will summarize it only briefly. Ebenezer Scrooge is a selfish and disagreeable miser. His only employee is the poor but optimistic Bob Cratchit, whose son, Tiny Tim, is even more jovial despite his severe illness. On Christmas Eve, three ghosts visit Scrooge. They show him a series of visions, including one in which Tiny Tim has died because Cratchit is unable to support his family on his meager salary. After the night's ordeal, Scrooge realizes how miserable his attitude to life has been, recovers his joie de vivre, and begins to treat kindly those around him. Tiny Tim lives to see another Christmas.

It is less well known that, in addition to being an ode to charity and compassion, Dickens wrote *A Christmas Carol* as a response to the great economic debates of his time. Versions like *Scrooged* (1988) and *The Muppet Christmas Carol* (1992) are hilarious renditions of this classic. *Scrooge* (1935) was influenced by German expressionism, and the 1970 version by Ronald Neame was a colorful musical adaptation. But the grim British film adaptation of 1951 is the one that most accurately portrayed Dickens' text and intentions and the economic context of nineteenth-century Britain.

In England in 1843, the Industrial Revolution was at full speed. Technical advances had created huge factories. People from the countryside were migrating *en masse* to the cities. Although a new middle class was forming, large sections of the population still did not benefit from the process. The wealthiest 5% held about 65% of the wealth (Lindert, 1986). Dickens read a parliamentary report on the appalling working conditions of children. After visiting schools and coal mines full of starving, illiterate infants, he decided to write a pamphlet denouncing their predicament. But Dickens then changed his mind. He had the sudden inspiration to write a fairy tale that would be more effective than any article he could write.

Dickens held responsible a new academic discipline for the deplorable situation of children. It was called Political Economy then. We call it Economics now. Political economists like David Hume or Adam Smith had set out to do with the social sciences what Isaac Newton had done with physics: to discover the laws that govern human behavior. Dickens created Scrooge as a caricature of the *homo economicus* described by Adam Smith, a man who thinks that "you have to be the strongest if you don't want to be crushed by someone else's ambition", as Scrooge says in the 1951 version of *A Christmas Carol*.

This analogy becomes even more apparent earlier in the film when Scrooge (Alastair Sim) is visited by two men who ask him for a charitable donation. His response is not surprising:

- Are there no prisons?
- Plenty of prisons.
- And the union workhouses – are they still in operation?

- They are. I wish I could say they were not.
- The treadmill and the Poor Law? They are still in full vigor, I presume.
- Both very busy, sir.
- Oh, from what you said at first, I was afraid something has happened to stop them from their useful course. I am very glad to hear it.

The treadmills, the Poor Law, and the workhouses Scrooge refers to were punitive measures imposed on prisoners and the poor in England at the time. Because the destitute were held responsible for their situation, they were required to work their way out of it. Any poor person could enter a workhouse where they received food in exchange for hard physical labor. In prison treadmills, inmates ran on a giant wheel to grind flour and pay for their stay. Under the Poor Law, a small debt meant prison, as is the case of the poor devil who at the beginning of the film begs for mercy from Scrooge to whom he owes £20.

Dickens took aim at another famous political economist. One of the men asking Scrooge for a donation tells him that some people would die before setting foot in a workhouse. The miser replies, "they'd better do it and decrease the surplus population". This sentence is an obvious reference to the Reverend Thomas Malthus, whose influential *An Essay on the Principle of Population* (1798) argued that the economy grows arithmetically while population increases geometrically, implying that war, famine, or disease eventually regulate "overpopulation". To be fair, Malthus wrote his *opus magna* just at the end of the economic stagnation that had characterized human history right until the Industrial Revolution. Between 1270 and 1770, the English economy had grown by an average of 0.2% per year (Broadberry et al., 2015). With the advent of the Industrial Revolution, the economy began to draw what is known as the "hockey-stick graph" because it boomed and traced a sharp upward curve after centuries of a flat pulse.

Dickens hated Malthus. For one thing, the reverend had been one of the most ardent supporters of the 1834 Poor Law, which tightened the workhouse regime. But the writer also suspected that in their quest to understand how the economy worked, political economists like Malthus had forgotten that they were dealing with people, not numbers. That is precisely Tiny Tim's purpose as a character: to put a face on the surplus population that Malthus was glad to let die with his utilitarian calculations.

A Christmas Carol suggests that the remedy Dickens advocated to solve the widespread poverty and inequality of his time was a form of proto-Keynesianism. Scrooge exemplifies what Keynes called the "paradox of thrift", which warns that an excess of saving leads to a reduction in aggregate demand and a contraction of the economy (and then to even more saving). Unlike his mentor Fezziwig (Roddy Hughes), who had dozens of employees and believed that "life is more than money", Scrooge has only one employee and pays him a pitiful salary. After the visit of the three Christmas Spirits, Scrooge expands his demand for labor and goods. He gives Cratchit (Mervyn Johns) a raise, pays a boy to buy the biggest turkey in the butchers, and gets a taxi to take him to the clerk's house. Scrooge has never been happier. He shouts, "I'm as light as a feather! I'm as happy as an angel! I'm as content as a child!". He is no longer a calculating and miserly man because, as Keynes wrote, "a large proportion of our positive activities depend on spontaneous optimism rather than on a mathematical expectation".[2]

CAN'T BUY ME LOVE

Rather than ghosts, the Scrooge's arc is often triggered by a female character who helps the selfish male protagonist open up to love or connect with his childhood. The paradigmatic case would be that of Humphrey Bogart and Audrey Hepburn in *Sabrina* (1954), which would serve as a template for romantic comedies such as *Pretty Woman* (1990), *Two Weeks' Notice* (2002), *In Good Company* (2004), and *A Good Year* (2006) among others.

Pretty Woman was Hollywood's response to Reaganism's economic excesses and individualism. The film is built on classic tales and myths such as Cinderella and Pygmalion to tell the romance between a good-hearted prostitute Vivian (Julia Roberts) and the handsome millionaire Edward (Richard Gere), a *corporate raider* who buys up troubled companies, dismantles them, and sells them on. Early on, the film conveys a critical view of stock markets and finance as useless and wasteful compared to the production of tangible objects. That is best summarized by the dialogue between Edward and his lawyer where the former says, "We don't do anything, we don't build anything", to which the lawyer replies "We make

---

[2] *The General Theory of Employment, Interest and Money*, [1936] (1953), p. 161. New York: Harcourt.

money" in typical Larry Garfield fashion. Edward, who is also haunted by his family past, is a sweetened version of Gordon Gekko, closer to James Garner's character in the elegant and naive *Cash McCall*. In fact, *Pretty Woman* does not hide its deliberate appeal to nostalgia for a better era. The film recycles the typical plot driver of the 1950s corporate films we will review in Chapter Four: the conflict between ethics and humanity versus efficiency and profit.

In addition to being rich, Edward is a workaholic. His schedule is so full he has no time for romance. He hires prostitutes at his convenience. He does not even have time to wait for his car to be returned by the valet after a party, so he borrows his lawyer's car and drives through Hollywood Boulevard on his way to his hotel. By chance, he runs into Vivian, who charges him for directions. Unlike Edward, she is a working-class woman who—the film makes it very clear—did not get the opportunities she deserved. Vivian needs all the money she can find because her flat mate spent her rent on drugs, and she wants to stay away from pimps. Edward rents Vivian first for one night, then for a week. In this sense, *Pretty Woman* reverses the classic romantic comedy plot in which sexual tension is the primary driver. Here, sex happens right at the beginning of their relationship, and it is the process of falling in love that comes next.

Although it soon becomes clear that their liaison is more than commercial in nature, Edward, true to his capitalist tendencies, buys Vivian's time as if he were buying a company. The scene in which they negotiate—Edward dressed, Vivian in the bathtub—offers a great example of the concept of consumer surplus, first proposed by the French economist Jules Dupuit. The consumer surplus is the difference between what the buyer is willing to pay for a good or a service and what he finally pays. As if it were a commercial transaction, Vivian offers to spend the week with Edward for $4000. He counteroffers $2000, and in the end, they close the deal for $3000. After the bargaining has ended, she admits that she would have accepted the $2000, and he would have paid the $4000. In other words, each has taken a surplus of $1000.

As their relationship progresses, the business aspects disappear, and a process of emotional transference takes place between them. Edward learns that it is not money but the warmth of human relationships that truly matters in life and finds himself as a person. He realizes that he does not want to scrap the shipping company he is struggling to acquire, which, unlike him, creates jobs and builds things. When the transference process between Edward and Vivian is complete, the millionaire decides to become an entrepreneur and build ships (destroyers for the US Navy, in fact) instead of destroying companies and rides to Vivian's rescue like a knight-errant in his shiny limousine wielding his sharp umbrella.

As Boozer (2002) suggests, *Pretty Woman* reflects the change in the social perception of financiers caused by the fall from grace of Ivan Boesky, Michael Milken, and their ilk. The widespread admiration guys like Gordon Gekko once attracted was gone. At least for the time being.

THE DEVIL AMONG US

On other occasions, the metamorphosis from *homo economicus* to *homo socialis* occurs when the Scrooge-like character leaves the solitude of his ivory tower, mingles with his employees, and becomes their friend. This is the case of the ill-tempered millionaire in the delightful *The Devil and Miss Jones* (1941) and the efficiency expert played by Anthony Hopkins in *Spotswood* (1992).

Early in *The Devil and Miss Jones*, four limousines bring four dapper men to the imposing New York mansion of JP Merrick (Charles Coburn), the richest man in the world. Through a ser of wide stairs, they enter a cavernous and gothic space that reminds us of Xanadu in *Citizen Kane* (1941). Merrick does not work. He is a rentier and financier who lives off his investments without any interest in the productive enterprises from which he profits. Merrick's character is deliberately based on JP Morgan. He is a gruff millionaire who gets furious when his acolytes inform him that the workers in one of his department stores have hung up a dummy with his face during their protests against their working conditions.

Irritated by his subordinates, who have failed to keep the unions out of his establishments and have not spared him from public mockery, Merrick decides to follow an unlikely plan: To pose as one of his employees and become his own informer. Because he has been secluded in his mansion for years, no one will be able to recognize him. But as soon as he sets foot in his department store, events take their own course. Merrick suffers the same appalling treatment his employees were protesting against. He is constantly humiliated by a sales manager who also takes undue credit for his subordinates' sales. Two female employees pity and befriend him: young Mary Jones (Jean Arthur) and Elizabeth (Spring Byington), a middle-aged shop assistant. Elizabeth takes him for a destitute who has just been fired from his previous job after years of service. They soon bring him to a union meeting and present Merrick as a helpless victim of management.

Merrick's attitude gradually changes. Not because he believes his employees' demands (now his colleagues) are fair but out of friendship. He grows fond of Elizabeth and Mary as he spends time with them. He even begins to like Joe (Robert Cummings), Mary's boyfriend and union leader. At the beginning of the film, Merrick was a miserable and lonely man as his new friends correctly thought of him when they met him. After living with others, vitality and a healthy appetite replace the frail health and lousy temper he had when he lived alone in his mansion.

Yet Merrick remains determined to break the union. He carries around a little notebook in which he compiles his blacklist with the union members' names. Merrick changes his mind when his romance with Elizabeth finally blossoms, and Joe rescues him when the police take the millionaire for a common thief by mistake. After a series of pure screwball comedy acts, Merrick finally takes the workers' side. He sits at the bargaining table as part of the union delegation and overrides every management's proposals by revealing who he is.

Spotswood is made from a very similar mold. The film is set in 1960s Australia, shaken by intense labor conflicts, and is therefore soaked in nostalgia for a better time. The Scrooge-like character is Errol Wallace (Anthony Hopkins), an "efficiency expert" called in by a shoe factory owner. The company was once thriving and active but is now in decline because of "Asian imports", that is, because of globalization.

Wallace, who has just overseen the dismissal of 500 employees at a car company, is underwhelmed by the quiet and unproductive workers at the shoe factory. They are primarily interested in talking about their personal lives, reading the daily newspaper, and competing in toy cars tournaments. The only exception is the ambitious salesman played by a young Russell Crowe. Wallace's first measures aim to reduce the interactions between employees by placing screens between them and organizing lunch shifts. But as the film unfolds, Wallace cannot help taking affection for the workers and learns to see his eventual victims as human beings who deserve a chance rather than a sacking. A key point is his realization that the factory owner is willing to sell all his assets to sustain the business a little longer purely out of appreciation for the people who made him wealthy with their hard work and loyalty during the good times. As in other economic films concerned with similar problems we will be discussing in Chapter Six, the happy ending comes through ingenuity, product diversification, and co-ownership with the workers.

A third variant of the Scrooge's arc occurs when the character has a family. The businessmen played by Nicolas Cage in *The Family Man* (2000) and *Lord of War* (2005) had to choose between confronting the lack of morality in their trade and abandoning their careers or continuing them at the price of losing their family and their humanity.

The Family Man was an update of *It's a Wonderful Life!* (1946). Jack, the carefree and egotistical Wall Street executive played by Cage, personifies capitalism, as one of the characters tells him. He only has time for himself and believes that love is like tax deductions; you file them for three years, and then you throw them into the bin. On Christmas Eve, Jack meets Cash (Don Cheadle), who at first seems to be a robber but reveals himself to be a spirit. Rather than showing Jack the past or the future, Cash transports Jack to an alternative life. The life he would carry if thirteen years earlier Jack had stayed with his college sweetheart Kate (Tea Leoni) rather than leaving her to take an internship in a bank in London.

His new life is full of problems. He is a car tire salesman, and Kate is a non-profit lawyer. They have two kids and look at every penny they spend. His new daughter is the only one who sees who he truly is; she thinks he is an alien who has impersonated his father—a very apt description of how cinema depicts the *homo economicus*: as a non-human creature. Horrified, Jack tries at first to go back to his previous life but eventually learns to appreciate his new predicament. He connects with his children, falls in love with Kate, and takes pride in being very good at his modest job. When his transformation into a human is complete, and Jack goes back to his old self transformed, the audience is left with a question: Why is it that the family life cannot be a bit more like Jack's bachelor life? Why is it that life cannot be a bit easier for everybody, families included?

The final variation of Scrooge's arc is the one where suffering catalyzes the metamorphosis of the *homo economicus*. It can be others' pain, like in the case of the diamond dealer played by Leonardo DiCaprio in *Blood Diamond* or the executive played by Stephen Dorff in *The Debt* (2015). Or it can be their suffering. Some Scrooge-like characters learn to reconsider their life priorities only after becoming the object of revenge one of his victims wants to enact on them. Three good examples are *Drag me to Hell* (2009), *Retribution* (2015), and *Money Monster* (2016), three films in which the economic crisis is little more than an excuse to revisit a type of plot that goes back at least as far as Edgar Allan Poe's *The Raven* (1845).

THE SECRET LIFE OF MONEY

Recent films about money such as *The Big Short*, *Money Monster*, or *The Laundromat* conjecture that the new forms of credit and currency have detached those who operate with them from the consequences of their transactions, thus creating new Scrooges. This idea vertebrates the mosaic of stories in *The Laundromat*, the satirical adaptation by director Steven Soderbergh and screenwriter Scott Burns of the dense non-fiction book *Secrecy World* (2017) by Pulitzer-winning journalist Jack Bernstein about the Panama Papers; the leak of 11.5 million documents about 200,000 offshore companies from the law firm Mossack and Fonseca by an anonymous source. *The Laundromat* can also be watched as an apocryphal adaptation of Gabriel Zucman's *The Hidden Wealth of Nations* (2013). Both books deal with the same subject: the massive tax evasion and money laundering that criminals and billionaires all over the world carry out in tax havens through shell companies, aided by high-profile law firms and banks.

After the prologue we already discussed at the beginning of this chapter, *The Laundromat* deals with the misadventures of a retired woman named Ellen Martin, played by Meryl Streep. She loses her husband in the Lake George tragedy, a boating accident in which 21 older people died. That is the beginning of her tribulations as she seeks to be adequately compensated by the boat operator. The insurance that the company has taken remains unresponsive because it belongs to a shell company, which belongs to another shell company based in a tax haven. Ellen discovers that no one is responsible for the insurance payment as she peeks into the complex and bizarre global network of shell companies.

At that point, the film plays with our expectations as an audience because one of Steven Soderbergh's big hits was Erin Brockovich (2000), the real story of a woman of great courage who took legal action against a multinational polluter. It seems that *The Laundromat* will do precisely that and will tell us how Ellen Martin carried out a similar crusade against Mossack and Fonseca. But the film follows an anthology structure instead, using a series of independent but subtly interconnected globe-trotting episodes featuring a variety of characters, from high-ranking members of the Chinese communist party to an African millionaire with family problems. *The Laundromat* is a Russian doll that seeks to create a fresco of global tax avoidance by emulating its very structure, a web of shell companies in which one is within another. All this whilst Mossack and Fonseca act as a Greek chorus and break the fourth wall in the intermissions to deliver very didactic lectures on international finance and economics.

The message of the film is quite apparent, and neither Burns nor Soderbergh try to hide it: the criminals and millionaires of the world have at their disposal potent financial mechanisms to dodge taxes. Their behavior has very tangible repercussions. Lower tax revenues are collected, leading to worse public services and infrastructures, worse roads and fire protection, worse education, and healthcare. Another consequence, as demonstrated by Helen's case, is that when something goes wrong, these companies are not accountable to anyone. They are not a democratically elected government that can be voted out. They are just a web of empty shells behind which there is ultimately a ghost, no one.

References

Boozer, J. (2002). *Career movies*. University of Texas Press.
Broadberry, S., Campbell, B. M., Klein, A., Overton, M., & Van Leeuwen, B. (2015). *British economic growth, 1270–1870*. Cambridge University Press.
Karl, A. G. (2008). Goldfinger's gold standard: Negotiating the economic nation in mid-twentieth century Britain. *International Journal of Cultural Studies, 11*, 177–192.
Kiyotaki, N., & Moore, J. (2002). Evil is the root of all money. *American Economic Review, Papers and Proceedings, 92*(2), 62–66.
Lindert, P. H. (1986). Unequal english wealth since 1670. *The Journal of Political Economy, 94*(6), pp. 1127–1162.

CHAPTER 4

Brokers, Bankers, and Boiler Rooms

Money inevitably leads us to finance, the backdrop of many economic films but ironically a small part of economics as a discipline. However, it must be acknowledged that financial markets have been a very fertile ground for plots of intrigue and suspense. The stock market often appears in cinema as a capricious god that can instantly make anyone rich or bankrupt. Films such as *Pi*, *The Bank* (2001), or *Limitless* (2010) represented financial markets as an arcane universe whose incomprehensible rules can be decoded only by mathematical geniuses. In contrast, the trading floor, filled with swarms of brokers frantically buying and selling stocks, is very cinematic. Films as early as *L'Argent* or *The Toast of New York* (1937), the biopic of notorious Jim Fisk, one of Wall Street's first robber barons, show the stock market as a human spectacle. In these films, "the stock market is nothing but a giant casino", as the protagonist of *Rogue Trader* puts it; winning and losing millions is just a matter of luck, and traders risk it all by doubling down on their investments. A casino populated by men of dubious morality willing to do anything to make a profit; scammers, tricksters, snake oil salesmen always ready to take advantage of the greedy or the unwary.

A Tricksters' Game

In 1959, George Goodman, a Harvard-educated American author and economics commentator known by the pseudonym "Adam Smith", wrote a searing and satirical novel entitled *The Wheeler Dealers*. A "wheeler-dealer" is an informal term used to refer to people who scheme to gain financial or political advantage in unethical or borderline illegal ways. Goodman would collaborate with Ira Wallach on the film adaptation of his novel, which followed the canonical path of the romantic comedies starring Rock Hudson and Doris Day.

The male protagonist is Henry Tyroon (James Garner at the height of his popularity), a speculator whose latest oil deal is about to ruin him; an eventuality that, as his accountant warns him, "a rich man like you can't afford". Henry is from Boston and graduated at Yale but fakes a Texan accent to appear as a naive and simple-minded millionaire. His main trade is to buy things—companies, taxis, restaurants, works of art—that he cannot afford, using a typical middleman's trick, simultaneous buying, and selling, which allows him to make a profit without using his capital. Henry designs his plans to avoid any tax obligations. As he admits when he is asked about his business failures, "I find a way for the government to take three-quarters of the loss". Henry travels to New York to convince a group of unsuspecting investors to bail him out. There he meets Molly Thatcher (Lee Remick), a securities analyst whose moronic but spiteful boss has just tasked her with an impossible mission: She has thirty days to sell the shares of a company, Universal Widgets, which has not declared a single sale since the turn of the century.

Henry sets out to seduce Molly by helping her to sell these assets and make some money along the way. He designs a perfect project on paper. It has no underlying fundamental, but the fake Texan just needs enough investors to fall for it. Henry creates the illusion that the "widgets" the company sells—the audience never knows what they are—are bullish and that Universal Widgets is the most promising stock on the market. It is a textbook definition of the animal spirits that, according to Keynes, govern the stock market. Henry tells Molly, "I know that the stock market is money and emotion. I know that the stock market is people [...] People need a reason to buy. The beauty of it is that that reason doesn't have to make sense!".

In the same way Rock Hudson's character in *Lover Come Back* (1961) creates a campaign for a non-existent product, Henry hires an advertising firm to publicize the widgets. He also moves one of his oil rigs to the company's headquarters to pretend some action is going on. Universal Widgets shares sell like hot cakes, even though no one knows what they are buying.

Ambition and deceit are also the key ingredients of *Trading Places* (1983). Directed by John Landis, this is probably the film that best describes the workings of financial markets. This caustic and cynical rendition of Mark Twain's classic *The Prince and the Pauper* (1881) starts with Louis Winthrope III (Dan Akroyd), a successful Philadelphia stockbroker educated in the best schools. He lives in a lavish mansion and is about to marry his beautiful fiancée. His future is bright. But his bosses, the tycoon brothers Randolph and Mortimer Duke (Ralph Bellamy and Don Ameche), decide to take all away from him. To settle an argument over whether nature or nurture determine people's lives, they make a bet on what would happen if they took Louis' job, girlfriend, and mansion. That day, the Dukes also rescue a street hustler named Billy Ray Valentine (Eddie Murphy), falsely accused of having mugged Louis. They give him everything their old employee, now destitute, owned and raise him to become a successful commodities broker.

After a series of ups and downs, Louis and Billy Ray learn that the Dukes have played with them. They team up with a prostitute with a heart of gold (Jamie Lee Curtis, reduced to a mere showpiece) to drive the brothers to bankruptcy and get rich in the process. Their plan involves trading in financial futures and manipulating the market for frozen concentrated orange juice. This product is traded in real stock markets, as crazy as it may sound.

In one great scene, the Duke brothers masterfully explain how commodity futures markets work. They meet Billy Ray over breakfast and teach him that they do not trade in physical commodities like bacon or orange juice. They deal in contracts, promises to sell or buy a specific commodity at a specific time at a price fixed in advance. These promises are nothing but bets on whether the product's price will go up or down. Billy Ray quickly understands how the market works, to the point of advising the Dukes not to buy pork futures because Christmas is round the corner and the brokers who have taken those futures will be anxious to get rid of them, make some money and buy presents for their families. As the supply of futures will increase then, the price of pork will fall. The Dukes can make a lot of money if they wait.

Louis and Billy Ray discover that the Dukes have bribed an official to obtain a copy of a government report on the orange crop that will give them inside information on the movements of the frozen juice concentrate market. The pair manage to steal the report before it reaches the Duke brothers. The forecast says that the orange crop will be good. That means the price of frozen juice will drop once the information is made public. Louis and Bill Ray replace the actual report with a fake one that says that the harvest has been bad. When the Dukes read it, they believe that the price of juice will rise and instruct their brokers to buy as many futures as they can regardless of the cost. In other words, they commit to buying liters and liters of frozen juice in a few months because they believe they will be able to sell it even more expensively when the report comes out. It might seem surprising but trading commodity futures on inside information obtained from the government was not illegal when *Trading Places* was released. It has been illegal only since 2010 when a special provision of the Dodd-Frank financial regulation law passed. In yet another example of how film influences economics, that provision is known among brokers as the Eddie Murphy Rule.

The stock market opens, and the Duke brothers begin to corner the market. Realizing this, other brokers start thinking that the brothers know something they do not and buy in a frenzy. The price goes up and up. Then Louis shouts, "I sell on April 30th at 1.42!" which means that he is offering a contract promising to sell juice in April at \$1.42 per unit. As all the other traders believe that the price in April will be even higher, the contracts fly out of their hands. That's when the Secretary of Agriculture appears on TV and reads the crop report. It has been good; there will be no shortage. The price of orange juice takes a nose-dive. Until a minute ago, traders were buying as much as they could. Now they need to sell if they don't want to lose their shirts. The price falls. When it reaches 29 cents a unit, Louis and Billy Ray agree to buy orange juice in April at that price. They bought at a low price and will sell at a high one. They are millionaires. The Dukes, who made the opposite bet, are entirely ruined.

Despite its accurate description of the stock market, *Trading Places* remains fascinated by its allure; Louis describes it as "the center of pure capitalism". Like many other films of its era, *Trading Places* depicts the stock market as a place governed by luck rather than a place where investors try to diversify risk, and the real economy is financed. Instead, it seems that skill and talent only matter if they help you cheat the system. The Dukes try to get rich(er) by stealing the government's report; Louis and Billy Ray succeed because they snatch it from them. It is also a world of fakery where no one is what they seem: Billy Ray is not disabled as he pretends to be at the beginning of the film, and the rich are not that smart. Even the Dukes are not infallible.

The film does not forget about economic inequality, though. The opening credits consist of a montage of scenes that take us from Louis' elegant mansion as he is woken up by his butler and has breakfast in bed, to the impoverished neighborhoods of Philadelphia, full of homeless people sleeping on the streets. It is no coincidence that the film was released at the height of Reaganism, a period which kick-started the rapid rise of inequality that continues unabated today.

A Giant Casino

Just three years after *Trading Places* was released, Margaret Thatcher deregulated the City of London, Europe's largest agglomeration of banks and financial services, abolishing the separation between commercial banks and stock market investors. Until then, banking in the United Kingdom had been a family business. Its managers belonged to the country's elites. The figure of the old patrician banker was replaced by that of a young, hungry broker, often of humble origin, interested only in making money.

Finance is an opaque orb that only a few understand. In cinema, the natural consequences of that unintelligibility are fraud and deceit. The stock market allows unscrupulous men, like the protagonists of *Dealers* (1989), *Rogue Trader*, *Owning Mahowny* (2003), *Boiler Room* (2000), and *The Wolf of Wall Street*, to get rich by masterminding large-scale swindles. These films on financial fraud are a variation of the caper genre, and their clockwork heists in the style of *The Sting* (1973) or *Ocean's Eleven* (2001). Finance offers an appealing backdrop for these criminal masterplans because everybody understands that everyone is trying to swindle everybody all the time in the stock market.

Nick Leeson was one of these amoral men, played by Ewan McGregor in *Rogue Trader*. Like many other young people of the 1980s, Leeson wanted to be rich and famous. He longed for the maelstrom of the trading floor. His bosses at the distinguished Barings Bank, one of the oldest in England with the Royals among its clients, would not allow him to do so. Barings was not very well managed, but Leeson was good at fixing the accounting books and managed to gain his superiors' trust. After helping the bank collect huge debts in Indonesia, Barings sent him to Singapore, one of the "Asian tigers". There, Leeson could finally trade on the futures market; he could finally trade on the stock exchange.

When he arrived in Singapore, he found an inexperienced team. A perfect excuse in the film for a good old infodump about how financial instruments work: Leeson and his team buy and sell options on assets at a future date at an agreed price. These futures do not involve physical commodities like the orange juice futures in *Trading Places*, but something completely intangible: the Nikkei index of the Tokyo stock exchange. Leeson's job was basically to bet on whether the index would go up or down.

Rogue Trader is based on Leeson's memoirs and therefore tends to exonerate him from what happens next. The film portrays him as a very charismatic individual who got into a colossal mess only because he wanted to protect others. That is why he opens his infamous 88,888 account to cover up the losses of one of his subordinates who has made a serious mistake in a transaction. But the real Nick Leeson was a narcissist with an incredible ability to deceive and manipulate others. Leeson deceived his bosses on the pretext that he needed funds for new client trades. In reality, that money was to meet the payments he had to make to the Singapore stock exchange to cover his bet on assets. The lie became bigger and bigger. When the 88,888 account was already 10 million in the red, Leeson doubled down. He bought even more futures under his current position in the hope that the market would turn around and he could recover all his losses. As we hear him say in voice-over, "when you double, you end up winning sooner or later". And so it happened. He was lucky and made millions, but he also lost whatever caution he had left.

Leeson goes on to operate with Barings' own money. He conceals the losses in the 88,888 account after altering the software to remain undetected. Meanwhile, Leeson asks for more cash injections to finance his ruinous operations. He is known as the King of Singapore, but the rogue trader has become the loser he never wanted to be. Leeson is now tens of millions of pounds in the red. When the Kobe earthquake sinks the Nikkei index, Leeson makes an insane decision: he uses the Barings' money to prop up the market by betting astronomical sums on the index rising. It is all or nothing. Of course, the gamble fails. And with it, a commercial bank with 200 years of history declares bankruptcy.

The truth of the matter is that Leeson's superiors at Barings never acted on his recklessness. As Bud Fox's bosses in *Wall Street*, they did not question the young broker while things were going well. Leeson's massive losses went unnoticed to the managers at Barings, who are shown in the film to be inept and rather uninterested in how their business works. *Rogue Trader* overlooks an important factor, though: Leeson's bosses decided to turn a blind eye even though the profits he was making were obviously impossible. They were not interested in where those figures were coming from. They chose to ignore all the red flags and the fakery of the profits their golden boy was reporting. They, too, felt an irresistible attraction to money.

Despite its formidable source material, *Rogue Trader* was caught between the need to explain the complexities of the futures markets and the need to give suspense and excitement to a story whose conclusion was well-known by the audience. The film is saved by Evan McGregor's performance, making us care for Leeson. McGregor had just made an international name for himself with *Trainspotting* (1996). His Nick Leeson can be seen as a continuation of the heroin-addicted Rent Boy he played in Danny Boyle's film: Leeson is addicted to the rush of the trading floor rather than to that of heroin. It would seem that when Rent Boy decided to "choose life" at the end of *Trainspotting*, he chose to become Nick Leeson.

Trades with Wolves

Addiction is also one of the central topics of *The Wolf of Wall Street*. Throughout his long career, director Martin Scorsese has been drawn to excessive anti-heroes. People who have fallen from grace and are vulnerable to addiction: the protagonists of *Taxi Driver* (1976), *Goodfellas* (1990) or *Bringing Out the Dead* (1999), fictional reflections of his own tormented biography, and successful people like Howard Hughes in *The Aviator* (2004), who harbored a self-destructive and asocial side. Scorsese's approach to these figures has always been one of understanding and empathy because he believes that these ways of being are a fundamental part of our society. That is why the Italian American director often uses voice-over narration by the protagonists, who guide us in the exploration of worlds where the concepts of right and wrong, of the repulsive and the attractive, are blurred and intermingled.

It was only natural that Scorsese teamed up with screenwriter Terence Winter, who worked as a stock market analyst in his youth, to bring that conviction of his to the world of finance. *The Wolf of Wall Street* adapts the autobiography of Jordan Belfort, an unscrupulous broker who ran an illegal and lucrative financial operation during the 1980s and 1990s. Through Stratton Oakmont, Belfort became a millionaire by selling penny stocks and manipulating the stock market until he was caught and sentenced to 22 years in prison for fraud and money laundering.

Belfort, played by Leonardo DiCaprio, started working at the prestigious Rothschild investment bank. When it fell after the Black Monday of 1987, he found Stratton Oakmont. This investment brokerage firm employed a "pump and dump" strategy to defraud millions of dollars from any unwary person his salespeople came across using their undeniably effective methods. We will come back to this type of scheme very soon.

As a result, the twenty-something Belfort and his crew lived permanently on the road of excess. Parties, sex, and drugs. Like *Goodfellas* or *Casino* (1995), *The Wolf of Wall Street* film becomes a dizzying, hyperactive, three-hour-long journey toward the collapse of a central character who takes his ambitions and addictions to their ultimate consequences. The film does not aspire to be a moral parable like *Wall Street*; it does not want to set itself up as a cautionary tale against unbridled capitalism. Rather, its purpose is to recreate a world where it is acceptable to lie and take advantage of others. As it is typical of Scorsese, that recreation also harbors a seed of sincere fascination toward a bunch of amoral characters.

When *The Wolf of Wall Street* hit the screens in 2013, comments about its relevance in the wake of the 2007–2008 financial crisis were inevitable. Scorsese himself claimed that the Belfort story and the style he chose to tell it were a way of making audiences question how Wall Street works. But the rise and fall of Stratton Oakmont had little to do with the dynamics that brought the financial system to the brink of collapse in 2008. Scorsese shows a complete disinterest in portraying the machinations of its protagonist. At one point, Leonardo DiCaprio's voice-over begins to describe the details of his activities only to stop shortly after that: addressing the audience, he states that what really matters is that the operation was illegal, not how it was done. This minimizes the bite of *The Wolf of Wall Street* as a satire of the day-to-day operations in Wall Street. As a result, the film is closer to *Pain and Gain* (2013) than to *Margin Call*. The reason is that a director as telluric as Scorsese probably finds it easier to depict the addiction, excesses, and greed of Belfort—little more than a salesman—rather than the complex operations of opaque financial institutions with hedge funds or collateralized debt obligations.

Perhaps the most appealing aspect of *The Wolf of Wall Street* as an economic fable is its exploration of the motives that might lead someone to invest their savings just because someone calls them on the phone offering insider information. Belfort's salesmen know how to exploit the stock market's popular image as an inner circle, as an esoteric realm where insider information is traded constantly and can only be accessed if you are an insider. Even so, it is not clear why, with the deluge of information available, anyone would be willing to entrust someone else with their money without investigating what is on offer. The answer can be found in the last scene of the film, where a Belfort-turned-lecturer teaches the art of selling to a devoted audience. Scorsese chooses to focus the final shot on that audience.

Every successful scam is based on the victim's greed, on their desire to make a quick buck. We have all received an email or seen a pop-up window in our browsers promising a too-good-to-be-true investment, based on some secret method or piece of information which is supposed to make us millions. These fraudulent forms of tele sales, which until the late 1990s operated by telephone and these days on the internet, are very old scams designed to take advantage of our greed. They come from the most sordid corners of the financial world, corners that looked very glossy in *The Wolf of Wall Street* but that were more realistically portrayed in *Boiler Room*.

The main character is the young Seth Davis (Giovanni Ribisi), who has just dropped out of college. All his life, Seth has wanted only two things: to become a millionaire and to earn his father's respect. On the first front, Seth is on the right track: he runs a small-time illegal casino in his basement where he fleeces posh college kids. On the second front, he is not doing too well: his father, an unsympathetic federal judge, disapproves of his life and activities.

To reconcile his two life goals, Seth joins JT Marlin, a seemingly legitimate second-tier brokerage firm in Long Island, a far cry from Wall Street. At first, all goes well. He learns quickly, rises through the ranks, and starts dating Abby (Nia Long), the firm's tough secretary who has to put up with abusive comments every day because she is an African American woman. But Seth is pretty smart—or so we are told—and he soon smells that something is rotten in Long Island: The commissions that the salesmen and brokers get for their sales are very high, too high, and the investments he recommends to his unsuspecting clients, usually family men, are all ruinous.

Seth does not yet know that JT Marlin is, like Jordan Belfort's Stratton Oakmont, a boiler room. A fraudulent investment firm that does business in small, dank spaces filled with desks and telephones where "brokers", usually unlicensed salesmen, make hundreds of calls in a single day. "No" is not in their vocabulary, and the only way to get rid of them is to hang up the phone immediately. Their hyper-aggressive style alternates between seduction, manipulation, and intimidation to get the unwary to invest in shares in a company that, according to the insider information the salesman claims to have, will go through the roof. The problem is that these shares are worthless. They belong to small, unlisted companies that no one has ever heard of but which, and this is the trick, Seth's bosses have bought in large volumes and rock-bottom prices. The brokers create an artificial demand that drives up the price of these otherwise worthless "penny stocks". When it has risen enough, the boiler room owners dump these assets and pocket the huge difference, leaving the poor unsuspecting investors without a penny. This is known as the "pump and dump" strategy.

The resulting huge profits pay for the hefty commissions that intrigue Seth so much. These attract more sellers, turning the firm's business model into something similar to a pyramid scheme. When the authorities get suspicious, companies like JT Marlin or Stratton Oakmont moved their operations to another equally derelict and dilapidated boiler room.

Boiler Room does not hide the heavy influence *Wall Street* exerts on it. Like Martin Sheen in Oliver Stone's film, Seth's father is the film's ethical pole, the force that constantly demands Seth to redeem himself. The relationship between them is the film's moralizing vector and by far its weakest point. The FBI also makes an appearance, but only in the final act to show that "crime never pays". *Boiler Room* also shows that film is not just a text; it influences culture and thus economic practices (Hunter, 2003). The brokers of JT Marlin have learnt how to do business by watching films. They are told to follow the "ABC" strategy from *Glengarry Glen Ross* (1992). The sellers memorize and recite the dialogues of Gordon Gekko in *Wall Street* as if they were amateur drug dealers learning the lines of Tony Montana in *Scarface* (1983) or small-time mobsters quoting *The Godfather* (1972).

Boiler Room director Ben Younger, who also writes the screenplay, worked for a time in a boiler room and interviewed similar intermediaries. That is why, in addition to exploring the fraudulent side of finance, the film makes a fascinating portrait of its fauna. JT Marlin's stockbrokers are competitive in every facet of their lives. They are violent, racist, and sexist. They will take on anyone and fight anyone who dares to stand up to them. The economic environment is transformed into a cultural climate: extreme competition in the marketplace leads them to constantly look for a way to outdo others, to prove that they are the best, the ones who sell the most, flirt the most, punch the hardest, and buy the best cars and the best houses, going into debt if necessary. There is a false sense of camaraderie among them that is based on greed and self-centeredness. These men live and breathe for money; they do not intend to have genuine relationships. They follow the mandate of their beloved Gordon Gekko: "if you want a friend, get a dog".

Selling the Intangible

In the first act of *The Wolf of Wall Street*, Jordan Belfort meets stockbroker Mark Hanna (a towering Matthew McConaughey), who buys him lunch at an exclusive restaurant overlooking the skyscrapers of Manhattan. Between vodka martinis and shots of cocaine, Hanna teaches Belfort how Wall Street works: "The number one rule of Wall Street: nobody knows if the stock is going to go up, down, sideways or in circles, least of all the brokers". He also confesses his view of the business: it is not about benefiting the clients; it is about taking their money. "We don't create shit, we don't build shit", he says. With this, Scorsese and Winter address explicitly, albeit briefly, a central idea that was also at the heart of *Rogue Trader*, as exemplified by the moment Leeson explains to his team of investors, "we don't buy or sell anything real; it's just numbers". Recall also the moment in *Pretty Woman* when Richard Gere's character admits that "we don't do anything; we don't build anything".

That central idea is that the modern economy has moved away from the tangible. That is a Copernican shift. When Louis and Billy Valentine trade with orange juice futures in Trading Places, they do not have the slightest intention to consume that product or facilitate its consumption. No orange juice is physically traded. The Nikkei index Nick Leeson gambled with and the money he transferred from one account to another were also an abstraction. The penny stocks Jordan Belfort traded with and the bubbles he feeds were unsubstantiated. All these transactions are air, a fantasy. They created wealth as quickly as it vanished. Rogue traders report profits that do not exist, generated by fake clients. Figures on a screen belonging to accounts and companies no one has heard about and who may or may not exist.

These films represent that fundamental change in financial markets toward the imaginary, toward the metaphor, from the thing itself to the word that represents it. The basis of financial and banking systems is the metaphor, the idea that a concept is represented by a different one. The character of Mossack describes financial instruments in *The Laundromat* as "Words. Invisible. Abstract". With this step toward the intangible, a gap opens up between what is being sold and the people affected by each financial operation. These films argue that the shift toward the abstract and the intangible removes those who operate in financial markets from the consequences of their actions, inevitably distorting their moral compass.

The activities of these traders from fiction are not only amoral. Recent films about finance emphasize that they are also worthless and socially wasteful. They do not create any real wealth. A recent movie highlighting this idea is *The Hummingbird Project* (2018) a very apt approximation to the world of High-Frequency Trading. This is a trading method that employs powerful communication methods to take advantage of infinitesimal differences in prices of assets across the globe. Vincent Zaleski (Jesse Eisenberg) is an ambitious and hyper-focused young man who has an idea that can make him millions: to build a fiberoptic cable in a straight line from Kansas electronic exchange to Wall Street, saving enough milliseconds to get ahead of their rivals. With that, Eisenberg repeated the role of market disruptor he had already played in *The Social Network*.

Zaleski works for Eva Torres (Salma Hayek), who is developing an alternative microwave system that will eventually make fiberoptic obsolete. That gives the film an excellent opportunity to explain what high-frequency trading is, including the response any lay person would give in the words of two potential investors Eva is pitching her ideas to: "Ah, you're just scalpers". As the film progresses and Zaleski's plan goes into shambles, the dichotomy between wasteful economic activities and the "real" economy becomes very clear. This theme is encapsulated by the moment where Zaleski tries to convince the leaders of an Amish community to let him drill through their property. The farmers' hard manual work and their refusal to talk about money contrast with Zaleski's financial hocus pocus and insistence on the idea that everybody has a price.

Maybe involuntarily, *The Hummingbird Project* deals with another implication of the economy's financialization: the misallocation of talent. Zaleski is obviously a very brilliant young man. But because high-frequency financial trading is very lucrative, he chose to use his talent in an activity with a very dubious social return. The character is reminiscent of the brilliant young analyst played by Zachary Quinto in *Margin Call*, a theoretical physicist by training who chose to work in finance, most likely because he had to repay a piling sum of student debt.

The Good, The Bank, and The Needy

Many films have portrayed banks in a negative light. A nameless and abstract bank harasses the honest farmers in *The Grapes of Wrath* (1941), *Country* (1984) and *The River* (1984). In the conspiracy thriller *The International* (2009), the big villain is a shadowy bank that did not hesitate to eliminate anyone who threatened to reveal its nefarious activities. The recent and formulaic *Crypto* (2018) tackled the topic of cryptocurrencies also in the form of a thriller where another bank played the role of the bad guy, one that uses this new form of money to cover up its operations with arms dealers, drug traffickers and ruffians of all sorts.

When banks are not shadowy entities and become personified, cinema has often mistreated them as well. In the Australian film *The Bank*, the evil banker played by Anthony LaPaglia sets the plot in motion when he pushes the protagonist's father to bankruptcy and suicide. His son takes revenge on him years later by employing a devious financial plan based on a wildly inaccurate interpretation of Chaos Theory. In the Spanish/Peruvian/US co-production *The Debt*, Stephen Dorff played a banker who deals in Peruvian government debt securities without caring too much about the fact that his operations will lead hundreds of small landowners to foreclosure. The character goes through the entire Scrooge's arc and eventually comes to understand the suffering that his bank is inflicting upon others.

That said, cinema has also featured bankers from a much more positive perspective. This is the case of two films by Frank Capra, *American Madness* (1932) and *It's a Wonderful Life!*, both set against the backdrop of the banking panics of the Great Depression. Bankers appear in both films as a positive force that helps funding the real economy by providing loans and liquidity to families and entrepreneurs. Nonetheless, negative speculative forces remain a threat, as we will see next.

The Crash of 1929 plunged the United States (and the whole world) into the Great Depression. One in four Americans became unemployed. The country's per capita income fell by a third. After a few years of counterproductive economic measures, Franklin D Roosevelt's election as president brought about a complete change in economic policy. The New Deal produced the most significant expansion of public spending the country had ever experienced, creating a de facto new economic system known as "mixed economy". This mixture of free markets and state interventionism improved the welfare of citizens, restored the country's prosperity, and ended up spreading throughout the world as the spearhead of the Keynesian doctrine, named after the great economist John Maynard Keynes, who argued that aggregate demand is the main propeller of the economy.

The pillars of the New Deal were regulation of product markets, industrial recovery, the improvement of workers' rights, and a reform of the banking system. Thousands of community banks had failed between 1932 and 1933, including healthy, cautious institutions that found themselves unable to repay their depositors in cash when they flocked to recover their savings, afraid of the crisis. *American Madness*, the first collaboration between director Frank Capra and screenwriter Robert Riskin, was released in this turbulent period. The film was pioneering in its depiction of Americans' fear and anxiety during the Great Depression, much more so than William Dieterle's dull melodrama *The Crash* (1932), which focused on the problems of the rich. *American Madness* was also the first in the series of films that would make Capra the ultimate herald of the New Deal and in which he presented his vitalist and benign vision of human nature. This vision linked economic recovery with the restoration of the values of solidarity and integrity championed by America's Founding Fathers.

The main character is Tom Dickson, the quixotic manager of the Union National Bank, played by Walter Huston, who not by chance had played Abraham Lincoln two years earlier in the biopic directed by DW Griffith. The first part of the film introduces us to Dickson, first through the praise of his employees, whom he treats as his equals, and then through the contrast with the bank's rapacious executives, who accuse Dickson of being too lax with his loans. The manager replies that he keeps the reserve deposits required by law but wants the rest to remain in circulation to stimulate the economy. Dickson delivers then a monologue that outlines point by point the arguments used at the time against the austerity policies of then-President Herbert Hoover, arguments that would inspire the New Deal: money must circulate so that the economy expands and must be lent to generate new businesses and prosperity. The opposite, that is, keeping the money in the bank's vaults, is nothing more than unproductive speculation.

Dickson also defends himself by arguing that thanks to his excellent eye for customers, whom he considers his friends, none of his loans has ever been defaulted on. Frank Capra acknowledged that he had based the character on AP Giannini, founder of Bank of America, who famously approved loans based on the applicant's character. Dickson appeals to social capital—empathy, trust—as a way of solving one of the fundamental problems in credit markets: incomplete information about the ability to repay those who apply for loans. The lack of information leads to a problem known as adverse selection: because they do not know the risk of default for each customer, banks must raise their interest rates to protect themselves against that eventuality. This, in turn, weeds out suitable applicants from the market, leaving only the riskiest ones. By knowing its customers well, Dickson can set low-interest rates and widen credit access.

Following this approach, Riskin's script establishes a double threat device that triggers a series of betrayals and misunderstandings that provoke a run on the bank. On the one hand, the executive board is conspiring to take control. On the other hand, the head cashier Cyrill Cluett (Gavin Gordon) is under the thumb of a group of gangsters who demand him access to the bank's vault to repay his mounting gambling debt. Finally, Dickson's wife, hungry for the attention of her altruistic but absent husband, feels flattered by Cluett, who is looking for an alibi for the night of the robbery.

Despite Capra's humanism, the film does not look at the average American with complacency. When the morning after the heist, the telephone operator tells a friend that the bank has been robbed, a chain reaction of rumors sets in motion. Capra masterfully depicts the process of spreading this lack of trust in a dizzying montage in which telephone indiscretions and whispers in bars, streets, and hair salons lead to a bank run. Crowds of depositors flock in front of the bank tellers. The queue reaches the street. Clients who until then had benefited from Dickson's generosity and trust no longer listen to reason. They just want their savings back.

In the end, the bank dodges bankruptcy thanks to solidarity. In the same way, Cluett's betrayal and false rumors brought the bank to the brink of collapse, a countervailing chain of favors and mutual help saves the day: friends, grateful customers, even the bank's directors contribute their deposits to restore public confidence in the institution. The bank run panic ends as quickly as it began. The robbers are apprehended, and Cluett is arrested. The Dicksons reconcile.

Despite its relative obscurity in Capra's filmography, *American Madness* is an engaging film. Its devilish editing and extraordinary narrative pace—which Capra achieved by having the actors speak much faster than was standard at the time—give the film a radical and electric modernity than its sugary descendant, the quintessential Christmas film *It's a Wonderful Life!* lacks.

Just in case the reader has managed to avoid this classic film every Christmas season, here is a brief summary of its plot: The main character, George Bailey (James Stewart), gives up his dreams of traveling the world and stays in Bedford Falls, the idyllic little town where he was born, to run a small community bank inherited from his father. All goes well until Uncle Billy (Thomas Mitchell) loses $8000 on his way to deposit the sum in the bank. The evil and very Dickensian real estate developer Mr. Potter (Lyonel Barrymore) finds the money but does not return it because he knows that the bank will fail without it. George will go to jail, and Potter will finally take over Bedford Falls. Thinking that the only way he can help his family is to pass away, George decides to throw himself off a bridge. But a fledgling angel named Clarence (Henry Travers), keen to earn his wings stops George from jumping. Clarence shows him a vision: how things would have been like in Bedford Falls if George had never been born. What he sees convinces George that it is better to continue living, and he returns home rejoicing to await his impending arrest. He does not know that his wife (Donna Reed) and Uncle Billy have rallied the townspeople and raised the $8000 needed to keep the bank afloat. George is rewarded for sacrificing his dreams for the dreams of others.

In addition to its humanist message, *It's a Wonderful Life!* develops the issues about the nature of banking and the availability of credit that Capra had explored in *American Madness* a decade earlier. In the famous scene in which Bedford Falls' citizens run to the bank to get their deposits back, George shouts, "The money is not here!" to their befuddlement. Banks make a profit by lending out their customers' money. The borrowers pay interest, which enables the bank to pay interest to its depositors (very low nowadays). In other words, banks create money. Their deposits are counted twice: as the bank's debt with its depositors and as the debt of borrowers with the bank. That also means that banks keep very little money in their vaults. They keep a small reserve that they use to cover their day-to-day transactions. This is the minimum cash requirement Thomas Dickson referred to. That reserve is enough as long as the demand for cash on any given day is not too high. But if there is a confidence problem in the bank or the banking system in general, a bank run ensues. The rumor that George's bank may be insolvent sends the citizens of Bedford Falls scurrying to retrieve their deposits, which they believe remain in the bank's safe. George has little choice but to employ his own capital to avoid bankruptcy; he manages to convince his fellow citizens not to take out all their money, only what they need.

When *American Madness* was released in 1932, the Federal Deposit Insurance did not exist yet. It was created by the Roosevelt administration a year later. The numerous banking panics that followed the Crash of 1929 were part of American audiences' daily lives then. In 1946, the year of the premiere of *It's a Wonderful Life!*, American savers knew that they could get their deposits back if there were any trouble, but bank runs were still fresh in the collective memory. Although deposit insurance is still in place today, it did not prevent the 2007–2008 crisis from triggering other panics and queues in front of banks driven to insolvency by overexposure to *subprime* mortgages.

Both films portray very well the disadvantages of what it means to be a "good" bank, namely, a bank that lends money to people who need it but suffer from excessive leverage, that is, a too high a ratio of loans to total deposits. Mr. Potter would prefer the bank to be "bad", in other words, one that is profitable because it supplies credit only at high-interest rates or only to solvent people with temporary liquidity problems.[1] Capra uses the dialectical confrontation between George Bailey and the stingy tycoon during the town meeting to exaggerate the opposition between the moral judgments inherent in these two ways of seeing how banking should be conducted. At one point, Potter asks George, "Are you running a business or a charity?" The choice Capra presents us with is exaggeratedly Manichean because these facets are not mutually exclusive. A bank

---

[1] "The Morality of Banking in It's a Wonderful Life", Bouree Lam and Gillian B White, *The Atlantic*, December 23, 2016. Last accessed March 30, 2021 https://www.theatlantic.com/business/archive/2016/12/its-a-wonderful-life-banking/511592/.

can help people achieve their financial goals and at the same time make a profit.

The film also explores several questions we still face today when debating who should get credit and on what terms. "Why would you give a loan to Ernie Bishop, the taxi driver? You know he's not going to pay it back!" Potter responds to George during their heated argument. Capra presents George as a good man who gives risky loans and forgives unpaid installments. But to be fair, he could also be seen as an irresponsible banker who competes unfairly with Potter by lending money almost for free.

On the other hand, Potter believes that the working class should be thrifty and wonders why people cannot be more disciplined and save money. But the reality is that there are many working-class people in Bedford Falls like Ernie, the taxi driver who cannot afford a house. Without George's bank, he and his family would be living under a bridge. The problem is that housing in Bedford Falls is prohibitively expensive because Mr. Potter has monopolistic control over its real estate market. And that issue should not be fixed by a bank. Not even if James Stewart runs it.

The more recent *The Banker* (2020) also addresses the issue of access to credit, this time from a racial standpoint, and depicts bankers in a similarly positive light. The film tells a little-known passage of American financial history. It is a biopic of Bernard Garrett (Anthony Mackie), a real estate developer who offered housing to African Americans like himself who were struggling to buy a new home. Garrett went later to buy a bank to help African American communities to prosper. He had to do it secretly because, in the early 1960s, Blacks could own a bank. Garrett had to become something of a con artist, as we shall see.

The film opens with Garrett as a boy in his hometown in Texas, shining shoes for a living. The clever boy sets up his little stall next to the town's leading bank. There he overhears the conversations of bankers and tellers without them noticing, learning from them financial concepts such as compound interest and capitalization rates. Something quite remarkable about *The Banker* is that it does not shy away from talking about financial mathematics concepts, making them relatively understandable. Little Garrett soon realizes that he will not be able to fulfill his dreams of greatness in his backward hometown, and as soon as he becomes an adult, he moves with his wife Eunice (Nia Long) to Los Angeles to set up a real estate business. He soon must face new forms of racial discrimination.

The film's central part is set in the mid-1950s and early 1960s. That was the time of the "white flight". Whites moved *en masse* to the suburbs whilst African Americans remained confined to ghettos in the inner cities. The level of racial residential segregation went off the charts. This is the same period in which the play *A Raisin in the Sun* (1959) by Lorraine Hansberry was published, adapted in 1961 as a very interesting film starred by Sydney Poitier. *A Raisin in the Sun* narrates the tribulations of the Younger, an African American family who have just lost their father. The family members are waiting to collect a large life insurance check. They live in Chicago, in a rather dilapidated flat. Among their plans is to move to a better neighborhood, to a suburb with reasonable housing prices but which happens to be all-white. Their future neighbors try to prevent the Youngers from moving by offering them a sum of money. It seems they will not be very welcoming if the Youngers refuse.

This is the context in which *The Banker* is set. Garrett is looking for real estate to buy, renovate and then offer to middle-class African Americans who want to get out of the ghettos. But he has a very hard enough time finding anyone willing to do business with him. Garrett must ally himself with an Irish real estate developer who sees his talent for business. He must be the one closing the deals even if Garrett is the brains behind the operation. He cannot show his face because he is not white.

Garrett later joins forces with Joe Morris (Samuel L Jackson), the savvy and cynical owner of the stylish jazz club The Plantation, impressed by his talent. Together they devise a most ambitious plan: to buy the so-called bankers' building, a building in Los Angeles that at the time served as the headquarters for most of the city's commercial banks. They reckon that is the only way to get the banks to pay attention to them; each time they try to get a new project loan, the banks do not even listen. At that point, *The Banker* becomes a very entertaining heist film. Neither Garrett nor Joe can appear as being in charge of the operation, so they coach a white high school drop-out named Matt (Nicholas Hoult) to pretend to be a wealthy and talented businessman, to act as the public face of their real estate empire. A hilarious montage ensues in which Garrett and Joe teach Matt financial mathematics, how to eat and dress appropriately, and how to play golf; that is, they teach Matt how to navigate white society, which is what they have been doing their entire lives.

Garrett comes up with an even more extravagant plan in the second part of the film. He remains bothered by the lack of access of African Americans to credit. Garrett realizes that only a bank owned by African Americans will give credit to Black communities. In the early 1960s, that was impossible, so Garrett and Joe need to get Matt to help them buy a bank. But not just any bank: Garrett is determined to own his hometown's leading bank.

The social commentary of this part of the film is obvious, but it is also very amusing. Garrett and Joe disguise themselves as chauffeurs and janitors to get into the banks and spy on Matt's meetings without being detected. The white boy is just a front; he does not know much about finance, even less about banks. They have to overhear the conversations—just like Garrett did when he was a shoeshine boy—so that they can later feed lines to Matt with what he has to say. They must dress like a chauffeur and a janitor—later Garrett 's wife disguises as a cleaner—because those were the only ways in which an African American could set foot in a bank at that time.

The plan does not go well because one thing is to buy a building and another thing is to buy a bank. There are too many interests at stake. The authorities come down on them because Matt is too greedy and reckless and because a bank employee soon rats on Garrett and Joe. In addition, they end up caught up in a political dispute over a new bill regulating the banking sector.

The story of the real Bernard Garrett and Joe Morris was more complicated than it appears in the film. *The Banker* opts for a gentle version. Both men wanted to get rich and succeeded. But it is less clear whether breaking down racial segregation barriers was also among their objectives. Thus, *The Banker* makes a questionable portrait of Bernard Garrett as a civil rights champion. It seems as if the film were advocating a less divisive alternative to the frontal civil rights activism depicted in films like *Selma* (2014) or *Loving* (2016): the path of making money.

Despite its problems, *The Banker* illustrates a pervasive phenomenon: the difficulty of ethnic minorities to access credit. Credit markets are imperfect, not only within developed societies but globally. The result is tremendous racial inequalities in wealth; in 2019 United States, a typical white family's net wealth was about ten times that of an African American family.[2]

Reference

Hunter, L. (2003). The celluloid cubicle: Regressive constructions of masculinity in 1990s office movies. *The Journal of American Culture*, 26(1), 71–86.

---

[2] "Examining the Black-white Wealth Gap", The Brookings Institution, *Brookings*, February 27, 2020. Last accessed March 30, 2021 https://www.brookings.edu/blog/up-front/2020/02/27/examining-the-black-white-wealth-gap/.

CHAPTER 5

Evil, Inc.

The villains of films about finance and banking are the product of a ruthless and greedy corporate culture. Corporations are most often portrayed negatively in contemporary cinema, as vast and unethical organizations that do not hesitate to commit crimes to increase their profits if necessary. Backstabbing and clashes of ambitions between employees are also rife, attaining Shakespearian proportions in Akira Kurosawa's *The Bad Sleep Well* (1960) and Aki Kaurismaki's *Hamlet Goes Business* (1987). This leads us to another subject matter that film often associates with economics: the world of business.

In an interesting article on the representation of corporations in Hollywood, Ribstein (2012) wondered why it is so negative. Science fiction has often depicted futures where giant corporations such as Weyland-Yutani, OCP, or the Tyrell Corporation have free reign and rule over dystopian societies like the Detroit in *Robocop* (1987) or Mars in *Total Recall* (1990). The sinister tobacco company that harasses the whistle-blower played by Russell Crowe in *The Insider* (1999), the evil pharmaceutical company of *The Constant Gardener* (2005), or the homicidal U-North in *Michael Clayton* were similarly evil. Ribstein found it ironic that major studios fund this widespread "anti-capitalist" attitude in cinema. He conjectured that filmmakers resent film producers for the latter's attempts to constrain their artistic intentions. Production companies and studios are aware of this resentment but allow directors and screenwriters to

© The Author(s), under exclusive license to Springer Nature
Switzerland AG 2021
S. Sanchez-Pages, *The Representation of Economics in Cinema*,
https://doi.org/10.1007/978-3-030-80181-6_5

"smuggle" their anti-capitalist views as long as they do not harm the box office and because filtering such messages would be too costly. In other words, according to Ribstein (2012), film studios face what we economists call a principal-agent problem.

This is a provocative argument, but one that probably places too much emphasis on film production processes and not enough on the economic and historical context in which films are made. Corporations have not always been portrayed unfavorably in cinema, as this chapter will show.

CORPORATE DRAMAS

If Ribstein's theory were true, one might wonder whether screenwriters and directors in 1950s Hollywood were less constrained by studios than those of later decades. Postwar American cinema had a reverential view of big business. The economic boom during World War II, which eventually brought the United States out of the Great Depression, was driven by massive public spending that helped industries expand. Large corporations played a vital role in this expansion. Driven by a boom in consumption, corporations grew in both size and complexity, becoming heavily bureaucratic and hierarchical. Big business became a haven of opportunity for wealth creation and lucrative careers. The Cold War tensions also helped to close ranks around corporations and contributed to their enormous social legitimacy. Cinema reflected these new social and economic conditions with a marked shift in perspective (Spector, 2008).

In the 1930s and the early 1940s, Hollywood took a critical view of corporate power and influence. Frank Capra's films such as *Mr. Deeds Goes to Town* (1936) and *Meet John Doe* (1941), or John Ford's *The Stagecoach* (1939) offered a view of business and businessmen that today some would call "populist". In these films, evil capitalists are greedy, dishonest, and amoral. Unlike good entrepreneurs, they have a complete disregard for families and communities (Rodriguez-Braun, 2011). In contrast, the corporate fiction of the 1950s glorified big business. Screenwriters across the political spectrum saw corporations as necessary institutions in a modern economy. The huge organizations at the center of *Executive Suite* (1954), *Patterns* (1956), *The Power and the Prize* (1956), and *The Man in the Grey Flannel Suit* (1956) were benevolent entities whose main aim was to serve consumers as best they could. These films offered reassurance to an audience fascinated by corporations but remained concerned about their motivations. Their managers and executives were portrayed as heroes who questioned their aging bosses' methods. The new breed of leaders of these complex and powerful giants was not greedy or amoral but trustworthy men of integrity. They were promoted to their new position on merit and were capable of incredible feats for the companies they worked for and society.

The pioneer of the subgenre was *Executive Suite*, an excellent drama about the struggles for power and vision among the executives of a huge corporation. The film was based on a popular novel by Cameron Hawley, an author key in the 1950s fictions about large companies and financial institutions (Rajski, 2011). Directed by the great Robert Wise, the film soon became canon; its influence would still be felt decades later in *Wall Street* and *The Hudsucker Proxy* (1994).

The president of the Tredway Corporation dies suddenly, and at first, only one of its vice presidents, the racketeering George Caswell (Louis Calhern), knows about it. He takes advantage of this inside information to short Tredway shares so he can cash in when the news hits the stock market and their price plummets. A power vacuum opens up in the company then. The late tycoon had built up the company by personally overseeing and controlling almost all its activities. It is a "one-man corporation", as Caswell mockingly puts it. The company has five vice presidents of equal rank. One of them will be the new president.

As the title suggests, the plot of *Executive Suite* takes place almost entirely within the corporation's headquarters, a huge skyscraper with gothic architecture, stone staircases, and stained-glass windows that make it look like a cathedral. The action unfolds over 24 dizzying hours in which we are presented with a very explicit debate about what should be the primary goal of a corporation. The struggle is divided into two camps. Loren Shaw (Fredric March), Vice President and Financial Controller, leads one. Don Walling (William Holden), Vice President of Design and Development leads the other. Both will try to win the decisive support of Julia Tredway (Barbara Stanwyck), daughter of the company's founder, who years ago committed suicide by throwing himself from the corporate tower.

Loren Shaw is the villain of the film. He is cruel and perspires constantly. But Shaw is no ordinary bad guy. Everything he does is for the good of the company. As he argues in his plea to become chairman of Tredway, a corporation is primarily a financial institution that must provide a profitable and safe investment to its shareholders. The furniture the firm produces and the jobs that it creates are only the means necessary to achieve that end. Shaw thus gives voice to Nobel Laureate Milton Friedman's ideas, who in *Capitalism and Freedom* (1992) argued that corporations should have only one responsibility: to increase their profits and those of their shareholders. Corporations that engage in "social responsibility" open the door to totalitarianism.

Socially responsible is precisely what Don Walling wants Tredway to be. He has joined the power race reluctantly. Walling is more interested in getting his hands dirty with new products and in his happy married life than in the company accounts. Ambition seizes him only after realizing that Shaw is likely to become the new president. Walling hates him for curtailing his innovations to cut costs. But Walling also cares about the workers at Tredway. When he left the factory earlier in the film, a group of them came up to talk to him, worried that the plant would close, and the hard times of the Great Depression would return. Walling, who know many of them by name, spoke to them calmly and reassured them, with an American flag in the background, like a halo that seemed to anoint him as a leader.

After Shaw's plea, Walling argues in a vehement speech that money is not what motivates CEOs or workers to do a good job. It is their pride in making quality products and keeping their company alive. The Tredway Corporation must undertake new business ventures to make its shareholders, employees, and executives proud. This new goal, which will require all vice presidents to work united, seems to offer the perfect alchemy between the pursuit of profit and social responsibility. His vision offers a promise of hope and delineates the positive social impact large corporations can have.

Patterns was less idealistic. Broadcast in 1955 as part of the Kraft Television Theatre and adapted into a film a year later, it is a brilliant corporate drama about the power struggles at the top of a giant corporation. It was written by Rod Serling, creator of the legendary series *The Twilight Zone* (1959–1964). In addition to Serling's electrifying screenplay, the film adaptation benefitted from a talented cast that included Van Heflin, who reprised his character of the honest but ambitious executive in *Woman's World* (1954), and Ed Begley as the elderly vice president struggling to survive physically and in his job.

Heflin is Fred Staples, a labor relations engineer who has just been brought to New York from small-town Ohio to take a critical executive position at the giant Ramsey Corporation. Its corridors and offices dazzle and mystify like those of an extravagant palace furnished by Kafka. Staples is unaware that the company's unpleasant but efficient president, Walter Ramsey (Everett Sloane), has hired him to replace his number two, the veteran Bill Briggs (Begley). Bill is an original member of the firm, founded by Ramsey's father, a businessman more level-headed and concerned for his workers than his son is. But Ramsey Jr, through aggressive acquisitions, has taken the company much further than his father ever dreamed. He detests Bill and his humanistic approach to business but cannot fire him because of his seniority. Ramsey plans to humiliate him again and again—in public if possible—until he resigns. However, Staples and Bill become friends.

The Ramsey Corporation is typical of its time. The executives are all white males, often plagued with health problems; Bill, for example, suffers from heart problems and an ulcer. Women take a back seat. Fred's wife is the ideal companion for a rising executive: she knows how to please his husband's bosses and is the perfect hostess. To help Staples, she passes Ramsey the report he wrote jointly with Bill but presents his husband as the sole author. The boss is impressed. Fred dislikes the idea of stabbing his friend in the back and berates his wife for her lack of ethics. But she reminds her husband that he also failed to mention that Bill had contributed to the report when Staple had the chance. Ambition overpowered his husband too.

This is one of the *Patterns*' greatest strengths: nuance. There are no villains. The characters are the product of the social and economic ecosystem they live in. It is not a Frank Capra film. Staples is not a knight without a sword. He is a human being who wants to be honest but is tempted by ambition. Ramsey is a perfect jerk, by his own admission, not "a nice man", but he does what he believes he must do to keep his firm in business within a fiercely competitive market. In one of the many arguments between them, Bill reproaches Ramsey for having laid off 900 workers. The tycoon retorts that restructuring the plant will increase profits and allow the company to hire twice as many workers later on. In a way, Ramsey occupies the thankless role that economists often take in economic policy debates when they advocate seemingly insensitive measures, such as reducing dismissal costs because they increase unemployment. For Ramsey, the problem with Bill's proposals is that they are a hodgepodge of good but ineffective principles. Fred's report impressed him because it turns those good intentions into proposals that could work. That should be the primary goal of economists.

Executive Suite and *Patterns* belong to a subgenre called *grey flannel suit*. The term came from *The Man in the Grey Flannel Suit*, a famous 1955 novel by Sloan Wilson. These fictions portrayed a new social class, distinct from owners and manual workers, who had taken the vows of organizational life. This "organization man", as William Whyte, editor of *Fortune* magazine, called this middle caste of professional managers in an influential essay of 1956, had the high level of human capital large corporations needed to compete successfully in the postwar economy. In return for their service, obedience, and loyalty, these giant companies rewarded these men as faithfully as the Church or the Army had done traditionally with their subordinates.

The hero of the film adaptation of *The Man in the Grey Flannel Suit*, directed in 1956 by Nunnally Johnson, is Tom Rath (Gregory Peck). He is the stereotypical organization man who feels his individuality threatened by the corporate environment. Rath is afraid of becoming one of those bright young men in grey flannel suits running around New York in a frantic parade to nowhere. "It seemed to me that they were pursuing neither ideals nor happiness, but a routine", he says. An expression of the discomfort of the middle class in the new suburbs. Rath discovers that the way to the top of the executive pyramid is fraught with obstacles. Many of them are domestic. His wife and children are disillusioned and complain that Tom does not spend enough time with them. The search for a balance between domestic and corporate commitments is one of the plot's main drivers.

Tom is presented in contrast to the character of his boss Ralph Hopkins (Fredric March), who has paid a high personal price for his success. Hopkins has devoted his life to run his company but has neglected his family. His 18-year-old daughter is about to elope with a middle-aged playboy, and his estranged wife blames him for that. Hopkins tries to justify himself to Rath: "Big business is not made for men like you. A 9-to-5 job, home, family. Without men like me, there would be no big business". Because of these personal issues, Hopkins wants to help Tom reconcile his work and family life. The tycoon's patriarchal role is also apparent in the campaign against mental health problems that he is sponsoring. Hopkins thus represents an entirely unproblematic from capitalism. *The Man in the Grey Flannel Suit* questions the idea that success in the workplace leads to success in life, but it never questions business leaders' morality and benevolence.

A common feature of the corporate films of the 1950s is their stark portrayal of the corporate structure as a demanding and heartless world where men struggle to keep their place and not be swept aside by their rivals. The dangerous fauna that populates the corporate offices and boardrooms of these fictions contrasts with their protagonists. These dynamic and ambitious executives seek power to improve the company and make it more humane. This new type of leader disavows his predecessors and pledge to make the company a more personable and honest place, that is, a place where American values can shine again. William Holden in *Executive Suite*, Gregory Peck in *The Man in the Grey Flannel Suit*, and Robert Taylor in *The Power and the Prize* become the champions of corporate responsibility.

The Power and the Prize deals with the struggles of ambitious men to climb to the top of Amalgamated World Metals. His president, George Salt (Burl Ives), dispatches his top vice president and protégé Cliff Barton (Robert Taylor) to London to acquire a British steel company. Cliff seems unconcerned with the fact that the deal will liquidate the firm. His father, a Presbyterian reverend, is worried about his son's lack of ethics since he joined Amalgamated. Once in London, Cliff's conscience begins to creep in as he cannot help but befriend the owner of the steel company. There, he also meets Miriam Linka (Elisabeth Mueller), a concentration camp survivor, pianist, and widow of a resistance fighter, a complicated and passionate woman. Cliff falls in love with her and neglects his corporate mission. Soon Salt calls to pressure him; if Cliff closes the deal, Amalgamated will be his. Defying Salt to preserve his newly acquired moral principles means jeopardizing his career and his relationship with Miriam once the tycoon threatens to expose her as a prostitute and a communist.

The author of the screenplay of *The Power and the Prize* was Robert Ardrey, a playwright trained as an anthropologist, who told this story of power struggles along the lines he would articulate a few years later in his influential essay *The Territorial Imperative* (1966). For Ardrey, humans are essentially aggressive animals. This evolutionary hunting instinct manifests in the modern world by acquiring businesses, land, and property. George Salt is the ultimate expression of this imperative. He is determined to make every decision for Cliff, including choosing whom he should marry. He wants Cliff to commit himself to the company so that he can then control him.

In the last act of the film, the figure of Amalgamated's owner emerges from behind the curtains. Mr. Eliot (Charles Coburn) is a frail but determined older man who helps Cliff against Salt. He does not do so out of any moral principle but out of self-interest. Eliot believes that Salt is no longer the best person to run the company and that Cliff's personality—honest and faithful to the point of jeopardizing his career—will be beneficial to Amalgamated. In Salt's final monologue after his defeat, he warns Cliff that the corporate cycle will inevitably continue, and that the day will come when someone vanquishes him. Cliff will then find himself defeated, powerless, not knowing what to do with the rest of his life.

Corporate Idiocracies

The transition from the 1950s to the 1960s brought a much more critical sensitivity toward corporations, proving that the real reason why they are viewed positively or negatively in cinema lies most probably in their cultural and economic context. The new social and political climate created by the civil rights movement, the second wave of feminism, and the anti-war movement replaced the reverential view of finance and corporations of the 1950s with a much more critical one. An early example of this new take on business was *The Solid Gold Cadillac* (1956), which showed that the goals of corporate managers often have nothing to do with the welfare of shareholders but rather with their own.

The Solid Gold Cadillac is a gentle satire of corporate ethics or the lack of them. The film adapts a play by Howard Teichmann and George S. Kaufman, the legendary screenwriter and playwright who wrote or directed at least one Broadway play every single year between 1921 and 1958. Abe Burrows wrote the film adaptation. Comedian, composer, singer, and pianist, Burrows would write *How to Succeed in Business Without Really Trying* years later, another satire of the business world—albeit a much more corrosive one; we will get to in a few pages.

The brightest star of the show is Judy Holliday. She plays Laura Partridge, an amateur actress who has inherited ten shares in the multinational International Projects. Laura takes the floor at the shareholders' meeting—until then a mere formality—and irritates the board of directors with her questions; for example, why their salaries are so high and what they do to earn them. Her character is the audience's surrogate. She is an ordinary woman who uses her common sense to dismantle the web of financial and accounting jargon hiding the nefarious activities of the executive board. It's a delight to see an actress so gifted for comedy as Holliday turning the plans of the inept and swindling executives upside down.

The Solid Gold Cadillac is a good illustration of the conflict of interest that underlies any moderately large company: the conflict between ownership and control. A company is owned by its shareholders. These are interested in the dividends they receive for each share they own. But the company is controlled by the executive board, which, as the Nobel Prize-winning economist Oliver Williamson described, has its own objectives: prestige, power, and status. And that is what the very cartoonish managers of International Projects do: raise their salaries, hire their brothers-in-law, indulge themselves with copious amounts of alcohol, and treat their mistresses to jewels and dresses. This portrayal of executives is a caricature, but recent corporate scandals show that this tension between ownership and control of corporations is as topical today as it was in 1956.

Laura continues to appear at shareholder meetings with her uncomfortable and inquisitive questions. Finally, the board does what any good capitalist wanting to silence dissent would do: buy her out. They offer Laura a job to ensure that she does not attend any future meetings: She will deal with the nonexistent queries of other small shareholders. What the executives do not suspect is that Laura will not sit idly. Soon she is in regular correspondence with other shareholders about their daily lives, families, and health.

When the company president's brother-in-law drives the company to the verge of bankruptcy by mistake, the board decides that it is imperative to obtain some government contracts. A romance blooms between Laura and International Projects' only honest executive, Edward McKeever, played by Paul Douglas, who had played a similar role in *Executive Suite*. The board members have noticed that Laura and McKeever are attracted to each other. They expect that, in addition to getting rid of her for a while, Laura will convince him to lobby the government, something McKeever had previously refused to do on ethical grounds.

But instead of convincing McKeever to betray his ethical principles, Laura persuades him to become president of International Projects. Then comes the Frank Capra moment of the film. Before the shareholders' meeting where the board of crooked executives is to be reelected, Laura and McKeever discover that the mail bags stored at the director's office are full of letters from small shareholders who, thanks to Laura kind and caring letters, have trusted her to vote on their behalf. It seems that, for once, decent people will beat dishonest businessmen.

A few years later, *The Apartment* (1960) made a more biting critique of the corporate world. Jack Lemmon's character rises through the company ranks because he supplies his bosses with alcohol and a quiet place where they can take their mistresses to. Unlike the heroic characters in the corporate dramas of the 1950s, he decides to quit the "rat race", a recurring theme in the 1960s culture.

How to Succeed in Business Without Really Trying (1967) would go even further by depicting the corporation as a full-fledged idiocracy in which mediocrity and flattery and not talent and effort are the quickest way to a promotion.

The term "American dream" is relatively recent. James Truslow Adams coined it in his essay *The Epic of America* (1931), in which he reviewed the history of the country and its rise to become a world power. His purpose was to distill the American essence into a single idea. Truslow described "that American dream of a better, richer, happier way for all our citizens regardless of their social rank". It was an eminently egalitarian vision based on strong social mobility, that is, on the real possibility that anyone could climb the social ladder by effort alone, regardless of where they started from. In that sense, the corporations of the 1950s and 1960s were the embodiment of the American dream. They offered a decent salary, an independent lifestyle, and room for social mobility in a country that had never been as egalitarian. In 1956 the number of skilled employees surpassed that of manual workers for the first time. The urban office worker became the epitome of the Golden Age of Capitalism.

From our twenty-first-century perspective, the corporate culture of the mid-twentieth century seems rather odd: it was very hierarchical and followed a strict code of etiquette. Office workers drank, smoked, flirted (and harassed) like there was no tomorrow. This was helped by Robert Propst's "action office", a design of desks and workspaces that encouraged freedom of movement to enhance productivity. In this free and efficient environment, it seemed that with hard work, talent, and determination, even the most modest employee (if he was a man, of course) could rise to the top.

In this triumphalist context, Stephen Mead wrote a fake self-help manual inspired by his own rise from errand boy to corporate executive. That little book was called *How to Succeed in Business Without Really Trying* (1957). It became a best seller. Mead shamelessly satirized rags-to-riches success stories like Benjamin Franklin's *The Way to Wealth* (1758) and the dozens of little novels written by Horatio Alger in the late nineteenth century. These served to cement the American notion that determination and courage can help any young man make his way from the mailroom to the boardroom.

In 1961, Abe Burrows adapted Stephen Mead's satirical manual into a no less satirical Broadway musical. Burrows built a story around the book, the story of Pierrepont Finch; a window-cleaner determined to succeed by following the instructions in *How to Succeed in Business Without Really Trying* to the letter. That is, by being a liar, an opportunist, and a suck-up who takes advantage of his superiors' weaknesses and incompetence. He climbs to become vice president of the company in a matter of days. The musical was a smash hit and ran for 1417 performances before ending in 1965. It won the 1962 Pulitzer Prize for Best Drama and eight Tony Awards, including Best Actor for its star, Robert Morse. Forty years later, Morse would return to corporate fiction as Bertram Cooper, the most eccentric of the partners in Don Draper's advertising agency in *Mad Men* (2007–2015).

Robert Morse would reprise his brilliant performance in *How to Succeed in Business Without Really Trying* in the 1967 film adaptation with choreography by Bob Fosse. As Pierrepont rises through the ranks of World Wide Wickets, he demonstrates that merit and effort, despite the lip-service corporate culture often pays them, matter less than nepotism and flattery. The higher he climbs, the more we see that the company is an idiocracy ruled by mediocre executives fearing a stab in the back and who know less than the lift operator about how their company works.

As seen today, the digs *How to Succeed in Business Without Really Trying* takes at corporate culture hold firm. But it is impossible not to notice the gender relations at the office and the subservient role working women were forced to play. Although the US Congress had passed the Equal Pay Act in 1963 with the hope of abolishing gender differences in pay, there was a yawning gap between the promotions to which men and women could aspire. Sexual harassment was an everyday reality, which the film treats joyfully with the song "A secretary is not a toy", including lines such as "her pad is to write in and not spend the night in". Working women's aspirations in the film are confined to hunting for a good husband. The role of Rosemary (Michele Lee), the romantic heroine, is comparable to that of Pierrepont Finch in terms of her manipulation methods, intended in her case not to succeed in business but to trap a man. In Chapter Seven, we will discuss at length how cinema has represented the role of women in the economy.

Much has changed since the 1960s. Inequality has increased, but social mobility is about the same today as they were then despite social and welfare policies. Only half of 30-year-old Americans earn more than their parents at that age. To make matters worse, who your parents are and how much they earn is more important to young Americans today than it was in the 1960s (Chetty et al., 2017); young Europeans are going the same way. Climbing the social ladder is no longer as easy as when *How to Succeed in Business Without Really Trying* was released. Today Pierrepont Finch would probably have to settle for being a warehouse operator or a telemarketer like the main character of *Sorry to Bother You* (2018).

Corporate Hell

In films set in the corporate world, such as *The Apartment*, *Saving the Tiger*, and *The China Syndrome*, Jack Lemmon played working men faced with moral dilemmas. Lemmon's physique lent itself well to reflect the anguish of choosing between what is best for you and doing what is best for others. But none of these films went to the extreme of *Glengarry Glen Ross* in representing corporate logic as dehumanizing and alienating.

In this splendid and devastating adaptation of David Mamet's original play, Lemmon plays Shelley "The Machine" Levene, a salesman for the real estate company Premier Properties, specializing in selling plots of land in Florida and Hawaii. The company's name evokes a future of luxury to seduce potential clients with the added financial appeal of real estate investments. This type of company, which proliferated in the United States from the 1960s onwards, sold land in swampy, desert locations for more than its real value. For that reason, they used face-to-face sales. They targeted blue-collar workers, immigrants, and retirees, people with aspirations for social advancement and financial security, but without the means to study in detail what they were being offered.

Shelley is desperate to get hold of a stack of index cards with the details of potential dupes willing to buy the overpriced plots the company is selling. His wife is seriously ill, and he cannot afford the medical expenses. Shelley reminds us of Willy Loman in *Death of a Salesman* (1949), but without his pathos. He is just a fool who talks too much. Nobody pays much attention to him. He enters a client's house by putting his foot on the door with the excuse of a fake prize. He calls another from a phone booth and pretends to be in the office by shouting orders to his nonexistent secretary.

Shelley is not the only loser working at Premier Properties. Moss (Ed Harris) is a nasty, unscrupulous grunt. Aaronow (Alan Arkin) is a good albeit dull salesman. The only one with any charisma is Ricky Roma (Al Pacino). He is the best of the four. We see him closing a deal with a customer he meets at a bar counter by seducing him with some subtle homoerotic flirting. The four salesmen despise their reptilian boss Williamson (Kevin Spacey) because he is not a true salesman and got the position thanks to his uncle.

The cocky executive Blake (Alec Baldwin) comes from the head office to motivate the salesmen in the film's best-remembered scene, the one brokers in *Boiler Room* learnt by heart. Blake insists on the "ABC" of sales in his prep talk: Always Be Closing. This imperative to close deals no matter what makes sense when selling plots of land of negligible value to unsuspecting clients. But it contrasts sharply with a more profitable and long-term perspective in which salespeople try to build a good reputation among customers by offering them quality products. The distance between Premier Properties and a scam is only as wide as a prison wall.

Blake also tells the salesmen that they will now work under a prize system. The best one will win a Cadillac El Dorado; the second-best will win a ridiculous set of knives. The other two will be sacked. Only those who stay will get the shiny new client cards. What Blake has implemented in effect is a tournament, an incentive system studied by economists Edward Lazear and Sherwin Rosen (Lazear & Rosen, 1981) in which the distribution of rewards and their value is based on the relative performance of workers. This scheme may be very good for sales, but it makes workers no happier. It establishes a new scale of social comparison between them based on monetary success. As Blake tells Moss before he leaves the office, "I made $970,000 last year. How much'd you make? You see, pal, that's who I am, and you're nothing. Nice guy? I don't give a shit. Good father? Fuck you! Go home and play with your kids".

Tournament theory tells us that salesmen should respond to this new incentive system by increasing their effort to win the prizes and avoid the sack. The four must compete fiercely in this zero-sum game that has been set up between them. But in response to these incentives, each of them reacts in different ways. Roma aims to consolidate his position by making an additional sale. The Cadillac motivates him, but he has little incentive to work harder because he is already the best seller by far. For the other three, things are not so simple. Reaching the top prize is impossible. Salvation hinges on gaining access to the good client cards stored in Williamson's office. Cheating seems the only way. But does the danger of getting caught outweigh the benefits?

For Shelley, there is really no option. He needs to earn more commissions to pay for his wife's medical bills. He knows it will not matter how hard he works. His performance will not improve. More effort is too costly for him. She has no other choice but to help Moss steal the client cards and then sell them to a competitor.

Glengarry Glen Ross is probably the bleakest corporate fiction ever produced. The four salesmen are trapped in a corporate hell with no choice but to act as they do if they want to avoid redundancy. Premier Properties has reduced them to a disposable factor of production. They have no choice but to dehumanize themselves.

In *Disclosure* (1994), Tom Sanders (Michael Douglas) lives in a similar corporate landscape. Digicom, the company he works is a glass-walled prison where everybody can observe everybody else all the time. However, backstabbing and scheming are rife behind doors. Sanders is a nice guy, described by his wife as "the only person I know who sucks up to his subordinates". That saves him at the end from the cabal his bosses have mounted against him. But Tom is not immune to the constant rumors and hypocrisy his colleagues use to undercut each other. The corporate culture at Digicom is one where bosses use fear and second-guessing to keep employees permanently on their toes.

Glengarry Glen Ross and *Disclosure* exemplify the depiction of corporations as inhuman places, as harvesters of souls. These films blame the heartless and authoritarian capitalists who control the means of production for this. But, perhaps involuntarily, these films also question who is really to blame—the companies and their profit motive or the petty, ambitious, and vindictive people who work for them?

Corporate Buffoons

Cinema has also used satire to "expose" the motivations and methods of those at the top of corporations. In *The Apartment* and *How to Succeed in Business Without Really Trying*, senior executives and managers are represented as dotty and incompetent buffoons that take advantage of their position for their own aggrandizement. If they do something right, it is just by chance.

The reaction to the "greed is good" ethos of the 1980s produced some satires along these lines. Among them was *Head Office* (1985), the first feature film produced by HBO, advertised with the slogan "Join the lunatics that run the world's most irrational multinational". This is what Jack (Judge Reinhold) does. He is a recent business graduate and the son of an influential senator. He just got a job at a multinational called INC. Despite his lack of ambition and effort, Jack keeps getting promoted. He soon realizes that the secret of his success is that the company's CEO (Eddie Albert) wants to impress his senator father. INC needs political support to offshore a textile plant from Allensville to South America, where labor is cheaper.

The most interesting part of *Head Office* is that INC is a nuthouse. Big stars show up, play over-the-top characters, and then get devoured by its corporate madness. The executive played by Danny DeVito gets caught up in an insider trading scandal and jumps through the window before the 30-minute mark. Rick Moranis plays a deranged PR executive who spends his day taking phone calls; he even puts his wife on hold when she tries to tell him that his father has died. Jane Seymour is a power-hungry boss who sleeps with any man who can help her climb through the corporate ladder. Even boxing promoter Don King appears in a cameo as an executive. Although *Head Office* fizzles in its second half, it effectively portrays the corporation as a buzzing chaos, a madhouse where blackmailing and backstabbing are rampant.

In *The Hudsucker Proxy* (1994), the Coen Brothers also satirized corporate culture from the perspective of a newcomer rapidly promoted through the ranks. Norville Barnes (Tim Robbins) is a goofy but ambitious dupe who arrives at the city from a small town with a degree in business under his arm. Like most recent graduates, the only job he can hope for is a low-paying one. He gets a position at the mailroom of the Hudsucker Corporation, a rambling cavern reminiscent of the vast and clunky offices of the dystopian *Brazil* (1985). Meanwhile, Mr. Hudsucker, the company's chairman, and major shareholder, inexplicably throws himself from the 44th floor, and his shares are put up for public sale. Terrified that the plebe might take control of the corporation, the managing board led by Sydney J Mussberger (Paul Newman, having a great time playing the villain) agrees to pick an incompetent chairperson to make the value of the company go down. As a result, he will be able to buy late Mr. Hudsucker's shares at a knock-down price. When Norville goes upstairs to deliver a mysterious blue letter to Mussberger, his ineptitude and clumsiness catch the executive's attention. He has found the new chairman.

Predictably, the news that the corporation is in the hands of an inexperienced young man makes the prices of its shares plummet. But the plan does not fool the audacious and outspoken journalist Amy Archer (Jennifer Jason Leigh), who tricks Barnes by posing as a fellow countrywoman in an amusing scene reminiscent of *How to Succeed in Business Without Really Trying*.

Norville is a happy fool. He just wants the board to heed his revolutionary invention, which he pitches to the board with a drawing of a circle and the exclamation "You know... For the children!" It is a hula-hoop. Convinced that it will be the final nail in his coffin, Mussberger and the board give his product the green light. Unexpectedly, it becomes a hit. Hudsucker shares skyrocket, and Mussberger and the board must change their plan.

The Hudsucker Proxy is a hyperpastiche, a collage made of the idealistic films of Frank Capra, the screwball comedies of Howard Hawks and Preston Sturges, and the corporate dramas of the 1950s. The intertextual references are very direct. The voice-over and Norville's suicide attempt on Christmas Eve refer to *It's a Wonderful Life!* while Hudsucker's jump and the chimes of the enormous clock at the corporation's skyscraper are taken from *Executive Suite*. The characters follow the tropes of Hollywood's Golden Age. Norville is a naïve goofball reminiscent of the protagonist of *Mr. Deeds Goes to Town*. The unsympathetic and talkative Amy is a copycat of the female protagonist of *Meet John Doe*.

While the message in *Executive Suite* was clear—men who value only their careers are doomed to an empty life—the Coens had no interest in criticizing the ethics of corporate capitalism. They aimed to create a modern fairy tale set in the corporate culture of the 1950s. Norville Barnes is not George Bailey; he is not trying to help his fellow citizens in the face of abuse by big business. On the contrary, power goes to his head, and he does not prove to be much better than Mussburger; he is not even opposed to approving large-scale redundancies.

Although devoid of any fantasy elements, *The Informant!* shares with *Head Office* and *The Hudsucker Proxy* a view of companies and businesspeople as ultimately absurd and ridiculous. Based on a nonfiction book by journalist Kurt Eichenwald, the film deals with one of the most notorious corporate collusion cases in recent history and with the man who uncovered it.

To clarify, collusion occurs when companies agree to keep their output low or set high prices. Then it is said they have formed a cartel. Even relatively cheap and common commodities can be subject to collusive agreements; recent cartels in the United Kingdom have distorted the prices of barbecue fuel, concrete, or water tanks.[1] But instead of opting for a corporate thriller in the style of *The Insider* or *The Firm* (1993), which *The Informant!* openly laughs at, Steven Soderbergh and screenwriter Scott Z Burns chose to create a comedy that mocked the conventions of the corporate crime genre.

Mark Whitacre (Matt Damon) is a biochemist by training and vice president of Archer Daniels Midland (ADM), a vast agricultural conglomerate and one of the 50 largest corporations in the United States, which appeared thinly veiled as the murderous U-North in *Michael Clayton*. Whitacre investigates some contamination detected in a project he is overseeing involving the synthesis of lysine; an amino acid used as a feed supplement for livestock. He concludes it is a case of industrial sabotage; he has received phone calls from a competitor claiming that a mole has injected a virus into the lysine tanks. The president of ADM brings in the FBI to investigate the case. But when Special Agent Shepard (Scott Bakula) meets Whitacre, he confesses that ADM has been colluding with its competitors for some time. The FBI recruits him as an informant.

In this first half, *The Informant!* explains very well how collusive agreements work. In one of his first meetings with the FBI agents, Whitacre didactically explains that ADM and its cartel partners restrict the quantity they sell to drive up the price of lysine. A later scene in which Whitacre meets with some Japanese competitors illustrates the fundamental tension that exists within any cartel: the fear that one of its members will break the agreement and lower its prices or increase its production to take over the market. These very same tensions were at the heart of the dispute over a bunch of tungsten patents in the backdrop of *Gilda* (1946) and the war between the criminal cartel of the Five Families in *The Godfather*. The discussion with the Japanese focuses on ensuring a minimum of trust

---

[1] "Business cartels: case studies", UK Competition and Markets Authority. Last accessed March 30, 2021, https://www.gov.uk/government/collections/business-cartels-case-studies.

and a fluid exchange of information between the members of the cartel to prevent anyone from cheating and remaining undetected. Whitacre sums up the inverted logic of cartels perfectly: "Consumers are our enemies. Competitors are our friends".

In the second half of the film, Whitacre's narrative appears to be full of disturbing contradictions. *The Informant!* becomes then a mixture between a farce and a psychological drama. From the very beginning, we have been listening to Whitacre's voice-over, a stream of banal and harmless thoughts that includes comments about neckties or how difficult it is to construct words in German. Little by little, this internal monologue reveals that he has lied compulsively. Is Whitacre lying about the existence of a mole? Is ADM really swindling consumers?

The answer to both questions is yes. ADM engages in anti-competitive practices, and Whitacre is a pathological liar. Budging to the pressure of his double life, he confesses that he has been embezzling money from his company by forging cheques. In the hilarious third act of the film, the increasingly perplexed FBI agents gradually realize the extent of their informant's lies. Who would attempt to forge a cheque while working side by side with the FBI? Did Whitacre sabotage the lysine tanks? Did he really expect to be rewarded with the company's presidency if he exposed his bosses? Did he steal 7 million dollars? 9? 11? It is impossible to separate truth from fiction in anything he says. *The Informant!* uses a confused and unreliable narrator to portray the confusing and duplicitous nature of corporate practices. Everything is a farce. ADM's collusion agreement and Whitacre's embezzlement scheme look like practical jokes. All business deals are conducted by executives with ridiculous hairstyles and hideous suits. It is a pity that Soderbergh's experimentation with genres, the soundtrack by the great Marvin Hamlisch (composer of the score for *The Sting*), and the cameos by famous American comedians like Joel McHale, Tony Hale, and Patton Oswalt in deadpan performances did not find more favor with audiences.

CORPORATE IRRESPONSIBILITY

In his provocative analysis, Ribstein (2012) highlights that Hollywood's antibusiness slant makes ultimately no sense because it is not in the self-interest of corporations to harm society. Quoting Adam Smith's famous passage from *The Wealth of Nations*, Ribstein concluded that "there is nothing inherent in the firm as a self-seeking profit-making entity that leads to socially undesirable consequences. [...] Firms have powerful incentives to build reputations as good corporate citizens to encourage people to buy their products, work for them, and trust them in other ways" (Ribstein, 2012, p. 237). Unfortunately, he left out of the picture the very real presence of negative externalities.

In the early 1970s, the existence of a global ecological crisis became evident. In 1972, the Club of Rome published the report *The Limits to Growth*, a warning of the imminent global collapse due to overpopulation, pollution, and depletion of natural resources were supposed to bring soon. This crisis challenged Adam Smith's ideas about the efficiency of markets: If consumers buy what they like and firms seek to maximize profits, the "invisible hand" of the market was supposed to allocate inputs and resources efficiently. This is known as the First Fundamental Theorem of Welfare, proven analytically by Nobel laureates Kenneth Arrow and Gérard Debreu in 1954.

But this theorem was based on several assumptions that are rarely fulfilled in the real world. One of these is the absence of what we economists call externalities, that is, the effects that some production or consumption decisions have on others' welfare. A negative externality is loud music at an evening party, which the guests enjoy, but the neighborhood suffers. Or the air and water pollution resulting from industrial production. The First Fundamental Theorem of Welfare tells us that markets are efficient because they tend to equalize the price of a good or service with the cost incurred in its production. But when the economic activity (making steel, for example) generates externalities (the pollution associated with its output), the private costs of the activity (the cost of producing that steel), and its social costs (the private costs plus the illnesses or environmental deterioration caused by that pollution) no longer equate. In that case, the price mechanism does not work, the market fails, and firms create excessive harm. The most obvious and worrying case of a negative externality is the greenhouse effect caused by the gases released in fossil fuels' burning and as a by-product of many production and consumption processes.

In the context of the 1970s, corporate greed began to be socially perceived as responsible for the environmental crisis. And rightly so. Without proper regulation, companies that generate negative externalities do not internalize the cost they cause to others and pollute more than what is socially desirable. Films such as *The China Syndrome* (1979) and *Silkwood* (1983), which applied the tropes of the 1970s conspiracy cinema to environmental issues, expressed this anxiety very clearly. These films, in turn, created a new template for the representation of businesses in film, a template that still endures. The evil corporations Julia Roberts, John Travolta, and Mark Ruffalo fight against in *The Pelican Brief* (1993), *Civil Action* (1998), *Erin Brockovich,* and *Dark Waters* resort to all kind of illegalities and unethical practices to cover up evidence of their polluting activities. These films are particularly attractive for audiences because they follow the classic narrative of David versus Goliath: An ordinary person (a journalist, a single mother, an employee, a lawyer) against a powerful corporate giant.

Erin Brockovich recounted a real case of pollution by a large corporation, Pacific Gas and Electric. The film was a success, and received several nominations for the Oscars, including Best Picture and Best Actress, which Julia Roberts took home. Although the film's intentions are eminently commercial, director Steven Soderbergh and screenwriter Susannah Grant produced an electrifying movie. Erin Brockovich (Roberts) is a single mother with no formal education and no job prospects. To complicate matters further, she is involved in a car accident and loses the resulting lawsuit. In desperation, she begs Ed Masry (Albert Finney), the grumpy and hard-nosed lawyer who handled her case, to give her a job at his small law firm specializing in personal injury compensation. Reluctantly, Masry agrees to help her because he feels guilty about her situation.

On a routine visit to a client, Erin stumbles across files showing that PG&E has illegally dumped chromium near its plant and then bought the land to cover it up. But the substance has leaked and poisoned the water supply, and residents have been getting seriously ill. After Erin's tireless insistence, Masry agrees to take the case. His small firm becomes involved in one of the largest civil actions in history. Against all odds, Erin and Masry end up winning on behalf of their clients and obtain a landmark settlement of over $300 million, which forced the company to internalize the externalities it was causing to residents. By making it pay for the medical costs its pollution had caused, the private costs of its activities are brought in line with the social costs, and the market failure partially corrects.

The film leaves no doubt about the company's guilt. Erin describes her battle between "right and wrong" as the battle between "David and what's-his-name". Soderbergh uses his technical prowess to reinforce the contrast between the two sides of the conflict. Erin and Masry are always well lit. She has a close, compassionate, almost maternal relationship with the plaintiffs portrayed with a palette of warm tones and soft lighting. The choice of Sheryl Crow for the soundtrack is no accident either. Erin's naivety, authenticity, and frankness contrast with the stern corporate lawyer she negotiates with at the first meeting with PG&E. Her slicked-back hair, furtive gaze, and masculine attire contrast with the colorful wardrobe and cleavage-revealing outfits Julia Roberts wears throughout the film. On the other hand, Ed Masry is nothing like the professional and slightly robotic lawyer John Travolta played in the similarly themed *Civil Action*. He is a rather shabby-looking man, afflicted by a life of illness and constant work, and who hides a heart of gold beneath his bad temper.

Erin Brockovich rather than *Civil Action* was a box-office hit because Erin Brokovich is a working-class heroine rather than a privileged lawyer. Stories of victories over unbending corporate villains have a strong appeal to audiences who want to find hope for their daily struggles. Economic hardships such as Erin's are familiar to a broad spectrum of people and are easy to portray on film, especially if the heroine is an ordinary person pitted against a shadowy, monolithic multinational.

The conflict between the environment and economic activity was also portrayed in a tender but incisive British comedy, *Local Hero* (1983). An executive travels to a small Scottish village where the oil company he works for wants to open a refinery. As he mingles with the quirky locals and soaks up the beautiful scenery, he and the audience come to realize that it makes no sense to destroy the environment for the sake of better economic prospects. *Local Hero* served as a template for other films in which a stressed and ambitious urbanite falls in love with a place of natural beauty. *The Promised Land* is one of them.

Although weighed down by the good intentions of writers and stars Matt Damon and Joe Krasinski and director Gus van Sant, *The Promised Land* contains several ideas that make it very interesting from an economic point of view. Damon plays Steve Butler, the son of an Iowa farmer who works for an energy giant, Global Crosspower Solutions. His job is simple: to convince farmers to lease their rights to exploit the natural gas that lies beneath their plots through the controversial process of fracking. Steve is about to be promoted when he is sent to a decaying town in Pennsylvania. Another easy job, he thinks, given the difficulties of a deindustrialized area in economic decline.

Steve is emotionally invested in his job. As a boy, he saw his hometown and family farm disappear overnight. He still longs for a life in small communities where everyone knows and helps each other. In fact, his background makes him a better salesman because he understands the needs of the farmers; he knows how to talk to them and convince them that the only way to avoid poverty is to accept the money from fracking. "I'm not selling them natural gas, I'm selling them the only way they can get back on their feet", he says. It is refreshing that Steve is portrayed as a good person who believes he is doing the right thing despite being, in essence, a corporate henchman.

His first meeting is with the mayor, who is aware of the dangers of fracking. Here comes the first dilemma: The politician may oppose fracking, but his resistance is futile if all the other towns agree to deal with Global and prosper. He will be thrown out of office and lose the hefty bribe offered by the company if he accepts. "Don't be the last to agree", Steve tells him. The mayor follows the advice and organizes a town meeting to tell his citizens about the project.

The meeting serves to present the pros and cons of a highly controversial form of natural gas extraction that has experienced exponential growth in recent years. Its benefits are mainly threefold. First, natural gas is cleaner than coal and oil. Second, it helps the United States be less reliant on oil-rich but unstable countries; as Steve points out to one of the farmers he visits, "we won't have to go abroad to fight and die for oil anymore". But the main argument in favor of fracking, and indeed the guiding theme of the film, is that the exploitation of this resource can revitalize depressed communities and provide livelihoods for farmers who can now barely survive. More jobs and more tax revenues to fund public projects can resuscitate towns that have been dying since the mining and manufacturing industries closed and relocated. No wonder locals embrace Steve's offer with enthusiasm.

But at the town meeting, Steve runs into retired scientist Frank Yates (Hal Holbrook), whose informed opinions turn the tables. Frank argues that fracking is not a panacea; it has serious risks. It involves pumping water mixed with sand and chemicals at high pressure into deep mineral strata to release the natural gas trapped in them as they break up. This process can contaminate water supplies and fields because some of the fluid used resurfaces, bringing harmful chemicals to plants and livestock.

Economics tells us that citizens must weigh the environmental costs against the benefits of gas drilling and compare the outcome with the value of continuing farming as usual. The irony is that the division of land into many plots means that each small landowner has little incentive to internalize the externality that drilling on his land will cause on their neighbors. This problem would be avoided if there were only one landowner. That is why the town meeting is an important collective action device: An association of owners uniting these dispersed interests facilitates a more efficient outcome.

Frank's arguments postpone the decision to a further vote. Things complicate for Steve when an environmentalist named Dustin Noble (Krasinski) arrives in town and turns popular opinion against Global. Steve does not know how to respond to the tactics of the witty and optimistic Dustin, who wins the propaganda battle. Damon plays the underdog well, and his reaction to so many setbacks endears him to the audience. That is precisely the most interesting nuance of the film. Steve questions fracking, his job, and even himself: is he telling the whole truth? Is he in the right job? Too bad the convoluted last-minute plot twist where Global shows to be another evil corporation portrays him as a moral hero, betraying the complex questions *The Promised Land* had raised.

The most recent example of this subgenre is *Dark Waters*, which recounts a 20-year legal battle between a lawyer and chemical giant DuPont. Based on a 2016 New York Times article entitled "The Lawyer Who Became DuPont's Worst Nightmare", the film is the result of Mark Ruffalo's personal effort to get the project off the ground. Ruffalo is a passionate activist for human rights and environmental protection. Thanks to his status as an international star, the project came to fruition. One more proof that cinema has a much broader reach than academic economists; I am sure that *Dark Waters* has had more impact than all my lectures on negative externalities combined over 20 years of teaching.

Director Todd Haynes had already directed an interesting and disturbing film titled *Safe* (1995), where the character played by Julianne Moore finds out that she has an extreme sensitivity toward everyday chemicals. In the case of *Dark Waters*, the harmful effects of chemical products are not a figment of a troubled mind, nor are they the result of a specific person's hypersensitivity. They are very real and affect us all.

The protagonist of *Dark Waters* is Rob Bilott (Ruffalo), a lawyer who usually defends petrochemical companies but is unexpectedly drawn to the case of a farmer from a town in West Virginia. The farmer shows up at his office and asks for help because his cattle are dying. He blames the nearby DuPont plant. Bilott has mixed feelings. On the one hand, he is from West Virginia and wants to help his fellow countryman. But on the other hand, he knows that DuPont has provided jobs in the area and supported it economically for many years. Still, he travels to the village. There he finds dying cattle with strange tumors, smiling children with blackened teeth, and parents with coughs and a suspicious tendency to die of leukemia. The wintry, desolate landscape, full of dilapidated farms, is depicted by Todd Haynes with a dark color palette that makes it seem ravaged by a color out of space.

Bilott soon discovers that, with the EPA's connivance, DuPont has been poisoning the area's water and the plant's workers for years with a type of chemicals called PFOAs. It's a "forever chemical" that does not degrade. *Dark Waters* tells us that PFOAs are present in almost all nonstick cookware and the bloodstream of 90% of the people on planet Earth.

From there, *Dark Waters* follows the formula of countless legal dramas. It employs all the tricks and twists of these films: a success against DuPont is soon counteracted by another trick the company takes out of its sleeve. The relationship between Bilott and his wife Sarah, played by Anne Hathaway, is also fairly conventional; she is worried to death by her husband's growing obsession with the case. Bilott puts everything at risk, his marriage, job, and even health. This is the point-by-point template of other films on corporate irresponsibility such as *The Insider*, *Michael Clayton,* and especially *Civil Action,* where John Travolta played another lawyer defending a community from an environmental crime.

Despite being formulaic, the case recounted in *Dark Waters* is quite remarkable. DuPont used PFOAs since the 1950s and knew very early on that these chemicals were highly toxic to humans. It was only in 2006, when it lost the case depicted in the film, that the company agreed to phase them out of its production. DuPont is one of the many firms which knew they were causing harm and yet continued doing so. Other examples include the big tobacco companies, who hid for decades the scientific evidence linking cigarettes to cancer, and Exxon and other oil companies who were aware of the greenhouse effects caused by fossil fuels since the late 1970s and yet decided to hide it. Unfortunately, that is a too common strategy when companies produce negative externalities. Their reaction is often to hide the truth and spend a lot of time and money on PR and lobbying. In fictions like *The Pelican Brief*, corporations even go as far as committing murder.

This brings us back to Ribstein's argument: Why do companies generate negative externalities irresponsibly? Is it in the interest of companies to poison their customers and workers?

The first reason why companies may choose to continue behaving in a socially irresponsible manner is apparent: Because the regulation needed to deter them from doing so does not exist, it is insufficient, or it is not enforced. Second, because the financial or reputational damages these companies expect are minor. The evidence suggests that companies do not take long to recover the losses they suffer when environmental violations come to light.[2] Another reason is the so-called "distance bias": A company's reputation does not suffer too much if environmental malfeasances occur far from where its shareholders live. A film like *Dark Waters* has become a feature film because the DuPont case harmed Americans. It is doubtful that we will see stars like Mark Ruffalo or Anne Hathaway starring in a movie about child labor in Nike or Nestlé factories in the Third World or about oil spills in the Red Sea.

Dark Waters most appealing feature is its contrast with other legal dramas that expose corporate or political corruption. Usually, these films have a happy ending that reassures audiences: Justice always prevails. But in this case, we do not get that satisfaction. Sure, DuPont had to pay substantial compensations. But we are left with a sense of deep unease. The "forever chemicals" are in us. We now know about PFOAs, but who knows what other chemicals may be interfering with our bodies, causing all sorts of illnesses. They can be everywhere. We cannot trust markets to operate on their own in the presence of externalities. Companies will not necessarily align their individual decisions with what is best for society. We are left with a feeling of unsolvable paranoia when the end credits of *Dark Waters* roll.

References

Chetty, R., Grusky, D., Hell, M., Hendren, N., Manduca, R., & Narang, J. (2017). The fading American dream: Trends in absolute income mobility since 1940. *Science, 356*(6336), 398–406.

---

[2] "Dark Waters: what DuPont scandal can teach companies about doing the right thing", Koen Heimericks and Irina Surdu, *The Conversation*, February 26, 2020. Last accessed March 30, 2021, https://theconversation.com/dark-waters-what-dupont-scandal-can-teach-companies-about-doing-the-right-thing-132480.

Lazear, E., & Rosen, S. (1981). Rank-order tournaments as optimum labor contracts. *Journal of Political Economy*, *89*(5), 841–864.

Rajski, B. (2011). Corporate fictions: Cameron Hawley and the institutions of post-war capitalism. *Textual Practice*, *25*, 1015–1031.

Ribstein, L. E. (2012). Wall street and vine: Hollywood's view of business. *Managerial and Decision Economics*, *33*, 211–248.

Rodriguez-Braun, C. (2011). Capitalism in six westerns by John Ford. *The Journal of Economic Education*, *42*(2), 181–194.

Spector, B. (2008). The man in the grey flannel suit in the executive suite: American corporate movies in the 1950s. *Journal of Management History*, *14*, 87–104.

CHAPTER 6

Disruptors

In the preceding chapters, we have seen that the typical role of businesspeople or financiers in cinema is that of the villain; greedy, heartless, and corrupt. They are the bad guys in countless corporate thrillers too. They mislead the authorities. They scam or murder their rivals, their employees, and their customers. They spoil the environment and commit all kinds of crimes to make a quick buck at the expense of anyone who dares to cross their path.

In contrast, innovators and entrepreneurs are generally represented in cinema as positive and progressive forces. Inventors and creators are portrayed as heroes because they develop new products or production processes, give consumers what they like, and anticipate what consumers want. Hollywood loves them. Their character arcs are stories of self-improvement and personal achievement against self-doubt or powerful players who seek to suppress these geniuses and steal their ideas. In films about evil businesspeople, these are brought to justice by a noble lawyer or politician. In contrast, innovators on the silver screen suffer unfair indictments brought up by an establishment member. In these films, "government is not the solution to our problems; government is the problem", as Ronald Reagan said during his inaugural speech. This contrasts with the crucial role the public sector had in real-life innovations such as the internet, GPS, or the COVID-19 vaccines.

In real life, entrepreneurial success requires almost complete dedication of mental energy, time, and attention, so the limits between the personal and the professional life tend to disappear. Innovators and market disruptors in film often face insolvable dilemmas between their family or their sanity on the one hand and their grand visions on the other. Creators and entrepreneurs usually must pay the price for achieving their goals, be it love, their family, social ostracism, or their sanity.

RANDIAN INNOVATORS

Alisa Zinovyevna Rosenbaum emigrated from Russia to the United States in 1925. She settled in California and changed her name to Ayn Rand. After she met Cecil B. DeMille by chance, the director got her a job as an extra in *King of Kings* (1927). He later asked Rand to write a screenplay based on a story called "The Skyscraper". Although Rand hated the characters and the plot, the story inspired her to write the novel that would make her famous, *The Fountainhead* (1943). It became a best-seller and was adapted as a film by King Vidor in 1949 with Rand as screenwriter.

The protagonist of *The Fountainhead* is an architect named Howard Roark (Gary Cooper) who refuses to budge an inch in his vision of how architecture should be. Rand uses the character to convey her philosophy, which she called Objectivism, whose central tenet is that humans should free themselves from all forms of political and religious control and guide their lives by self-interest alone. Rand believed that she could "objectively" demonstrate that capitalism is superior to other economic systems such as feudalism or communism because it is based on voluntary exchanges between rational individuals interested only in their own happiness. In the words of Alan Greenspan, chairman of the US Federal Reserve for 20 years, Rand proved that "capitalism is not only efficient and practical but also moral".[1]

Howard Roark—a fictional version of the celebrated architect Frank Lloyd Wright—is a typical Randian hero because he acts on his creative impulses, disregarding others' opinions. Vidor used visual elements such as hydraulic drills, modernist skyscrapers, and Cooper's imposing physique to portray the character's genius and virility. Opposite to him is Peter Keating (Kent Smith), a social parasite always happy to pander

---

[1] "Greenspan, Economist, Is Believer in Laissez-Faire Capitalism", *The New York Times*. July 24, 1974.

to the majoritarian opinion, incapable of an original idea. Between the two men we find Gail Wynand (Raymond Massey), a William Randolph Hearst-inspired populist press magnate who becomes Roark's friend when they discover that they have a lot in common.

We have encountered Randian innovators before. Because the ant colony rewards submission and tradition and discourages individuality and innovation, Flik's fellow ants in *A Bug's Life* consider him an extravagant fool and mock him and his inventions. In Howard Roark's case, his refusal to capitulate to others' tastes scares away any potential clients, and he is forced to work in a quarry to earn a living. When Roark finally persuades some clients to trust his designs, he encounters his nemesis, Ellsworth Toohey (Robert Douglas), an influential columnist who prides himself on defining the masses' aesthetic standards. Toohey successfully conducts a smearing campaign against Roark, who becomes an outcast again.

The Fountainhead aims to tell a fable about the triumph of the individual over the forces of mediocrity and collectivism. Like the Austrian economist Friedrich Hayek, Rand was reacting against the New Deal and the increasing government intervention in the economy during the 1930s, which they both saw as an open door to socialism. Toohey wants to destroy Roark only because he is an unbridled innovator, an individualist who cannot be tamed. Vidor underlines this menacing atmosphere by using expressionistic devices, shadows, and angles reminiscent of *Metropolis* (1927) and the film noir genre (Schleier, 2002). Here, the threat in the shadows is the masses ready to pounce over the individual creator.

In the last act, Keating is commissioned to design a major social housing project, Cortlandt Homes. Unable to complete the job, he asks Roark, once again an outcast, for help. He agrees on the sole condition that his project is not to be altered (the same condition Rand imposed to write the film's screenplay). Predictably, Keating gives in and lets the government impose its stylistic criteria. There is only one solution left for Roark: To blow up Cortlandt.

In Roark's lengthy plea during the trial against him, Rand summarizes her thoughts on the civilizational role of innovators: "The creator requires independence. He neither serves nor rules others. He relates to other men by free exchange and by voluntary choice". Roark argues that he chose architecture not to help others but because he loves it and wants to be the best, even if that means challenging the establishment. "History is full of men who took the first steps on new paths armed with nothing but their own vision", he says. Roark ends up triumphing in the light of day, on top of his new building, a colossus standing tall in the clouds.

Rand was right to point out that the creators of new products or designs accept financial and personal risks and are one of the main drivers of economic progress. But it is also true that any sensible innovator's goal should be to satisfy consumers, not to ignore them as Roark does. Discovering and meeting your potential customers' needs is at the very heart of the market economy. This is what true market disruptors do.

One of them was Preston Tucker, an American entrepreneur who attempted to disrupt the automobile industry in the late 1940s. In *Tucker: The Man and His Dream* (1988), Francis Ford Coppola used this true story to tell another fable about innovation in imperfectly competitive markets. The film opens with some colorful commercials for the Tucker Corporation that sum up the beginnings of Preston Tucker (Jeff Bridges), first in the automobile industry and then working for the military. Tucker produced a high-speed armored car that turned out to be too fast. But its turreted machine gun could be reused in bomber aircrafts. This is how he made his fortune. After the commercials, Tucker promises to put the three big car manufacturers based in Detroit (Ford, Chrysler, and General Motors) out of business in five years. That is his challenge.

Tucker had a vision for a revolutionary car that incorporated innovations commonplace today such as seat belts, disc brakes, safety windscreens, and automatic transmission. But he faced a big problem: the mass production of a car requires a gargantuan up-front investment, access to skilled labor, raw materials, and design talent. So, he has a great idea: He advertises his "car of tomorrow" in a popular magazine to attract the attention of consumers and potential investors. The response is overwhelming. He then meets Abe Karatz (Martin Landau), a cautious capitalist who shares his vision. Tucker specializes in selling cars and Abe in trading stocks. They hire a former Ford executive as president of the new corporation and begin raising capital by selling a car that only exists on paper so far. Tucker manages to lease the country's largest manufacturing space because the government wants to repurpose plants for military production to civilian use.

Director Francis Ford Coppola portrays Tucker as a compulsive optimist, an idealistic visionary with the ability to inspire others even in the hardest of times. But he also reveals his lack of business and financial acumen. Driven by his enthusiasm, Tucker tells the press that the Big Three are not interested in the safety of their vehicles and that "they are guilty of negligence" and "should be charged with manslaughter". The comment backfires on him. Michigan Senator Ferguson (Lloyd Bridges), who functions as Tucker's main antagonist, refuses to help him develop his project.

The film illustrates how market entry barriers serve to eliminate competition and innovation. Companies already operating in an industry use various tactics to scare away new entrants. Some of these barriers are legal. That is the case with patents and advertising. Others are illegal, such as predatory pricing (setting prices below the cost of production that are unaffordable for potential competitors) or industrial espionage, a tactic that his competitors used against Tucker in real life.

One of the most common ways of raising barriers to entry is by capturing the regulator, that is, by influencing lawmakers to pass regulations that prevent new firms' entry. The post-war period was particularly conducive to this form of lobbying as economies were adjusting to peacetime, and governments played an essential role in this process of resource reallocation. In *Tucker: The Man and His Dream*, the anti-competitive forces are personified by Senator Ferguson, who protects the interests of the Detroit automakers. Just as the inventor is on the verge of achieving his dream, the senator prompts the US Securities and Exchange Commission to charge him with financial fraud.

The film's last act deals with the ensuing trial, which Coppola uses to portray the entrepreneur as a visionary embarked on a moral crusade against big government and big business. The Italian American director does not hide his intention to update the films of Frank Capra, *Mr. Smith Goes to Washington* (1939) in particular, although Tucker's final plea is closer to Howard Roark's in *The Fountainhead* than to James Stewart's in Capitol Hill. His speech is a passionate defense of the innovative entrepreneur as an expression of the American dream: "If big business closes the door on small businesses with new ideas, on us, we will not only be closing the door on progress, we will be sabotaging everything we have fought for, everything this country stands for". Thus, the film's thesis is that for new ideas to bloom, it is necessary to prevent the collusion of economic and political power and eliminate all barriers to market entry.

The innovations the real Preston Tucker introduced in his cars were incorporated by major automakers years later, but only under pressure from Japanese competitors, consumers, and regulators. The Big Three argued that introducing seat belts would be tantamount to admitting that their cars were unsafe (Booze, 2002). But the truth is that they did not need to improve their vehicles because they had market power. Their mentality is well described by the Tucker Corporation president when he testifies against Tucker in the trial; he states that Tucker was spending too much money on research and development because "as everyone knows, that is only necessary when there is competition".

Some critics have argued that Coppola probably saw himself reflected in Tucker. In the film, he is presented as a creative force, liberated from the pettiness and short-sightedness of established capitalists. Like filmmakers, entrepreneurs are powerful creators dedicated to noble and artistic endeavors. The difficulties Tucker faces are parallel to the problems Coppola went through to complete the film, a project he began to develop in the early 1970s. He had to postpone it due to the financial difficulties his Zoetrope production company suffered until Coppola found his own visionary capitalist: George Lucas.

Years later, Martin Scorsese felt similarly drawn to Howard Hughes's figure, the aviator and tycoon who disrupted both the aviation and film industries during the 1930s and 1940s. Scorsese saw in Hughes a perfectionist and independent filmmaker like himself who would go to all lengths to achieve his vision.[2] The *Aviator* (2004) recounts the first half of Hughes' life following an almost identical template to *Tucker: The Man and His Dream*.

Faithful to his obsession with complex and tortured characters, Scorsese used the tycoon to explore a trope common in films about innovators: the blurred line between genius and madness. Hughes suffered from mental health problems, but his intelligence and talent allowed him to succeed in anything he set his mind to. He was able to anticipate new technologies and consumer demands. For instance, after Hughes finished directing his first film—*Hell's Angels* (1930)—he reshot it almost completely to add dialogues because he realized that the public no longer wanted silent films. Similarly, he anticipated that travelers would demand more comfortable aircrafts and faster intercontinental travel.

Scorsese portrays Hughes as a pure Randian innovator. He is a perfectionist who keeps remolding his products—films or airplanes—until they fit his expectations, constantly pushing the frontiers of the possible, always unwilling to compromise for a solution inferior to the one he wanted.

---

[2] *The Aviator: A Screenplay by John Logan* (2004). New York: Miramax.

Hughes is depicted as a hero (he even served as a test pilot for his own planes), always ready to take risks and invest all his money in his projects to the brink of bankruptcy. He is at odds with society. Hughes finds himself misunderstood by the public, who disapproves of his eccentricities, and pitted against Hollywood and the aviation industry, who see him as an intruder.

Like *The Fountainhead* and *Tucker: The Man and His Dream*, *The Aviator* ends with a legal confrontation between a heroic creator and the forces of collectivism, represented in this case by Senator Owen Brewster (Alan Alda). The senator is in the pocket of Pan Am's President Juan Trippe, who embodies the entrenched business establishment that can muster the help of the government to maintain its market dominance. Hughes threatened Pan Am's monopoly over transatlantic routes, and Trippe used his influence to make sure things continued that way. During a private lunch, Brewster argues that "one airline can do it better without competition", suggesting that the airline industry is a natural monopoly and that it is socially efficient that only one firm operates in the market to avoid cost duplication. The tycoon prevails because he shows that Brewster is not serving the public interest; he is using government power to serve the interests of Pan Am. To be fair, Hughes' challenge against Pan Am's monopoly was not born out of a desire to increase consumer welfare but his drive to attain his vision of a fast and reliable intercontinental flying.

The New Economy

After the success of *The Fountainhead*, Ayn Rand built up a small following around herself. Among her entourage was a tall, taciturn young man named Alan Greenspan who, by his own admission, was deeply influenced by her ideas. During the 1990s, Rand's novels were widely read, especially among young Silicon Valley entrepreneurs working in networks, software, and biotechnology. One of them was Larry Ellison, creator of Oracle. Others named their companies and even their children after Rand characters and created reading groups devoted to her books. They saw themselves as Randian heroes, independent thinkers who made new products and for whom work was their life and their reward.

The 1990s were witnessing a period of rapid progress in information technologies. The arrival of the internet at home seemed to open up countless new opportunities for economic expansion. Dozens of so-called "dot-com" companies proliferated, offering unprecedented products and services. A bubble grew around these companies, fueled by cheap money, financial deregulation, and pure speculation. A "bubble" is defined as a process of rapid escalation in the price of a commodity above its fundamental (true) value. Processes of "irrational exuberance", that is, the unbridled enthusiasm of investors who bet on an asset, usually cause bubbles. The term was coined by Alan Greenspan in a 1996 speech called "The Challenges for Central Banks in Democratic Societies", which is often regarded as the starting signal for the dot-com bubble.

Venture capitalists, eager to find new territories, saw a massive opportunity in dot-com companies. They promised huge profits, even though their valuations were based on candid projections and business models of uncertain functionality. These companies went public through Initial Public Offerings (IPOs), often without clear revenue-generating models and fully ready products. Still, they generated enough buzz to catapult their share prices. Analysts linked to the banks underwriting these IPOs and companies issuing these shares fed the bubble. The NASDAQ index peaked on March 10, 2000; it had doubled in just one year. In this climate, traditional media companies felt also tempted by the dot-coms. The giant Time Warner acquired AOL and Telefónica bought Lycos for astronomical sums; Telefónica would recover less than 1% of the investment when it sold Lycos 10 years later.

Right at that market peak, investors panicked. Within a few weeks, the stock market lost 10% of its value. The dot-coms with faulty business models began to run out of start-up capital. When their liquidity problems became evident, their stock market value collapsed. The financial crash after the 9/11 attacks was the final straw for these companies. Most were delisted from the stock market before the end of 2001. Billions of dollars of capital evaporated overnight. A technological backlog ensued, resulting in the disappearance of otherwise viable companies.

That is the backdrop to *August* (2008). The action takes place in August 2001, when the dot-com bubble had burst, and the dot-com companies were in free fall. The plot centers around two brothers trying to save the company they both founded, Landshark. Tom Sterling (Josh Hartnett) is charismatic and egotistical, a snake oil salesman who manages the company's business aspects. His brother Joshua is the "techie", a quiet and brilliant software engineer, and family man. This deliberate contrast places the film as a moral parable like *Wall Street*. Tom has a troubled relationship with his brother and parents, sixty-something college professors, and especially with his father, with whom he has a tense exchange when he questions his son's work. "So, what do you do? Explain it to us". In case the moralizing intention in Howard Rodman's script was lost to the audience, there is another source of contrast: Tom's ex-girlfriend (Naomie Harris), an architect. As they resume their love affair, the opposition between them becomes clear: she designs natural objects, he designs immaterial products. In fact, it is never explained what Landshark sells. Tom's lectures are full of buzzwords like "new paradigm", "consumer-driven navigation", or "personalized web experience". Carefully broken down, his speeches say very little, though. This is a conscious decision by the screenwriter to reflect a time and place where the more obtuse a sales pitch was, the more likely it was to succeed because obscurity was taken as a signal of superior information.

Unlike in *Wall Street*, we do not witness the rise and fall of an amoral and ambitious young man in *August*, but his downward spiral. Tom is meant to exemplify the typical dot-com CEO. He is an arrogant twenty-something entrepreneur who became a millionaire in the blink of an eye. His lifestyle is frenetic. Booze, women, and fast cars. But Tom is not prepared, financially or emotionally, for the impending collapse. Landshark is now worth a negligible fraction of its valuation a few months earlier. As the share price continues to sink rapidly, Tom scrambles to find new investors before time runs out and he loses everything. One of *August*'s most compelling points is watching Tom's struggle to survive in the weeks leading up to the attacks on the Twin Towers, which subtly appear on a couple of occasions as an ominous reminder of what was to become of the city and the utopian dream of dot-coms.

At the end of the road, to deliver the final blow, old money awaits, personified by David Bowie in a brief but intense cameo. Lifelong potentates come to clean up the mess created by self-serving young entrepreneurs. Tom is left with nothing. He is forced to abandon the company and sell his shares at abysmal prices to save his brother. We would have to wait for *The Social Network* to see how the tables were turned and the old money ended up giving in to the second wave of tech companies.

In 2004, a Harvard student had an idea for a new social network. He designed it, built it, and made sure it worked every step of the way. From Harvard, the network spread to other universities and then to the public. That college student's name was Mark Zuckerberg, and the network was

Facebook. Today, with two billion users, it is the most important social network in the history of humankind. And Zuckerberg is a billionaire, the youngest in the world.

Aaron Sorkin had the idea of writing a screenplay for a film based on Ben Mezrich's book *Billionaires by Accident: The Birth of Facebook* (2009). The film was to be directed by David Fincher, who, with his unmistakable style, infused it with a breakneck pace and a formidable visual apparatus. The alliance between these two titans gave rise to one of the key cinematographic works of this century and an acerbic portrait of the new economy.

The film opens with a long dialogue scene in a Harvard campus bar in the fall of 2003. Zuckerberg (Jesse Eisenberg), a sophomore, is having a beer with his girlfriend Erica (Rooney Mara). He converses with her in a tone between witty and offensive. The argument escalates until Erica has enough and breaks up with him. Zuckerberg's response is to go back to his room drunk, turn on his computer and hack into the university's database to create Facemash, a website where users can rate the physical attractiveness of Harvard students.

From here, two lawsuits underpin the film's plot. The first one is filed by Cameron and Tyler Winklevoss (both played by Armie Hammer), two wealthy WASP twins. These two insiders, arrogant and handsome sons of old money, smell an opportunity in the web created by this introverted, resentful Jewish boy, an outsider excluded from the university's elite clubs. They hire him to create Harvard Connection, a website that, they thought, would become what would eventually become Facebook.

The other lawsuit is filed by Eduardo Saverin (Andrew Garfield), Zuckerberg's partner and only friend, who brought money to the fledgling company and worked tirelessly to increase its advertising revenue. Eduardo is sidelined by Zuckerberg because he disagrees with the wild expansion of Facebook's operations. His business model seems obsolete compared to the ambitions of Sean Parker (Justin Timberlake), a start-up veteran and co-founder of Napster who, after being kicked out of Silicon Valley, sees Facebook as an opportunity to get back into the business.

It is never clear whether Parker managed to make Eduardo leave Facebook and whether Zuckerberg stole the idea for Facebook from the Winklevoss twins. Fincher and Sorkin are clever enough to construct a multitude of perspectives by turning the narrative into a courtroom drama. The action is constantly interrupted by Zuckerberg, Saverin,

Parker, and the Winklevoss's statements during the pretrial hearings. The only thing their testimonies make clear is that they all distrust their ex-partners and are fighting among themselves for the ownership of a global company worth billions of dollars.

Probably the most crucial scene in the film occurs when the Winklevosses meet with then Harvard chancellor Lawrence Summers—a controversial economist and Treasury Secretary under Bill Clinton—in an attempt to use their family connections to crush the irreverent Zuckerberg. Summers condescendingly brushes them aside. He suggests to the twins that they should better develop some other invention on the web, one of their own makings for a change. We are actually watching a form of capitalism based on prestige, chivalry, and inheritance being demolished by a new form of business devoid of class privileges. Neither Summers nor the twins, used to always winning, understand what is happening. They lost.

Zuckerberg created Facebook for less than a thousand dollars and without needing the permission of his internet provider or the authorization of Harvard, Yale, Princeton, or Stanford. Nor anyone else's. The internet provided him with an open and free platform. Like him, many others would have the opportunity to invent their own social network and launch it to the world.

Zuckerberg's innovation was a meteoric success because it exploited network externalities, the increase in the value of a product or service that occurs when its number of users grows. If everyone else is on Facebook, that is where you want to be too. The more sellers on eBay, the more buyers will use it. The more friends, family, or business colleagues use Whatsapp to communicate, the more likely you are to use it too. Facebook also represented a new model of online commerce. Because it was free, it reached such a large number of users that advertisers flocked to it.

The Social Network can also be seen as the story of a small company that became a huge business much faster than the friendship between the two people who created it could resist. Zuckerberg and Saverin are two friends who achieve success together and end up separated by ambition and ego. It is also the story of a boy who is inept at interpersonal relationships and who, drunk and spiteful, creates the biggest social network in history to take revenge on his ex-girlfriend. A pathetic irony that hitting F5 over and over cannot erase.

Aaron Sorkin would take a shot at another tech giant in *Steve Jobs* (2015). The film was to be directed again by David Fincher, but the deal fell through, and Danny Boyle took his place at the helm. As with Zuckerberg, Sorkin draws Jobs (played by Michael Fassbender) as a visionary whose insensitivity alienated almost everyone around him. Both films flesh out the unsavory qualities of their genius protagonists by contrasting them with a nobler counterpart. If Zuckerberg had his better version in Eduardo Saverin, Steve Wozniak (Seth Rogen) plays here the role of earnest friend betrayed by the innovator in his road to success.

Sorkin's script highlights very explicitly that, unlike Zuckerberg, Jobs was not technically gifted. He was neither a coder nor a good designer, nor an engineer. The film describes Jobs (through his own words) as a different type of disruptor. Not as a technical wizard or a business genius but as an "orchestra conductor". Someone who does not play an instrument but has the talent to coordinate with other people and to envision concepts any of his collaborators or the public cannot possibly fathom. Jobs had the ability to persuade people to believe his ideas were possible.

"People don't know what they want until you show them", he says in the film. Actually, *Steve Jobs* is full of one-liners like "People should be overcome" or "I guarantee whoever said 'the customer is always right' was a customer" that could come from the pages of an Ayn Rand's novel and show the character's individualism.

Creative Destruction

In *Capitalism, Socialism, and Democracy* (1942), Austrian economist Joseph Schumpeter redefined the Marxist term "creative destruction" to refer to the continuous process of technological innovation that characterizes capitalism. Entrepreneurs and inventors create and adopt new technologies or ways of doing things, replacing older productive processes and goods. For example, the emergence of the internet meant the end of the CD (which in turn had killed cassette tapes), of travel agencies, and, before long, of the written press. Released a decade barely after Schumpeter coined this idea, the delightful satirical comedy *The Man in the White Suit* (1951) gave an apt depiction of the process of creative destruction and the natural backlash from those it harms.

Ayn Rand could have well written the first part of *The Man in the White Suit*. Sydney Stratton (Alec Guinness) is an obsessive genius inventor employed in a textile factory. He sneaks out whenever he can to continue his chemical experiments to pursue a revolutionary new fabric type. After being discovered and fired by his bosses, he is hired again at the Birnley factory, where he catches the eye of Daphne (Joan Greenwood), the daughter of the company's president, who persuades her father to give Stratton access to the research lab. Hilarious scenes ensue in which Sydney is on the verge of blowing up the factory with his experiments. He finally achieves his goal: a new fiber that never gets dirty or wears out. At first, President Birnley (Cecil Parker) is enthusiastic. "Think of the profit potential!" he says. He allows Sidney to manufacture a prototype suit, which glows in the dark, and calls a press conference to present it to the world.

But things soon go wrong. The textile industry bosses blame Birnley for allowing Sydney to drive them to bankruptcy: Once people buy clothes made from the new fabric, they will never need to replace their dresses or shirts. There will be no demand. "I admit that some will suffer", Birnley replies in defense of the invention, "but I will not stand in the way of progress". The factory workers go on strike because they are also afraid that once the national demand for clothing is met, the company will be forced to close. Both sides chase Sidney, and he has to run for his life. Unfortunately for him, a fluorescent white suit is not the best of camouflages.

The Man in the White Suit was one of the most successful satires to emerge from the famous Ealing Studios, responsible for a series of comedies that mocked the institutional inertia and cultural stifling in postwar Britain. Their stories followed a "the common man vs the establishment" template. In this case, the protagonist is pitted against the textile plutocrats, represented as a bunch of old money-grubbers, and the workers represented as petty and lazy unionists. Capital and labor allied against progress.

The *Man in the White Suit* also touches on a very topical issue among consumers: planned obsolescence. One of the workers at the Birnley factory wryly observes that the economy would not work if products were too good. "What do you think happened to all the other things? The razor blade that never gets blunt, the car that runs on water with just a pinch of something. No, they'll never let your stuff on the market in a million years", he tells Sydney. This dialogue refers to revolutionary inventions—electric motors, immortal light bulbs—that never made it to the market because they threatened established industries. "Vested interests. The deadly hand of monopolies", replies Bertha (Vida Hope), Sydney's best friend among the unionists.

When a company sells a durable product (a fridge, a television, a textbook), it is in a way competing against itself. Consumers who buy the product now will not need it again for a long time. This means that durable goods tend to sell at decreasing prices. When the iPod was launched in 2001, it costed about $400; three years later, only $250. Companies selling durable goods often respond to this problem by releasing new versions that make older versions obsolete to a greater or lesser extent. The extreme of this strategy is planned obsolescence: the deliberate design of a product to reduce its useful life.

Economists have conflicting views on whether planned obsolescence is real. One case that has recently received a lot of attention is that of printers that run much slower after printing a certain number of pages or that stop printing when ink cartridges are not official products.[3] But it is difficult to discern whether this reduction in product quality results from a deliberate strategy to sustain sales. Typically, in markets, we find a mix of lower and higher quality products, known as vertical differentiation. Planned obsolescence may make sense in a monopolistic market, but not when there is competition; consumers who bought that short-life printer are likely to switch brands the next time they need one. But this argument ignores that companies form cartels, which, like the textile geezers in *The Man in the White Suit*, agree to prevent the introduction of longer-lived products. A real example was the Phoebus cartel, which carved up the world market for incandescent light bulbs during the interwar period and actively prevented the production of long-lasting bulbs.

Technical change and creative destruction were also the basis of *You've Got Mail* (1998). As a matter of fact, romantic comedies are very often articulated around the social and economic tensions of the period in which they are set. This Nora Ephron's classic is no exception.

A modern-day adaptation of Miklós László's play *Parfumerie* (1937), the film tells the story of two people in love by correspondence who hate each other in person. Joe Fox (Tom Hanks) is the owner of a large book chain. Kathleen Kelly (Meg Ryan) is the owner of a small independent bookshop called The Shop Around the Corner, a nod to Ernst Lubitsch's 1940 adaptation of László's play. Joe and Kathleen have met in an internet

---

[3] "Ink-Stained Wretches: The Battle for the Soul of Digital Freedom Taking Place Inside Your Printer", Cory Doctorow, The Electronic Frontier Foundation. November 5, 2020. Last accessed March 30, 2021 https://www.eff.org/deeplinks/2020/11/ink-stained-wretches-battle-soul-digital-freedom-taking-place-inside-your-printer.

chat room and have become intimate via email to the point of falling in love. When they meet in person by chance, they do so without knowing that they have stumbled upon their pen pal. The result of their encounters is cataclysmic. Joe is about to open one of his shops very close to Kathleen's, and the competition will drive her out of business. Thus, the film transforms the economic conflict between chain stores and small shops into a romantic one.

The Shop Around the Corner offers a unique product. Kathleen is an avid reader who has inherited her late mother's enthusiasm for books. She runs the shop together with two employees who are also book-lovers. Her specialty is children's literature. Kathleen has an appreciative and loyal customer base to whom she offers personalized and expert recommendations. The Shop Around the Corner is a very welcoming place that invites customers to spend time there. The product she sells is not just the book itself; it is also the experience of finding and acquiring it.

Kathleen is confident that the new Fox Books store will not kill her business because they are not selling the same product. Fox Books is characterized by its variety, its unbeatable prices, and by its modern café space in which customers can read and be seen reading. But Fox stores are also anonymous, noisy, and massive; shop assistants know almost nothing about books and literature.

The new bookstore has the upper hand, though. As a large chain, Fox Books has market power. It can offer hefty discounts because publishers offer better prices to bulk buyers. Its large size allows the chain store to achieve economies of scale, have a large inventory, and expand into the sale of related products such as stationery, coffee, and cakes.

Sales at The Shop Around the Corner drop precipitously. Kathleen starts a press campaign to defend her shop against the "big, impersonal" Fox Books. Many loyal customers help her and even speak out in her favor. But reality sets in. Sales do not pick up because New Yorkers value low prices more than Kathleen's dedication to her customers. It's business as usual.

This process of creative destruction has the obvious positive outcome of consumers having to pay less for the same product. Another creative aspect is a reallocation of resources to better uses. Kathleen receives several offers to become a children's books editor and an author herself. One of her employees accepts a position at the dreaded Fox Books and revolutionizes her department for the better. The premises left vacant by

The Shop Around the Corner will not remain empty but will be occupied by other shops.

With the benefit of hindsight, *You've Got Mail* also has something to say about the disruptive effects of technological change on markets. A few years later, after the film was released, the online book-selling giant Amazon entered the scene. If *You've Got Mail* were to have a sequel, it would be one where Fox Books is about to close because the very same technology that brought Kathleen and Joe together has almost wiped out physical bookstores.

Sports films also lend themselves to tell stories of conscientious individuals who challenge established conventions and innovate. Films such as *Jerry Maguire* (1996), *The Damned United* (2009), or *Draft Day* (2014) provide excellent business cases for managers who aim to get the best out of their employees and the budget they have. But one stands out for its representation of the disruptive effects of innovation.

Moneyball (2011) adapted Michael Lewis' best-selling book about the real-life struggle of Billy Beane (Brad Pitt) to lead a modest Major League Baseball team, the Oakland A's. Tired of not winning, faced with the loss of his best players and a tighter budget than most of his competitors, Beane decides to try something new. A new way of understanding baseball. Instead of maximizing individual talent, he seeks to maximize the team's winning potential. The first step is to analyze why teams win by crunching countless statistics. The result of the analysis defies common sense because it gives importance to aspects of the game that almost everyone ignores. Still, Beane goes for it. It works. It does not just work. It changes baseball forever.

Moneyball is one of the greatest economic films ever made. It deals with a multitude of economic concepts. The use of empirical methods is one. The analysis of data using statistical techniques allows economists to evaluate public policies and interventions, and to understand the state of markets and countries. Data analysis is (or should be) key to improve regulation, laws, and business operations. Beane encounters a young Yale economist, Peter Brand (Jonah Hill) while negotiating players' transfer. Peter wants to apply empirical analysis to baseball to build a better team. "It's about getting things down to one number. Using the stats the way we read them, we'll find value in players that no one else can see". Peter's approach is to find the factors that count most in a player's productivity.

If, as it was the case, those factors are undervalued by "common sense"—that is, by the market—a small team like the A's can succeed by acquiring all that overlooked talent.

Traditional baseball scouts, who we see surrounding Beane early in the film as they plan the new season, used subjective judgment to evaluate players. Their old-fashioned methods included criteria such as "he has a baseball body", "he's clean, has a good face and a good jaw", or even "his girlfriend is ugly". Brand proposes a radically different model that, although it does not work at first, becomes a massive success once Beane can finally implement it fully. This new model reallocates human capital within his organization to improve productivity. We see this in the subplot devoted to Scott Hatteberg (Chris Pratt), an insecure, injury-riddled player whom Beane wants to put in a position he has never played in but where the data says he will contribute the most.

The technological change Bean and Peter bring to baseball generates a wave of Schumpeterian creative destruction. They replace old, inefficient methods with more effective ones. As in *The Man in the White Suit*, this process is not linear because it threatens the ways of doing and understanding baseball of many. The film's central dramatic tension is once more the hostility and rejection that Beane must face when he introduces his new methods. The fans do not understand them. The players are baffled. The scouts, who have become irrelevant under the new model, rebel against it. As the Red Sox owner tells Beane toward the end of the film, "every time that happens, whether it's the government or a way of doing business or whatever it is, the people who are holding the reins, have their hands on the switch. They will go batshit crazy. I mean, anybody who's not building a team right now and rebuilding it using your model, they're dinosaurs".

Moneyball was meant to be directed by Steven Soderbergh. However, the producers decided to fire him at the last minute because they felt that the director had become too involved in the script. Soderbergh, hurt by the experience, retired from filmmaking. But it did not take him long to get back behind the camera, and in 2018 he directed *High Flying Bird*, another film about sports and innovation, both in its plot, production, and distribution.

Actor and producer Andre Holland plays the protagonist, Ray Burke, a basketball player's agent who is in trouble. The reason is that the NBA is in a lockout like the one that took place in real life in 2011. The teams' owners have decided that there will be no more games until they reach a satisfactory agreement with players about sharing revenues from broadcasting rights. The lockout is having a domino effect because players do not get paid if they do not play, and if they do not get paid, their agents do not get paid either. Ray Burke has only 72 hours to navigate the crisis.

The team owners have colluded to form a monopsonistic cartel. They are the only ones who can employ these players who are now dry-docked. The owners can thus dictate a new sharing of the revenues. The players and the players' association try to negotiate, but they are on the weak side of the market. As several characters say literally, the NBA is "a game above the game". There is also a race dimension to the dispute. The screenplay by African American playwright Tarell Alvin McCraney emphasizes that the NBA is run by white men who want to control a sport in which those who excel and generate value are primarily black.

But Ray Burke has it all figured out, although it does not seem so at first. In those dazzling 72 hours, we see his plan unfolding to perfection: He plans to broadcast basketball games through pay-per-view streaming sites and mobile phones. With that innovation, he achieves what seemed impossible: to upend professional basketball by changing the ownership of the means of production and buyers' and sellers' relative bargaining power in the industry.

It is no coincidence that *High Flying Bird* is about someone using new technologies to disrupt an established industry. This argument has obvious parallels with Steven Soderbergh's dismissal from the set of *Moneyball*. He was fired for trying to take the film into his creative territory. He then withdrew from the "game" and soon came back as an independent filmmaker. The same happens in *High Flying Bird*. Ray Burke takes on the NBA owners and uses an innovation that disrupts the current market structure. He does it in a way that echoes how the film itself was produced and distributed. *High Flying Bird* was shot with an iPhone 8, albeit with a special lens, in 15 days and on a minimal budget. Soderbergh edited the film himself and acted as director of photography. The film was distributed on the streaming site Netflix in search of a bigger audience than if it had gone through the usual distribution channels. This is analogous to Ray's plan, who, in a metatextual wink, wants to have the basketball games streamed on Netflix.

Innovators vs The World

In *Wealth and Poverty* (1981), the book that would lead him to become one of the best-known champions of trickle-down economics, George Gilder argued that low taxes, minimal state intervention, and business deregulation are the best recipes for economic growth. He also argued that capitalism is moral. An entrepreneur is a generous person, an adventurer, who dares to offer a product or service that does not yet exist but that people need. In other words, capitalists make the world a better place.

This is largely the representation of entrepreneurs and innovators in cinema, as we have been discussing in this chapter. That said, they are also portrayed as oddballs and complex characters. As Howard Hughes in *The Aviator*, innovators are often depicted as eccentric and stubborn geniuses. They must be determined because they have to face a world that will not simply accept their innovations. Sometimes, they are rebuffed, like Preston Tucker or Billy Beane. On other occasions, rivals try to steal their ideas from them. This is the case of Willy Wonka in Tim Burton's adaptation of the Roald Dahl's classic Charlie and the Chocolate Factory and of Robert Kearns, whose life is recounted in *A Flash of Genius* (2008).

Willy Wonka is an extravagant character obsessed with inventing new sweets and new methods of producing them, like a giant chocolate cascade that gives his products a unique texture. His revolutionary innovations made him a de facto monopolist and led his competitors to the verge of bankruptcy. To break Wonka's dominant position, his rivals planted spies in his factory posing as employees. That is how they stole his recipes from him and marketed his designs. Sales of Wonka products plummeted. The chocolate genius fired all his workers, including Charlie's grandfather, and closed his factory to the outside world so that no one could ever take his ideas away from him again. It was a logical reaction: When intellectual property rights cannot be defended, creativity no longer offers a competitive advantage, and innovators have little incentive to keep inventing.

In *A Flash of Genius*, Greg Kinnear plays Robert Kearns, a Detroit college professor and inventor. In 1967, Kearns filed a patent for an intermittent windshield wiper drawing inspiration from the human eye. For years, the major automakers had been trying their own prototypes. Ford seems interested in the device and agrees to buy the wiper from Kearns' new company. However, Ford cancels the deal at the last minute. The corporation starts using intermittent wipers in their new models soon after, to Kearns dismay. The inventor then launches a 20-year legal battle against Ford.

A Flash of Genius condensates this story in about two hours and builds it following a David vs Goliath structure. The title of the film comes from one of the defining elements of a patent according to US law: the inventor must have a "flash of genius" while developing the idea to be patented. With that, the film perpetuates the very cinematographic narrative that a spark of genius is an essential part of any innovation. Because the events portrayed in the movie are relatively well known, its interest lies mainly in its portrayal of Kearns as an increasingly obsessive man. Kinnear does an outstanding job at playing Kearns as a difficult and stubborn man who alienated his wife, children, business partners, and lawyers. The legal proceedings also took a toll on his mental health; Kearns had to spend some time in a mental hospital. He even refused a $30 million settlement offer from Ford because the company was unwilling to admit any wrongdoing. In 1990, a jury declared that Ford had unwilfully infringed on Kearns' patent and awarded Kearns a $10 million compensation.

As it is customary, *A Flash of Genius* ends with a courtroom scene where the inventor is finally vindicated. After losing almost everything, Kearns' six children become interested in their father's case and help him in his crusade. Predictably, Ford appears as the villain. The film suggests openly that the company stole Kearns' concept for an intermittent wiper. As stated in the film advertisements, corporations "have time, money and power on their side". The film implies that Ford took Kearns' idea simply because it was confident it could get away with it. Kearns was just one man fighting for an invention he felt was a part of him; "to me, it's the Mona Lisa", he says in the film.

Other films about innovators and entrepreneurs show them as disturbed and difficult geniuses. Tom Sterling in *August* behaves as if he is always the smartest guy in the room. Thomas Edison played by Benedict Cumberbatch in *The Current War* (2017) is arrogant and dismissive and has no time for pleasantries or small talk. The innovators in Aaron Sorkin's biopics are also good examples of this. In *Steve Jobs*, the creator of Apple is shown as a paranoid egomaniac. Before the launch event of the Apple Macintosh, he claims to be "surrounded by enemies", then boasts that he does not "have the time to be polite or realistic" and threatens one of the engineers with the sack using a Russian roulette's analogy. When Wozniak tells him, "Your products are better than you are, brother", Jobs retorts

"That's the idea, 'brother'", admitting that he is trying to overcome his deep personal flaws through his products.

Steve Jobs encapsulated George Gilder's view of innovators as adventurers. With that, the American author seemed to have solved the distinction Israel Kirzner had made a few years earlier between businesspeople and entrepreneurs (Kirzner, 1973). The former focus on making profits, while entrepreneurs look for new opportunities. The separation between the two is, in part, the dramatic conflict at the heart of *The Social Network* and *Steve Jobs*. John Lee Hancock's *The Founder* explored this distinction further and provided a critical view of Gilder's entrepreneur/adventurer.

The film is a biopic of Raymond Kroc (played by Michael Keaton), one of America's most unorthodox and famous entrepreneurs. We join him when he still is a veteran traveling salesman specialized in those seemingly revolutionary objects advertised on the info commercials. But he has little success. His dream of making money from these products has made him a running joke among his friends. But he does not give up. "You don't have a blender because you don't sell milkshakes, or you don't sell milkshakes because you don't have a blender?" he asks one skeptical customer, who does not seem to understand that Ray is just stating Say's Law: Supply creates its own demand. His wife (Laura Dern) is sympathetic to her husband's efforts but tries to dissuade him from his stubbornness. Kroc listens to recordings of motivational talks and believes in himself 100%, but that does not seem to be enough. Then something happens that transforms his life: He visits McDonald's.

McDonald's was a single establishment back then. A modest burger joint in San Bernardino, California, without golden arches. It had been founded by Richard and Maurice "Mac" McDonald (Nick Offerman and John Carroll Lynch). According to Kirzner's definition, the McDonald brothers were innovators (Staley, 2018). They offered an affordable, efficient, family-friendly alternative to the dingy, run-down fast-food restaurants of the time. They experimented with new ways of doing things until they perfected a new system focused on quality control and reinvented restaurant kitchens. However, the McDonald brothers were not so successful in expanding their business. The franchises they granted ended up offering a product of negligible quality.

Kroc arrives in San Bernardino because the McDonald's have placed a massive order for the mixers he sells. What he sees there amazes him. Kroc has an epiphany: To franchise McDonald's. He manages to convince the brothers. The deal they strike allows the McDonald's to maintain strict oversight over the restaurants' design and product quality. Kroc's role is to oversee finances and franchising. He is a Kirznerian businessman.

From there, *The Founder* tells the story of an improbable and spectacular success. The story of a 52-year-old entrepreneur who, despite being on the verge of despair, creates the global brand we know today. His rise is meteoric, but it exemplifies that not all entrepreneurs are the valiant heroes Rand or Gilder depicted. Kroc's tactics exploit the grey areas of business ethics.

After opening a few establishments, Ray realizes that Dick and Mac were right: franchising leads to a drop in quality. The financial hole becomes unsustainable. He is now convinced that he has given too much control of the business to the McDonald's and tries to renegotiate their deal. But his ambition clashes with the parsimony and solid principles of the brothers, who would rather lose their restaurant than alter their concept.

On the verge of bankruptcy, Kroc meets Harry Sonneborn (BJ Novak), who makes him realize that the real business is not the restaurants but the real estate they occupy. Kroc's vision—grow, build a global brand, monetize it—is as uncompromising as the McDonald's. He pursues it to the point of breaking the spirit of his agreement with the brothers. And he succeeds. That is why, even today, McDonald's is one of the most real estate-rich companies in the world.

Innovation alone does not create social value. Innovations need to diffuse and spread to change an industry and benefit society. The McDonald brothers lacked Kroc's business acumen to build a brand and expand it. Without him, their vision would not have gone beyond that little restaurant in San Bernardino. Kroc, in turn, could not have succeeded without the McDonalds. Without their innovation, he had no product to sell.

Director John Lee Hancock tiptoes somewhat over this tension. Watched superficially, *The Founder* might look like just another biopic of yet another larger-than-life and inspirational entrepreneur like Preston Tucker or Howard Hughes. But the film, perhaps involuntarily, also opens the backdoor to the canon of ruthless and amoral businesspeople in cinema. On his way to success, Kroc becomes a buccaneer. He is someone who, in his own words, would not hesitate to "put a hose down my competitor's throat when he's drowning". He takes what he wants and does not stop until he gets it. It may be someone else's wife, someone else's ideas, or someone else's name. Rather than the successful and generous adventurer George Gilder drew in the pages of *Wealth and Poverty*, Ray Kroc in *The Founder* is more of a cannibal.

REFERENCES

Boozer, J. (2002). *Career movies*. University of Texas Press.
Kirzner, I. M. (1973). *Competition and entrepreneurship*. The University of Chicago Press.
Schleier, M. (2002). Ayn Rand and King Vidor's film *The Fountainhead*: Architectural modernism, the gendered body, and political ideology. *Journal of the Society of Architectural Historians, 61*, 310–331.
Staley, S. R. (2018). *Contemporary film and economics*. Routledge.

CHAPTER 7

The Path of Workers

In addition to the environmental crisis, there is another reason why companies do not enjoy a very good standing in today's cinema: the gradual worsening in the quality of jobs. This phenomenon is due to two significant changes that have been represented on the big screen tangentially. One is the global competition from emerging countries and the resulting offshoring of many industries. The other has been automation.

These two large-scale trends have eroded the position of middle-skilled or routine workers in Western countries, who since the 1980s have been competing against robots and cheaper manufacturing in developing countries. The policies of market deregulation and privatizations adopted in response to these pressures—often referred to as neoliberalism—helped perpetuate corporations' role in cinema as villains. Capital was the most obvious culprit of stagnant wages and increasingly precarious jobs. Companies sieged by competition and freed from labor regulations started asking for more and more sacrifices from their employees while offering them less and less in return. One recent example is the soul-destroying telemarketing company where the protagonist of *Sorry to Bother You* works, exploiting its employees with a carrot-and-stick technique.

Cinema about work and labor conflicts have received considerable analysis.[1] This is not the place to survey the dozens of related films in detail. Instead, I will discuss how this filmography dialogues with pressing issues for workers worldwide: the increasing precariousness of work, unionization, automation, and mass migration.

WHITE-COLLAR BLUES

Fight Club, American Beauty, and *Office Space*, all released in 1999, conveyed the anxiety of white men who found that their personal and work lives did not match their aspirations (Hunter, 2003). *Fight Club* was a radical manifesto against advertising, the culture of consumerism, and the cycle of work and spending that these sustain. In *American Beauty*, the main character frees himself from the chains of work and the state of sedation he has lived in for years. Finally, Mike Judge's *Office Space* offered a hilarious satire of corporations and their new forms of management, their inefficiencies, and their alleged disregard for workers' welfare. Less viscerally than David Fincher's film, *Office Space* also questioned the role of employment in defining and validating our existence. Finally, it also offered a crash course on the importance of incentives.

Peter Gibbons (Ron Livingston), is a programmer at Initech, a software company more idiotic than evil, was not much better. It rewards mediocrity rather than hard work and treats its workers like manure, continually harassing them with all kind of stupid regulations. As the first 15 minutes brilliantly show, Peter hates his job and life, a daily struggle against the alarm clock and traffic jams every morning. We see him arriving at his aseptic cubicle where Initech workers go about their work under the stale fluorescent lights and the electronic hum of copiers and computers. His bosses parade around to pester him for something as silly as not having included a front page in his latest memo. To top it all off, it is Monday.

The only co-workers he tolerates are his friends Michael Bolton (David Herman)—no relation to the singer—and Samir (Ajay Naidu). They hate their jobs too, of course. The main target of their animosity is their boss, Bill Lumbergh (Gary Cole), a nasty bore full of disdain which he dresses up with his constant use of corporate-speak. We soon learn that

---

[1] See Zaniello (2003) for an authoritative survey.

Lumbergh has hired two efficiency experts to evaluate all employees and decide on layoffs. Stress levels at the office skyrocket.

As if that was not enough, things are not going well for Peter on the love front either. His girlfriend, with whom he is about to break up, urges him to visit a hypnotherapist, who hypnotizes him into blissful ecstasy. But the man dies before he can be released from this state, and Peter is left in a nirvana of zero worries. He stops doing what he does not want to do. Peter ignores the alarm clock, hangs up the phone on his girlfriend, and ignores work calls. He goes fishing, sporadically pops into the office, and knocks down one of his cubicle walls so he can look out of the window.

In his meeting with the two experts, Peter confesses with beatific candor that his working day consists of arriving late, remaining in a stupor until lunchtime, and pretending he is working until it is time to leave. "I'd say I only do about fifteen minutes of real work a week", he concludes. The consultants love his honesty, as if Peter were a version of the upstanding and authentic corporate employee Gregory Peck had played 40 years earlier in *The Man in the Grey Flannel Suit*.

Peter says that his only motivation is the fear of losing his job and being picked on for trifles by his eight bosses. The pay is not good, either. The efficiency experts ask him if the problem would improve if workers received stock options or a share of the profits. "I think so", he replies. This issue also comes up in conversations between Joanna (Jennifer Aniston), the waitress at the coffee shop Peter goes to every day, and her boss. It is a house rule that the waiters must wear colorful badges with slogans and symbols that "express their personality". The mandatory minimum is 15, exactly how many Joanna wears (chosen at random, though). Her boss admonishes her because he expects her employees not to be satisfied with the minimum. These scenes illustrate that the workplace has become a purgatory where your bosses expect workers to exert more effort but do not do much to motivate them or gain their loyalty.

As the main characters in *How to Succeed in Business Without Really Trying* and *Head Office*, Peter is surprisingly promoted after his change of mind. But he learns that his friends Michael and Samir are about to be fired. The plot takes then a crazy twist: The three friends install a virus on Initech's servers that deposits the cents rounded up in daily transactions into an account. When they meet to discuss the plan, we see how much Peter has changed since the beginning of the film: he now feels confident, autonomous, and empowered (albeit for unethical reasons).

The mid-century corporate fiction narrated the trials and tribulations of middle managers trying to avoid the conformity of organizational life. *Office Space* shows that at the turn of the millennium, the workplace had transformed into a space where workers hate what they do, are in a state of permanent anxiety, and do not know what their actual job is or who to trust. It is not surprising that *Office Space* became a cult film and influenced the British series *The Office* (2001–2003), its US version, and movies like *The Promotion* (2008), and *Horrible Bosses* (2011).

Human resource management, increasingly perceived as insensitive and arbitrary, has also become the target of several films reflecting the growing unrest at work so pertinently described by Richard Sennett in his seminal essay *The Corrosion of Character* (1998). One example of this trend is *Exam* (2009), which disguised as a sci-fi thriller the anxieties that new corporate recruitment and personnel management processes produce among an increasingly precarious workforce.

On the other side of the Stygian river of white-collar work awaits unemployment. This is the dramatic conflict in several films starring well-paid workers dismissed by the capricious and impassive corporation they have served for years. These films describe the ordeal of long-term unemployment or job downgrading because those who suffer it are aging executives with wives and children to support. *The Axe* (2005) tackled this theme using black humor, while *Time Out* (2001), *Tokyo Sonata* (2008), and *The Measure of a Man* (2015) took a more introspective route to explore the crisis in male identity that arises when men are no longer the breadwinner. The flexibility and permanent availability required from workers have blurred the old divisions between work and family, between the public and the inner self. In this context, losing one's job is a world-shattering event that goes beyond the loss of income or social status. It is tantamount to the self's collapse, defined as a productive and successful individual.

Jason Reitman's *Up in the Air* (2009) differs from these films in that it takes the point of view of the "executioners". That would bring it closer to French films like *Heartbeat Detector* (2007) or *Corporate* (2017) were it not for the fact that *Up in the Air* is entirely uninterested in establishing a connection between corporate logic and evilness. Instead, the film uses bittersweet comedy to depict the drama of job termination.

The protagonist of *Up in the Air* is the handsome and charismatic Ryan Bingham (George Clooney), a "termination expert" hired to fire the employees of companies that have chosen to outsource this unpleasant task. Ryan does well when everyone else crashes. He flies from city to city and stays as little time as necessary to deliver severance packages to those he lays off. But Ryan does not just lighten his clients' wage bills. He has made an art out of it. Ryan never uses the word "redundancy" with his hapless victims; he tells them that they are going to "talk about the future", that their company is "letting them go", and that they should not take it personally. As he explains to his inexperienced but ambitious colleague Natalie (Anna Kendrick), "we're here to make limbo tolerable".

Ryan embodies an economic transformation that is taking place on a grand scale. Thousands of people have been affected by so-called biased technological change: the increasing use of new technologies in routine tasks. This change has produced a polarization in employment. In other words, it has eliminated jobs in the middle of the wage distribution, while workers performing abstract tasks—those earning the most—and those in manual occupations—those earning the least—have been less affected. It is the jobs in between that have been most frequently eliminated. These are the ones Ryan gives the sack to. At one point in the film, he lands in Detroit to lay off the employees of a car company. Their in-screen responses are believable because Reitman chose real people who experienced a similar job termination to play these characters. In the background, we see a union poster, a reminder of America's industrial past, of a time when united workers were able to extract concessions from their employers because their businesses were still profitable. There is little economic prosperity to share when two of the three American auto giants—Chrysler and General Motors—are on the verge of bankruptcy. Still, the employees accept their dismissal with resignation. Indeed, none of them expected to work for the same company all their working lives. Times have changed. Job insecurity is no longer an injustice to be responded to with rallies and strikes but an inescapable fact of life like taxes or death. Even large corporations seem to be at the mercy of vast, impersonal global forces.

But none of this is a problem for Ryan. He loves his lifestyle. His real home is in airports, VIP lounges, and car rental offices. He enjoys no-strings-attached affairs with numerous mistresses waiting for him in every city and dreams of becoming the seventh person in America to reach ten million frequent flyer miles. In short, Ryan feels like a winner in this new economy.

But even he is beginning to wish for something more permanent. Besides, his travels all around the country are starting to prove too costly for his employers. As the cutbacks loom, it is clear that he will be unable to adapt. When Natalie proposes doing the layoffs by video conference instead of in person to cut costs, Ryan reacts with the same outrage he has so often encountered from those he laid off: "You don't know anything about how I do my job". Seeing his precious way of life threatened, he runs to complain to his boss.

At the end of *Up in the Air*, it remains unclear what will become of Ryan. Surely, his future will be the same as that of the people he fired. A season in limbo. A bitter closure that reminds us that losing the job is heartbreaking. In contrast, at the end of *Office Space*, Peter leaves Initech and gets a career in construction, suggesting that white-collar workers only have two options: burnout or quit. He finds his new life invigorating: physical exercise, fresh air, decent pay. The film seems to tell us that blue-collar workers are happier than the office guys. But are they?

Solidarity Forever

Recent films like Dardenne Brothers' *Two Days, One Night* (2014), the satire *Sorry to Bother You*, and Ken Loach's *Sorry We Missed You* (2019) show that the deterioration in the job conditions of the average worker has gone hand in hand with the decline of the unionization. *Sorry to Bother You* echoes the recent strikes and union votes at Uber and Amazon and satirizes these champions of the new economy, with a less than stellar record at providing decent conditions for their employees. *Sorry We Missed You* takes a similar stance against the so-called "gig economy", which Loach and his usual screenwriter Paul Laverty portray as a new form of slavery.

Ricky (Kris Hitchen) has had a million jobs of all kinds of sorts. He and his family have not recovered yet from the 2008 financial crisis. The collapse of Northern Rock took away their savings. Rick starts working a delivery company as an independent contractor to make ends meet. As Maloney (Ross Brewster), the hypermasculine and ruthless owner of the franchise, tells him, "You don't get hired here; you come onboard. You don't work for us; you work with us. You don't drive for us; you perform services". This litany of double-speak where Rick is supposed to be now "self-employed", the "master" of his own destiny and a "warrior" rather than a loser hides a reality of endless shifts and a lack of a formal contract, paid leave, holidays, and even bathroom breaks.

This type of freelance work has become increasingly controversial as it has become more important in our economies. About 15% of US workers are employed in gig economy jobs. Like Ricky, these workers use gig work when facing financial difficulties due to job loss or reductions in hours (Koustas, 2019).

Ricky's wife Abbie (Debbie Honeywood) is a home healthcare worker who faces similarly draconian shifts. She is meant to provide to her "clients" the care their families are often unwilling to provide. Abbie also faces stereotypical gender roles within her household. Ricky's insistence on being the breadwinner means that she must sell her car so he can buy a van and start working as a freelance driver. Abbie must now spend hours navigating the unreliable public transport network. When they both get home after their 14 hours shift, Abbie and Ricky are exhausted and snappy, unable to care for their children and each other.

This is the other main theses Loach and Laverty try to convey in the too often too melodramatic *Sorry We Missed You*: That under the pressure of mounting debt and eternal shifts, gig jobs have a deleterious effect on workers and their families. Because of their parents' absence and stress, their teenage son Seb (Rhys Stone) drops out of school and runs afoul of the police while their smaller daughter's mental health deteriorates. Tensions at home and work mount. It is a relentless slippery slope where things only keep getting worse with no end in sight.

For Ricky and Debbie, trade unions and their fight to protect workers' rights are a thing of the past. They are isolated and cannot expect any solidarity from anyone. One of the older women Abbie cares for shows her pictures from the days she fed pickets during the miners' strike of 1984–85. Those days are now long gone. The lady is shocked to hear the conditions Debbie works under and asks her, "What about the eight-hour day?".

It is very telling that the present-day issues of overwork, low pay, and job insecurity that *Sorry We Missed You* and *Two Days, One Night* deal with are very similar to those portrayed in films about labor conflicts set during the Industrial Revolution and at the beginning of the twentieth century.

One of them is the critically acclaimed *Comrades* (1986), which poetically reenacted the story of the Tolpuddle Martyrs, six English agricultural laborer's who were sentenced to transportation to Australia in 1834 because they had formed a trade union. Although unions were legal at the time, they were charged under an old law that made oaths illegal.

It is not by chance that making the film, which took writer and director Bill Douglas eight years, ran parallel to Margaret Thatcher's successful dismantling of the union movement. The Tolpuddle Martyrs were a milestone in Britain's labor movement and deserved recognition and a beautiful film like *Comrades*.

In *The Organizer* (1963), Mario Monicelli's masterpiece, the professor played by Marcello Mastroianni, acts as a spark for the employees of a textile factory in Turin at the end of the nineteenth century to go on strike demanding a reduction in working hours. The priest protagonist of the Belgian biopic *Daens* (1992) also acts as a galvanizer for the workers of a nineteenth-century textile factory sacked by their employers and replaced by their wives at lower wages. Meanwhile, their children are crushed to death by the looms on which they work from dawn to dusk.

The Organizer, *Daens*, *Matewan* (1987), and *Norma Rae* (1978)— which we will discuss in detail in the next chapter—, used a typical narrative arc: an outsider arrives to organize manual workers and leads them to strike. We owe this plot to Emile Zola and his novel *Germinal* (1885), which dealt with the mining conflicts in Northern France during the crisis of 1866. In fact, mining cinema—almost a subgenre in itself— serves well to illustrate the vicissitudes that industrial workers have suffered over the last century and a half, from the early struggles to be heard and treated with dignity to the strikes aimed to prevent the closure of the mines, which had become loss-making due to high extraction costs and competition from other energy sources.

Claude Berri's 1993 film adaptation of *Germinal* recounts the conflicts between miners and pits owners at the dawn of the labor movement. The miners' attempts to organize themselves failed more often than not and were rife with deep internal divisions contradictions. The labor disputes in Sergei Eisenstein's *Strike* (1925), *The Organizer*, and *Germinal* end in tragedy when the army is called to intervene a historically frequent twist which illustrates the thesis of economic historians Robert Heilbroner and William Milberg (Heilbroner & Milberg, 2008), who argue that the accumulation of capital necessary for industrialization came at the expense of workers. The Industrial Revolution was essentially a process of capital accumulation. Thanks to the new machines, buildings, canals, and railways, labor productivity increased considerably. But for this process of accumulation to take place, the owners of the means of production needed to pay low wages. This sacrifice was not achieved through market forces alone; it also required government intervention in the form of violent repression whenever necessary.

Several films have featured workers' responses to employers' use of force. Martin Ritt's *The Molly Maguires* (1970), centered on a clandestine organization of Irish American miners in nineteenth-century Pennsylvania. John Sayles' *Matewan* (1987) recounted a violent event that took place in West Virginia during the "coal wars" of the early twentieth century in the United States. In the latter film, the main character is again a fictional union organizer whose perspective allows the audience to witness the conflict between the miners of Appalachia and the gunmen and Pinkerton detectives sent by pit owners to quell their demands. A more recent example is *In Dubious Battle* (2016), adapted from John Steinbeck's novel inspired by the labor conflicts of the Great Depression.

James Franco, who also directs, plays Mac, a member of "The Party" who helps workers organize strikes demanding better conditions. Jim (Nat Wolff), a new recruit, joins him. Together, they travel to California to infiltrate the fictional Torgus Valley's apple pickers. Mac is very experienced and has already been involved in several strikes, while Jim is more naïve and idealistic. One of the key drivers of the first part of the film is the relationship between them and how Jim learns from his older partner the tricks of their unusual trade.

Earlier in the film, we have seen Bolton, the landowner played by Robert Duvall, announce to the pickers that he will pay them one dollar a day instead of the three dollars he promised. His excuse is that "times are tough". A dollar a day was not enough to live on, even in 1933. The workers demand that Bolton keeps his promise. He refuses because he knows he has the upper hand. Bolton enjoys a monopsony position, a situation where there is only one buyer but many sellers—of labor in this case. Bolton can thus dictate the wage.

Monopsonies arise in labor markets when workers have few alternatives because there are only one or few employers, and mobility restrictions prevent workers from seeking better options. Monopsonies have always existed. One example is Luchino Visconti's classic *La Terra Trema* (1948), adapted from an 1881 novel, the story of a family of impoverished Sicilian fishermen who work for a handful of wholesalers controlling the market for fish and therefore its price. One of them, Toni, tries to get the fishermen to organize and set up a cooperative, but he is unsuccessful. Instead, he tries to become his own boss and invests all his and his family's money in buying a boat. When a storm destroys it leaving Tony with nothing, he has no other option but to swallow his pride and fish again for the wholesalers.

Newsies (1992) offered a surprisingly apt and entertaining depiction of monopsony based on an actual event: the 1899 strike of newsboys against Joseph Pulitzer and other publishers, who colluded to push down the boys' wages. The "newsies" did a job no one else wanted. They could be exploited easily as the high rates of child poverty and illiteracy meant an army of futureless kids would take their place if some decided to strike. Disney transformed this somber subject matter into a brilliant and joyful musical. The negotiations between Pulitzer (Robert Duvall) and the newsies' head (a very young Christian Bale) offer excellent insights on concepts such as self-interest, social capital, and the value of reputation.

Monopsonies have become increasingly important in recent years. Some of the forces that for many years counterbalanced monopsonistic power, such as trade unions and minimum wages, have eroded. Other reasons are the proliferation of temporary employment agencies and the clauses imposed by franchise companies banning franchisees from hiring workers from other franchises (Krueger, 2018). Agreements of this kind between independent firms are illegal, yet they exist. A recent example is the 2015 lawsuit won by a group of 64,000 software engineers against Google, Intel, Pixar, Lucasfilm, and other companies, which agreed to cap their employees' wages and pledged not to poach workers from their competitors.

In *In Dubious Battle*, Steinbeck explained very well how monopsony power works. Because James Franco's adaptation is very faithful to the novel, so does the film: During the Great Depression, workers were desperate and had little choice. Mobility was difficult; hardly any of them had a car, unlike the Joads from *The Grapes of Wrath* (1939). The Californian valleys were isolated, and therefore the pickers had little chance to exert any pressure on the farm owners to improve their situation. Moreover, they lived in houses owned by the landowners and had to buy essential goods at inflated prices from them.

The situation at Torgus Valley is a tinderbox. At first, the pickers want nothing to do with Mac because fighting against the status quo is too dangerous. That was a time when going on strike could cost you your life. But after a minor incident, the pickers decide to stop working temporarily. Bolton soon brings in a trainload of scabs. Then, the situation explodes. In the train comes an old party colleague of Mac's, played by Ed Harris, an older man who stands up and makes a fiery speech in favor of workers' rights. A company sniper shoots him and kills him on the spot. That is the final spark that leads the pickers to strike. But that is only the beginning. The landowners will have no qualms about resorting to violence to break the strike.

The pickers' situation is dire because the landowners also control the local credit market. Even if other landowners were to offer better terms to the workers, the control that the big farmers exerted through banks deterred them from doing so. We see this through Mr. Anderson, the farmer played by Sam Shepard in the film. When Mac asks him to allow the strikers to camp on his land once Bolton has thrown them off his farm, we learn that the Torgas Finance Company, the landowners' bank, mortgages Anderson's farm. If he gives shelter to the striking workers, he will defy the more powerful farmers, and his property may end up foreclosed. In the end, Anderson allows the workers to stay on his farm in exchange for harvesting their crops for free so that he can make more profit to pay off his debt.

One of the main ideas *In Dubious Battle* explores is that the strikers' violence was the predictable result of the strategies that the landowners used to reassert their control over the economy of the valleys. This led to a spiral of violence; when the big farmers brutally repressed the pickers, these responded in kind. None or almost none of these strikes were immediately successful. However, they were crucial to the passing of the Wagner act in 1935, which guaranteed workers the right to join trade unions and bargain collectively.

Unions on the Screen

The arrival of the New Deal and its progressive policies did not improve the image of trade unions in American and British cinema, which between 1933 and 1941 produced a handful of films influenced by the Red Scare. In *Black Fury* (1936), *Riffraff* (1936), and *The Proud Valley* (1940), for example, the strikers were gangsters and the unions a bunch of subversives. In *How Green Was My Valley* (1941), John Ford longed for an idyllic past, unsullied by labor strikes. One of the reasons for this negative portrayal of unions on film was that Hollywood studios had already encountered their good deal of labor conflicts at home after writers, actors, and technicians had unionized during the 1920s.

Contrary to popular belief, the first film to show sympathy for workers' demands was not *Salt of the Earth* (1954), but *The Devil and Miss*

Jones (Rogin, 2002), the delightful comedy of interclass entanglements we already talked about in Chapter 2.

Set against the backdrop of a labor dispute in a department store inspired by the struggle of Woolworth's employees in 1937, *The Devil and Miss Jones* previews many of the elements that will become tropes of the films on labor strikes: the company mole, the blacklisted workers, the union meeting that serves to expose their grievances, the picket lines, etc. The workers in JP Merrick's department store may be "pink collar" and have little in common with the industrial proletariat. Still, they are also willing to fight to improve their working conditions. *The Devil and Miss Jones* also touches on an aspect that was not very common in later films: older workers' fear of being replaced by younger and cheaper ones just at the point in their career when they were going to achieve the job status they aspired to. We would need to wait for a rom com like *In Good Company* and the comedy *The Internship* (2013) to see again represented on the screen the anxiety of middle-aged workers, now in the context of the new digital economy.

Also pro-union, *Salt of the Earth* is one of the most controversial American films of all time. Not because of its violent or obscene scenes but because of its political content. Almost 70 years after its first release, *Salt of the Earth* does not enjoy an entirely normal commercial distribution yet, even though it remains as relevant as it was then. At the heart of the labor struggle narrated in the film, there is a trio of conflicts that still exist today: race, class, and gender.

The film is based on a true story: the strike organized in 1951 by Mexican miners working in the pits of the Empire Zinc Company in Grant County, New Mexico, fed up with the discrimination they suffered at the hands of their employers. Ramón Quintero (Juan Chacón), one of the most prominent union leaders, decides that a strike is the only way to force the company to meet their demands for safety and wages. Their conflict is class-based because it is directed at their bosses, but it is also race-based because Ramón and his men are demanding the same working conditions the "Anglo" miners enjoy. The third conflict is gendered: Ramón's wife Esperanza (Rosaura Revueltas), the film's narrator, is confined to housework and childcare. Another child is on the way. Ramón feels powerless in front of the company, and Esperanza lacks power at home. The miners ignore their wives' demands on practical issues such as lack of sanitation and hot water. Ramón denies his wife small comforts such as a radio but does find money to drink at the tavern. In short, the women are treated with the same contempt and condescension that the Anglo managers and supervisors display toward the miners.

This situation gradually changes as the strike goes on. After seven months of hard struggle, including picket lines, anti-scab patrols, and harassment by the police, a court order arrives forbidding the miners to prevent others from entering the mine. The women of the community, led by Teresa Vidal (Henrietta Williams), decide to replace their husbands on the picket line to circumvent the order. But this means that the men must take over the domestic chores. The role reversal that occurs when women take the lead in union affairs disturbs Ramón and his fellow workers who feel their masculinity and position threatened.

This triple conflict makes *Salt of the Earth* extremely fascinating and powerful even today. The film confronted prejudices with a message denounced as communist. It also brought gender equality to the fore in a way that almost no other movie had done before. The changes in the domestic sphere brought about by the strike and the overcoming of the old ways, represented in the problematic relationship between Ramon and Esperanza, serve as a small-scale model of the labor rights and women's rights issues taking place in developed nations. We will explore in more detail how cinema has represented the upheaval in household mores due to labor conflicts in the next chapter.

Despite its obvious budgetary limitations, *Salt of the Earth* displays a wonderfully expressive use of editing. Director Herbert Biberman, who had learned a lot from Eisenstein, combined elements of the miners' daily routine and their wives to illustrate the hardships of life in the mine. In one dramatic sequence, the montage alternates between Esperanza's delivery and Ramón's beating at the police officers' hands. This scene also marks the point at which their roles switch, with Esperanza becoming increasingly involved in the strike and Ramón reluctantly agreeing to take over the domestic duties. Biberman shows a preference for the use of angles in the composition of close-ups, which vary depending on whether the focus is on a male actor, a woman talking to men, or Mexicans talking to their Anglo bosses. Medium shots appear when there is equality between the characters in the frame.

Salt of the Earth was a battered film. McCarthyism blacklisted its director, producers, and screenwriter for their communist sympathies. It was banned from distribution in the United States for much of the 1950s. Biberman hardly worked in Hollywood again, while Revueltas was deported to Mexico during filming. Screenwriter Michael Wilson was uncredited to avoid financing problems. Fortunately, the Library of Congress did the film some justice and in 1992 included it in its register of culturally significant works. Salt of the Earth remains wildly influential. The film's focus on a family's daily struggles to exemplify big economic and social issues is a device Ken Loach would use in most of his movies years later.

Unions were also represented positively in *The Garment Jungle* (1957). This modest but entertaining film noir addressed the criminal activities of union-busting gangsters in the textile industry. The better-known *The Pajama Game*, a romantic musical comedy produced by Warner Bros that adapted Richard Bissell's wildly popular novel, *7½ Cents* (1953), turned into a Broadway musical with Bob Fosse as a choreographer and the legendary Richard Adler and Jerry Ross as composers. *The Pajama Game* deals with the cheerful but disgruntled workers of SleepTite, an Iowa textile mill, who expressed their class solidarity and labor demands in musical numbers that would become famous like "Once there was a man" or "Hernando's hideaway". Leading the group was the intelligent and determined head of the union grievance committee, Catherine "Babe" Williams, the show's heroine.

The musical was a success. In 1955, *The Pajama Game* received a Tony Award for Best Musical. This atypical comedy centered on the labor struggles in a pajama factory caused a sensation because it connected with the time's social and economic climate. That same year, the two most powerful unions in the United States had merged: the American Federation of Labor and the Industrial Organizing Committee joined to form the AFL–CIO, the first nationally based American union. *The Pajama Game* appeared in perfect synchrony with these changes in industrial relations.

For the film adaptation, Warner Bros. turned to Stanley Donen, the now legendary director of classic musicals such as *Singin' in the Rain* (1952). Donen worked with George Abbott and Richard Bissell to write the script and employed the same creative team as the Broadway version. The only significant change was the addition of the scintillating Doris Day in Babe's role.

The film opens with the arrival of Sid Sorokin (John Raitt) as the new factory superintendent. Sid and Babe immediately fall in love, but their romance seems impossible because they are on opposite sides of the labor dispute. *The Pajama Game* thus follows the conventions of classic Hollywood storytelling with its use of a dual plot, one centered on a heterosexual romance and the other related to labor, war, a mission, or a quest, in this case, the dispute between factory management and the union over a pay rise.

When the union grievance committee learns that the factory is the only one in the industry that has not received the 7½ cents an hour wage increase agreed to in the new collective bargaining agreement, the workers threaten to strike. Mr. Hasler (Ralph Dunn), the gruff and unpleasant boss, blames the uproar on communist agitators. After he refuses the pay rise, the employees' sabotage production spurred on by Babe, who deliberately breaks a machine. Sid fires her, precipitating the strike and the breakup of their relationship.

We know very little about Sid. He recently arrived from Chicago, where he was a factory worker, and got the job of superintendent despite lacking credentials. In this sense, *The Pajama Game* anticipates *How to Succeed in Business Without Really Trying* in that the male protagonist uses deception to get his job. But unlike the protagonist of the former, Sid is not a cheat. He is in between management and the workers. This allows him to understand both sides. He knows the business well, and we even see him roll up his sleeves to repair broken machinery. Sid succeeds in work and love because he respects the workers and because, unlike Mr. Hasler, he genuinely cares about the smooth running of SleepTite.

In the film's final scenes, Sid discovers that the company has conceded the pay rise, but his boss has been pocketing the difference. So he blackmails Mr. Hasler into accepting the deal. Sid rushes to the union meeting where the workers have just performed the song "7½ cents", in which they have calculated how much money they could save with the raise and what they could buy as a result. It is a charming number that shows the importance of living wages in sustaining demand and economic growth.

"7½ cents", they sing. "Give it to me every hour, 40 hours every week, and it will be enough to live like a king!" By saving the increase for five, ten, or 20 years, without spending it, they could amass more than $53,000! And that does not take into account the interests they could get on those savings. The figure is large enough to finance their dreams—washing machines, travel, cars—which in turn would stimulate the economy.

The corrupt boss reluctantly announces that there will be a rise (albeit not retroactively). Babe shouts, "We won!" and everyone dances. It is a celebration of decent, honest work, an ode to American enterprise and its traditional values. The workers are thrilled to be back at work. Even

Mr. Hasler joins in the fun. There is no resentment for his corrupt ways. Class differences disappear, disagreements are forgotten. Sid and Babe are together again. She has found her blue-collar prince with whom, presumably, she will fulfill her domestic destiny.

But the cinematic representation of trade unions has not always been so positive. *Salt of the Earth* and *The Pajama Game* are the exceptions to the rule. The 1950s were abundant with films that dealt with themes of corruption and disappointment among workers (Zieger & Zieger, 1982). The most famous of them was *On the Waterfront* (1954). This iconic film kickstarted a very heterogeneous set of imitations: A bunch of sensationalistic B-movies—*Inside Detroit* (1956), *Chicago Confidential* (1957), and *Portland Exposé* (1957), the gangster film *The Big Operator* (1959) with Mickey Rooney, a British rehash of On the Waterfront entitled *The Angry Silence* (1960), the Boultings' satire *I'm All Right, Jack* (1959), and even a musical with James Cagney, *Never Steal Anything Small* (1959). Later films like *F.I.S.T.* (1978) and *Blue Collar* (1978) helped consolidate the narrative that trade unions are intrinsically corrupt and mafia-like organizations. *F.I.S.T.*, the fictional biopic of a Jimmy Hoffa-like union leader, is slightly more sympathetic. The film goes back to the violent labor conflicts of the 1930s, tinged with racial tensions between WASP capitalists and immigrant workers. The film suggests that workers resorted to mobsters to gather support after the police and management hired gunmen to repress them. *Blue Collar* is much more negative. Paul Schrader's script represents unions as hypocritical and corrupt institutions that only help their leaders advance their ambitions.

But as the intensity of narratives about inflation caused by excessive wage growth started to recede in the mid-1980s, things started to change with unions on the screen too (Shiller, 2019). As the turn of the century approached, films on labor conflicts integrated themselves into the broader theme of the deindustrialization of the West and its consequences for employment. *Brassed Off* (1996), *Billy Elliott* (2000), and *Pride* (2014) were feel-good comedies set during the British miners' strikes of the 1980s. All three stand alongside *Raining Stones* (1993), *The Van* (1996), and *Full Monty* (1997) in a venerable tradition of British films in which those affected by deindustrialization seek a way to escape the ravages of long-term unemployment.

Unions were gradually seen in a better light as the consequences of neoliberal policies became apparent. The widespread use of the term "neoliberal" since the 1990s became associated with two global economic processes. The intense financial deregulation that was taking place at the time, and globalization, accelerated by the free movement of capital. At this point, I must warn the reader that few economists believe that the term "neoliberalism" means much or that it is well defined. Critics of economics and film critics alike have abused the term to the point it is used to refer to any economic policy or idea considered pernicious. But as Dani Rodrik has rightly pointed out, the term has been used as a straw man does not mean that it is irrelevant or inappropriate (Rodrik, 2015). It is hard to deny that, since the 1980s, the world economy has undergone a marked shift in favor of markets, and fiscal progressivity has gone down.

The neoliberal doctrine is contained in the so-called Washington Consensus, a decalogue published in 1989 by the economist John Williamson that served as the basis for the policies of the International Monetary Fund and the World Bank since then. The ten points include fiscal discipline, clear property rights, liberalization of trade and finance, openness to foreign investment, deregulation of markets, and privatization of public enterprises. There is nothing wrong per se with markets, private initiative, or the proper use of incentives. Thanks to them, humankind is currently enjoying a prosperity level never seen before. But this is not to say that the neoliberal policies have no problems. *The Navigators* (2001) addresses one of their most disastrous applications: the privatizations of railways in 1990s Britain.

In 1996, British Rail, the state-owned company in charge of Britain's railways, was privatized by John Major's Conservative government after a bitter parliamentary battle. Its operations—passenger services, freight transport, equipment repair, track maintenance, ticketing, catering—were sold to private interests. The railway network was left in the hands of several competing companies. The immediate consequences were the dismissal of many workers and a severe deterioration in safety, leading to half a dozen serious accidents resulting in more than 50 deaths and almost 400 injuries. In fact, the filming of *The Navigators* began days before the Hatfield accident, which had its echo in the film.

Set in Yorkshire in 1995, *The Navigators* follows a group of five railway workers. Director Ken Loach aimed to show the precariousness of working conditions and the waning of solidarity among these workers. The story's believability rests on the screenplay written by Rob Dawber, a railway worker who died just after the film was finished as a result of exposure to asbestos while working on the tracks. Loach's improvised group scenes and a cast of nonprofessional actors give the film a documentary style. Comic vignettes of its five main characters' personal lives serve as relief of *The Navigators*' bleak subject matter.

After British Rail is privatized, the five members of the gang go to work for East Midlands Infrastructure, one of the companies now competing in the sector. The men who used to work together can no longer collaborate. They are not even allowed to talk to each other for fear of industrial espionage. Relations with management also deteriorate. The new manager—who Loach caricatures as a heartless and fatuous man—thinks union members are troublemakers and breaks the agreements that have been in place for years between workers and management. He is also quick to renege on a new deal he has signed when it suits him. "The days of a job for life are over", he tells his employees in a motivational video. Faced with this new situation, many men opt to take their severance packages and leave. One of them is Len (Andy Swallow). Another is Paul (Joe Duttine), burdened by the need to pay child support to his ex-wife. John (Dean Andrews) follows suit. Mick and Gerry (Tom Craig and Venn Tracey) try to dissuade them, believing they will lose the union's protection. Eventually, their workshop is deemed inefficient and closed. They all end up on the dole.

The only alternative is the temp agency, which offers them sporadic employment under much worse conditions. The five friends will no longer have paid sick leave and must pay for their transport, equipment, and compulsory training courses. There are no proper negotiations anymore. The bosses now have the upper hand. Without unions, any quarrel over safety conditions, for example, leads to the "troublemaker" being blacklisted. The agency no longer calls him in.

The Navigators deals with a recurring theme in Ken Loach's films: economic forces beyond their control dominate the working class's lives.[2] The dilemma they face is between holding on in the face of uncertainty and selling their jobs in exchange for severance pay. When Paul decides to take the money and run, Gerry reproaches him: "You're playing right into their bloody hands, they're putting us in a position where we've got no choice". Paul replies, "Exactly, we've got no choice". The erosion of workers' living conditions, their solidarity, and class consciousness leads

---

[2] "The Navigators", Ros Cranston, BFI Screenonline. Last accessed March 30, 2021, http://www.screenonline.org.uk/film/id/556980/index.html.

to a tragic end in which they are forced to face a new dilemma: help one of their own or ensure their livelihoods. Their choice is as grim as it is inexorable.

WAITING FOR THE ROBOTS

In 1960, Nobel Prize-winning economist Herbert Simon wrote, "Machines will be capable, within 20 years of doing any work a man can do".[3] And here we are. Automating the most routine tasks and the digitalization of the economy have rendered entire sectors obsolete and destroyed jobs. But the productivity gains that this process has generated have also increased income and demand for goods and jobs in other sectors. Whether the balance is positive or negative depends on the economy's ability to provide new jobs for the people whose jobs have been automated.

Cinema has often expressed the understandable anxiety society feels in the face of these changes. Humans have been worrying about "technological unemployment" for at least 500 years, ever since we discovered that machines could save us labor. When William Lee invented the weaving machine in 1588, Queen Elizabeth I of England refused to grant him a patent because she feared it would cause mass unemployment in the textile industry. During the Luddite riots in the early nineteenth century, textile workers destroyed mechanical looms. No wonder that these concerns appeared in cinema as early as Charles Chaplin's *Modern Times* (1936), Robert Siodmak's *The Whistle at Eaton Falls* (1951) and *Desk Set* (1957).

Modern Times was Chaplin's last silent film and his iconic Charlot's last appearance. The film is perhaps the most iconic expression of the anxiety created by job automation. The inspiration came to Chaplin during his 1931 European tour. He witnessed the intolerance, unemployment, and poverty that the Crash of 1929 had brought to the continent. In an interview he gave just after he returned, Chaplin said that "unemployment is a vital question. Machines should improve the welfare of mankind instead of causing tragedy and unemployment".[4] The first title card in *Modern*

---

[3] *The New Science of Management Decision* (1960), p. 38. New York: Harper & Row.

[4] "Filming Modern Times", *Charlie Chaplin.com*. Last accessed March 30, 2021, https://www.charliechaplin.com/en/articles/6-Filming-Modern-Times.

Times already tells us that it is "a story about industry and individual initiative, the human crusade in search of happiness".

The first image is of a herd of sheep superimposed on a group of workers entering a factory, a montage of straightforward symbolism that would have delighted Sergei Eisenstein. An extended scene follows where Charlot goes about his work on the assembly line. The expressionistic prominence of the conveyer belt and the workers' mechanical movements, which make them look like limbs of the machine, convey a sense of profound dehumanization. The influence of *Metropolis* is evident, although it seems that Chaplin was paying homage to Rene Clair's *Freedom for Us* (1931).

The factory president reads comic books for entertainment and monitors his employees like Big Brother, using a closed-circuit television that even reaches the toilets. He wants to increase productivity by maximizing working time at the expense of lunch breaks. To do this, he plans to use more machines. In a hilarious scene, a crazy contraption maltreats Charlot, a robot that is supposed to feed workers lunch while working.

This first segment of *Modern Times* is a parody of Fordism, the mass production system introduced in 1914 by Henry Ford. It generated an unprecedented increase in productivity and became the standard operating procedure of industrial production. Chaplin had visited a Ford plant in the 1920s and was deeply disturbed by what he saw there. His refusal to use no dialogues underscores the sounds of machines at work. Technology mediates the only voices we hear: the boss giving orders through the screen while the feeding machine speaks through a phonograph.

The atmosphere of dread and alienation reaches a point where Charlot suffers a panic attack. Prostrate on the conveyor belt, the assembly line swallows him like Jonah by the whale. He is transported through a maze of cogwheels while his companions try to get him out. When they succeed, Charlot starts desperately looking for objects to tighten with his spanners as if they were nuts: buttons on clothes, noses, hydrants. A Luddite impulse possesses him. He pulls mechanisms and levers, causing the central control to explode and the factory to grind to a halt. *Modern Times* returns to the theme of machinism toward the end of the film. He is now the assistant to the factory's veteran mechanic. Charlot tries to repair some machines strikers have sabotaged. His fight with the apparatus ends with the gear swallowing up the older man in another clear metaphor of Chaplin's preoccupation with the effects of technological progress. Chaplin characterized "modern times" as a new period where people have been left at the mercy of machines.

The Whistle at Eaton Falls is a film that is rarely discussed despite it was pioneering in articulating several economic anxieties that still worry us today, such as automation, global competition, and deindustrialization. It also underscored the importance of technological innovation. The Whistle at Eaton Falls was a somewhat atypical film for its time, halfway between a stance favoring workers and mixed forms of company management and the negative view of unions On the Waterfront exemplifies. The film tries to be balanced and even-handed, which might have led to it being mostly forgotten.

Brad Adams (Lloyd Bridges) is the union leader at Doubleday plastics factory in the fictional town of Eaton Falls. The documentary style of the first scenes tells us that another essential factory in the city has just closed. Doubleday is the only one left standing. It is Eaton Falls' primary and only source of economic activity. Its whistle is the one that now determines the start and end of the workday.

Brad Adams is called to the offices of Mr. Doubleday (Donald McKee), a firm but fair businessman, who tells him that the company is losing ground in the market because its costs are too high. Doubleday has purchased new machines that will reduce production costs dramatically. However, fewer employees operate these machines. Half of the staff will be made redundant.

Of course, Adams flatly refuses and declares that the union will not accept it. Doubleday responds with a reasonable argument: the adjustment will be temporary. The adoption of the machines means that Doubleday will lower its prices. The company will then receive more orders, and this increased demand will allow the company to hire back the dismissed workers. In the conversation between Adams and Doubleday we can hear echoes of an economic debate today. If we believe that there is a fixed number of jobs in the economy, then automation necessarily means that machines will displace humans. However, the number of jobs in an economy is not fixed. With automation, workers adapt, upgrade their skills, and take over robots' maintenance. In addition to this change in job composition, automation leads to an expansion of demand because goods are now cheaper to produce. With this new demand, unemployed workers can be hired again. Of course, the critical question is the net effect of automation. The answer given in The Whistle at Eaton Falls is that the net impact for Doubleday plastics will be zero in terms of jobs but ultimately positive because the factory will not close.

Another interesting aspect of the film is the plot twist that follows. On a trip to get a big order to save the company, Doubleday is killed in a car accident. Out of all the possible candidates, his wife chooses Brad Adams as the company's new president. But the union-leader-now-president is in a tough spot. The day before, Adams refused to adopt a new technology that would save the firm but dismiss half the workforce. Now he realizes that the company's situation is dire and that he will have to do something about it. If Adams brings in the machines, he will have to lay off half of his colleagues and lose their respect. But if he does not, the company will almost certainly disappear. This plot twist is designed to make Adams and the audience realize that there are no simple solutions to labor problems and that protesting and going on strike is not one of them.

Doubleday and Brad Adams represent the noble side of this dispute; they are opposite sides, but they always treat each other respectfully. Both have a darker counterpart, however. In the case of Adams, it is the most belligerent faction of the union, formed by men portrayed as troublemakers, extremists, communist agitators. But management also has a dark side. Doubleday is a paternalistic figure who has his employees' best interests at heart. Still, his right-hand Dawkins (Russell Hardie) is ruthless and utterly uninterested in his employees' welfare. He is ready to sell the company without remorse. In fact, there is a point in the film when these two extremes work together. With this, *The Whistle at Eaton Falls* tells us that neither the Darwinian capitalism represented by Dawkins nor recalcitrant and obtuse unionism can make an economy prosper.

How is this conflict resolved? Adams and his friends manage to reduce production costs by innovating. The plastic parts had to be cut out of their frames by hand until then. They modify the machines they already have to cut these parts, thus saving labor in a much less drastic way than what the new machines would do. As Doubleday prophesied, this will allow the factory to lower prices, get more orders, and even run three consecutive 8-hour shifts 24 hours a day.

The Whistle at Eaton Falls thus anticipates the two solutions cinema has put forward to save industrial workers from the threat of automation and market competition: Innovation and employees' (co-)ownership. In *Spotswood*, which we discussed in Chapter Two, the shoe factory at the center of the film survives from the competition of Asian imports thanks to product diversification. *Kinky Boots* (2005) recounted a similar story, this one based on the real-life case: a shoe factory dodges the deindustrialization of Northern England by reinventing itself to produce boots for drag queens. In *New in Town* (2009), which we will discuss in detail in the next chapter, a female executive saves a food factory in a small town from automation and then offshoring by developing a new line of products and turning the plant into a cooperative.

Take This Job and Shove It (1981) had already used a similar plot decades earlier but took it to a radically different conclusion. Frank Macklin (Robert Hays) is a successful executive who returns to his hometown in Iowa. His mission is to automate the brewery there. Of course, the corporation he works for is heartless and does not care about massive redundancies. Frank hides this from his old buddies, who admire him. But they could not have grown more apart from each other. Frank is an individualistic and sophisticated winner typical of the 1980s, whereas his old pals are gregarious and happy with the life they have. Frank tries to use a computer to reallocate workers more efficiently, but the attempt fails. When he succeeds using friendlier methods, the plant becomes so profitable that the owner wants to sell it. At that point, Frank completes his Scrooge's arc and persuades his friends to raise enough money to buy the factory and run it together. But *Take This Job and Shove It* refuses a conventional ending. When supervisors talk workers out of the cooperative idea, they understand they cannot do anything about the whole thing and quit. They leave the plant empty and happily. It is their bosses' problem now.

Desk Set shows that machines can replace even white-collar workers. It was adapted from a Broadway play and turned into a romantic comedy by Phoebe and Henry Ephron as a vehicle for Katharine Hepburn and Spencer Tracy. The Ephrons' rom coms—her daughter's Nora's included—, featured an underlying social conflict in which each member of the leading couple represented one side of the argument. *Desk Set* is an unusual example of this canon because the main dispute is both gendered and economic. The film offers a highly entertaining and fascinating snapshot of 1950s social anxiety toward automation, which serves as the source of comic and romantic tension between its protagonists. The humor in *Desk Set* still works today because contemporary audiences share with 1957 audiences a growing concern about the implications of technological progress for jobs.

The film was a blazing big-budget production shot in glorious Cinemascope. It takes place in a Mondrian-inspired design office belonging to a television network in a gleaming New York skyscraper. Bunny Watson (Hepburn) heads the company's all-female Reference Department, devoted to fact-checking and researching abstruse data such as how much the Earth weights. Almost nonexistent today, reference libraries were once an essential part of print and television media but were made obsolete by information technologies. Bunny and her colleagues work in an office that is not entirely outdated. They communicate with other departments through reports and memos sent by physical mail; they use typewriters rather than computers, big as a room back then.

In the 1950s, citizens in developed countries increasingly encountered computers in their interactions with bureaucracies and banks. Soon, they reached the workplace as well. As a result, massive, powerful, and intimidating machines appeared everywhere in popular culture, promising more leisure and mass unemployment. *Desk Set* was pioneering because it addressed the consequences of automation on high-paid workers in general and in women's incipient labor market participation in particular. Clerks, secretaries, librarians, and operators saw their livelihoods endangered by these new technologies. The film was also quite progressive in its depiction of a feminist workspace: its stance toward computers is ambivalent, but its female characters are independent and excellent employees.

Richard Sumner (Tracy) enters this warm, friendly, feminine workspace. A computer pioneer, an efficiency expert hired by the company to automate various departments. We know he is a clueless genius but not of a fool: When the network's president comments how unimpressive Sumner looks, he replies, "Wait till you see my bill. You'll be impressed". It seems Sumner is going to install EMERAC, an "electronic brain", at Bunny's department. He has already installed one in the payroll department, leading to half the staff's sacking. But his exact plans are a mystery to all. He swarms around the office, measuring the spaces and observing the librarians' work, making Bunny and her colleagues increasingly anxious about the possibility of being replaced by EMERAC. In and out of the office, Bunny and Sumner banter and flirt, though she tries to cool her growing attraction to him for fear that he is a wolf in sheep's clothing.

Desk Set wants to reassure audiences that automation will be positive for female workers. EMERAC is not as perfect as it seems. As demonstrated by the monumental mess that the computer at the payroll department makes by mistakenly firing all employees in the network, it needs human help. EMERAC also saves librarians a lot of effort. Finding the Earth's weight is precisely the kind of numerical operations a computer can perform instantly. Automation can free up workers' time, relieving them of routine jobs, time they can then spend on more satisfying and intellectually stimulating tasks. That said, EMERAC caused the dismissal of a good number of employees. Not everybody will go home happy at the end of the day.

Despite the tectonic changes automation has brought to the twenty-first-century economy, including to the very definition of work, so far, only science fiction has dealt with this issue directly. One exception is Tim Burton's 2005 adaptation of *Charlie and the Chocolate Factory*, where themes of job displacement feature both explicitly and implicitly.

Willy Wonka's successful innovation in the candy market provokes a cascade of what economists call general equilibrium effects. The increase in chocolate consumption leads to more children having tooth decay problems. That, in turn, leads to a rise in demand for toothpaste. Thanks to the new profits, the toothpaste company where Charlie's father worked screwing the caps on the toothpaste tubes could afford to buy a machine to automates that monotonous task. Mr. Bucket thus becomes another victim of technological unemployment. Because the country in which Charlie's family lives does not seem to offer subsidies to unemployed workers or active employment policies allowing them to acquire new skills, they are all forced into an existence of hardship and cabbage that they cope with as best they can.

Another knock-on effect of Wonka's success is that his rivals plant spies in his factory posing as employees. When he finds out all his secret recipes have been stolen, the chocolate genius fires all his workers, including Charlie's grandfather, and closes the factory to the outside world. No one enters for fifteen years now until Charlie and the other lucky finders of the golden tickets gain a factory tour. There they discover that Willy Wonka's sweets have continued to be a global success because of a key innovation: the Oompa Loompas. While traveling the world searching for new flavors, Wonka meets them in the jungle. The Oompa Loompas are a tribe that worships cocoa. Wonka offered them a deal: work in his factory in exchange for an infinite supply of cocoa beans. It was a mutually advantageous transaction. For the Oompa Loompas, cocoa was precious, and Wonka needed a workforce that would not betray him.

Seen metaphorically, Oompa Loompas are a form of automation. As Fromer (2019) argues, information technologies fueled by large databases have become the new Oompa Loompas, guardians of industrial secrets. Cloud computing, machine learning, and task automation make it easier to confine sensitive information within companies' confines by reducing the need to share software with customers, the demand for labor, and the risk of information leaks.

We do not yet know whether automation will lead to more jobs by increasing productivity and expanding the economy. Some data suggest it is not the case. This is known as the "productivity paradox", coined by Nobel Laureate Robert Solow: From the 1950s to the mid-1990s, computerization did not lead to a substantial increase in productivity. Although most recent studies fail to find conclusive evidence that productivity has grown faster in the most technology-intensive industries, the debate continues among economists.

Freedom of Movement

Interpreted straightforwardly, the Oompa Loompas are a form of immigrant labor. Roald Dahl's original story described them as small and dark-skinned people, which seems to corroborate that interpretation.[5] Willy Wonka employs the Oompa Loompas to make his products more competitive. Their wages are lower than those he paid to his former employees. As a result, Wonka's production costs go down, and sales recover.

Immigration is a pressing issue in Western democracies. Massive migration flows have accompanied the globalization process. About 3.4% of the world population reside outside their country of birth; 5 million people migrated to OECD countries in 2016 alone. There are 150 million migrant workers worldwide; 5 of them are victims of forced labor.[6]

Economic films have explored the issue of immigration, mainly from the perspective of migrant workers. These films illustrate migrant workers' poor working conditions and the marginalization they regrettably experience. The movies we will discuss next also show the rejection of migrants face from natives who fear that they will get jobs are their expense.

---

[5] Tim Burton's version softened both the original and the previous film adaptation, *Willy Wonka & the Chocolate Factory* (1971), where Wonka kept the Oompa Loompas under a feudal regime, offering them protection and sustenance in exchange for work.

[6] Data from the UN International Office for Migration. Last accessed March 30, 2021, https://www.iom.int/global-migration-trends.

Louis Malle's *Alamo Bay* was one of the first films to deal with the economic and cultural consequences of immigration. The film's context is the arrival of Vietnamese refugees who settled along the Texas Gulf Coast after the Vietnam War. Most of these migrants were fishers. Local shrimp fishers, many of whom were Vietnam vets, resent their presence. Violence ensued.

At the beginning of *Alamo* Bay, we learn that the economic situation of native fishers is not good. Shang (Ed Harris) has trouble paying off his boat and hates his new Vietnamese neighbors because he feels they are taking away their sustenance. The underlying conflict between these two communities is the Tragedy of the Commons problem we discussed in Chapter One: the "Anglo" fishermen believe that the refugees are overgrazing the shrimp stocks. They fear that the resulting increase in the supply of shrimp will decrease its price and ruin them.

Alamo Bay also offers the perspective from the other side. Dinh (Ho Nguyen) is a young Vietnamese who, like so many other migrants, is joining his relatives in the new land. As it is common in the cinema about immigration, the film depicts Dinh as a hard-working individual trying to live peacefully in his new country. He gets a job at Wallies, the local fishermen employer who is under intense pressure from the "Anglo" fishermen for renting boats to the Vietnamese.

The two groups collide after Shang misses some payments and loses his boat. He then becomes desperate and turns against Dinh and the refugees. The other locals join him, and tensions rise. Violence breaks out when the Ku Klux Klan and its nativist rhetoric show their ugly head.

A landmark in Hispanic cinema, *El Norte* (1983) told the story of Enrique (David Villalpando) and Rosa (Zaida Silvia Gutiérrez), a Guatemalan brother and sister fleeing their country's military regime. They travel to the United States searching for a new home. The first two acts of the film illustrate vividly the travails of economic migrants crossing borders on their way to the North. In the last act, they arrive in Los Angeles. Enrique and Rosa do not go long without work. They follow the typical path of migrant workers. They take menial jobs that natives do not want, usually jobs where language skills and personal interaction are not essential. Enrique as a busboy in a restaurant and Rosa as an ironer. The jobs migrant workers do often complement the natives', thus helping the economy grow. For example, by taking a job as a busboy, Enrique frees time for others, which translates into more work for natives as waiters or managers.

Irregular migrants like Enrique and Rosa tend to concentrate in manual, labor-intensive occupations such as slaughterhouses, agriculture fields, and heavy construction. They satisfy the need for cheap labor of these industries because their employees save the cost of paying them benefits. This, in turn, places migrant workers in a very vulnerable situation. This vulnerability is another common theme in films about immigration. Migrants are at the mercy of exploitative smugglers. For instance, in *El Norte*, a Mexican immigrant hustles jobs for new migrants for a fee; he finds a job for Rosa in a textile factory ironing clothes for only 30 cents a garment.

Migrants also work under the constant fear of deportation, which often means death or starvation in their home country. When the immigration services agents ("La Migra") raid Rosas's factory, she must run to avoid being deported back to Guatemala, where her father was killed for attempting to form a labor union. *El Norte* also shows that migrant workers try hard to adapt and regularize their situation. Enrique takes English classes, which lands him a foreman job and a chance for a green card.

El Norte was pioneering in putting a face to the shadow population of undocumented migrant workers who are a vital element of Western economies. In *Bread and Roses* (2000), Ken Loach would explore this issue. The film recounts the "Justice for Janitors" campaign in Los Angeles that seek the unionization of service employees, primarily migrant workers, in the 1990s.

The main character is Maya (Pilar Padilla), a brave and strong woman. At the beginning of the film, she has just arrived in Los Angeles after illegally crossing the border. Maya is reuniting with her sister Rosa (Elpidia Carrillo), searching for a better life in the United States. Thanks to Rosa, Maya finds a job cleaning the offices of law firms and Hollywood agents downtown. She soon discovers the vulnerable position migrants like her are in. Like all non-unionized janitors, Maya earns only $5.75 an hour and has no health insurance.

Then she meets Sam (Adrien Brody), a young union organizer. Following *Norma Rae*'s template, Sam encourages Maya to challenge her supervisors and fight their intimidation tactics. When the bosses fire a co-worker for refusing to snitch on others, Maya and Sam lead a protest against the building owner. It seems the moment is ripe for a union. But their attempt fails because Maya's sister betrays them.

Like in so many other characters in Ken Loach's films, Rosa faces a dilemma. She has an ailing husband and cannot afford to lose her job for joining the protest. In the film's most heartbreaking moment, the idealist and naive Maya confronts her older sister. Then she finds out that Rosa slept with the supervisor to get her a job as a cleaner and worked as a prostitute for years to pay for Maya's education. "I've been whoring all my life, and I'm tired", Rosa concludes.

The variety of explicit and implicit transactions of migrant workers have to enter into and their invisibility in the economy is also at the root of Richard Linklater's *Fast Food Nation* (2006), his complex but flawed adaptation of Eric Schlosser's best-seller. The film employs a series of vignettes to portray the economic interconnections between the food industry, migrant workers, and consumers.

A plotline follows two Latina sisters who have just arrived in Colorado after crossing the US–Mexico border guided by a coyote. Sylvia (Catalina Sandino Moreno) takes a job as a motel housekeeper while her sister Coco (Ana Claudia Talancon), along with Sylvia's husband Raul (Wilmer Walderrama), go to work at a meatpacking plant. Work there is brutal and gruesome. It is a nightmare. One of their jobs is removing kidneys from slaughtered cattle. They must work at inhuman speed, and a simple slip may result in fecal contamination. The migrant workers are terrorized by Mike (Bobby Cannavale), a sadistic supervisor who demands sexual favors from her female subordinates. When Raul is badly injured in an accident at the plant and becomes unable to work, Sylvia is forced to have sex with Mike in exchange for a job at the infamous "kill floor". In the last scene of the film, Sylvia ventures into that heart of darkness where migrants and cattle become the invisible inputs of the fast-food industry.

A few years earlier, Stephen Frears' had already explored the commodification of migrant work and flesh—human in this case. The title *Dirty Pretty Things* (2002) eloquently captures the idea that the "the pretty things" that users of the service economy enjoy hide the "dirty work" Migrant workers do. This idea is also encapsulated in the customer service motto of the Baltic Hotel, where the two main characters work: "Our guests leave dirty things, we make them pretty things".

Okwe (Chiwetel Ejiofor) is a Nigerian doctor working as a cab driver by day and as a desk clerk at the Baltic Hotel by night. He illegally shares a flat in London with Senay (Audrey Tautou), a Turkish Muslim woman who works as a chambermaid at the Baltic and as a sewing operator in a sweatshop. Although they are asylum seekers and are not legally entitled to work, they both work endless hours.

After Okwe finds a human heart clogging a toilet, he and Senay discover that the sleazy hotel manager Señor Juan (Sergi Lopez) is part of an organ trafficking ring. He takes advantage of desperate illegal immigrants willing to exchange their organs for a forged passport. Migrant women are also goods to be transacted. Senay is eventually coerced to prostitute herself with the disgusting sweatshop owner in exchange for protection from immigration authorities. Later she trades sex with Señor Juan for a passport to America. Thus, the film's thesis is that migrant bodies are literal commodities, wholesale, or by parts.

The janitors in *Bread and Roses*, the meatpackers in *Fast Food Nation*, the cab drivers and cleaners in *Dirty Pretty Things*. These films underscore that immigrant workers in the service sector are invisible and interchangeable commodities. Frears shot *Dirty Pretty Things* in London but refused to show any recognizable landmark in order to recreate a side of the city that natives and tourists never see. Migrants, as Okwe puts it very bluntly in the film, "We are the people you do not see. We are the ones who drive your cabs. We clean your rooms. And suck your cocks".

References

Fromer, J. C. (2019). Machines as the new Oompa-Loompas: Trade secrecy, the cloud, machine learning, and automation. *New York University Law Review*, 94, 706–736.

Heilbroner, R. L., & Milberg, W. S. (2008). *The making of economic society*. Pearson-Prentice Hall.

Hunter, L. (2003). The celluloid cubicle: Regressive constructions of masculinity in 1990s office movies. *The Journal of American Culture*, 26(1), 71–86.

Koustas, D. K. (2019). What do big data tell us about why people take gig economy jobs? *AEA Papers and Proceedings*, 109, 367–371.

Krueger, A. (2018). *Reflections on dwindling worker bargaining power and monetary policy*. Federal Reserve Bank of Kansas City Economic Symposium, Jackson Hole.

Rodrik, D. (2015). *Economics rules: The rights and wrongs of the dismal science*. W. W. Norton & Company.

Rogin, M. (2002). How the working class saved capitalism: The new labor history and The Devil and Miss Jones. *The Journal of American History*, 89(1), 87–114.

Shiller, R. J. (2019). *Narrative Economics*. Princeton University Press.

Zaniello, T. (2003). *Working stiffs, union maids, reds, and riffraff: An expanded guide to films about labor*. Cornell University Press.

Zieger, G. P., Zieger, R. H. (1982). Unions on the silver screen: A review-essay on F.I.S.T., Blue Collar and Norma Rae. *Labor History, 23*(1), 67–78.

CHAPTER 8

Women at Work

Despite the public debates and increasing awareness, there is still a lack of effective equality for women in the workplace. Gaps in wages and promotion opportunities translate into an under-representation of women in positions of responsibility and decision-making, both in private companies and public institutions. For example, only one in four board members in large European corporations is a woman.[1] The differences in labor market outcomes between men and women have part of their roots at home. Motherhood and the unequal sharing of child-rearing are some of the reasons for this "glass ceiling" and the lower earnings of working women (Kleven et al., 2019). Social norms that deem women's careers of lesser importance and relegate women to homemaking also drive the lower female participation in the labor market. There is also discrimination in the workplace. Men tend to hire and promote other men (Reuben et al., 2014), so women's lack of representation in senior positions is self-perpetuating. Harassment at the workplace also falls disproportionally on women. The majority of working women in the United States have experienced sexual harassment.[2] Evidence shows that workplace

---

[1] Database on women and men in decision-making, European Commission, April 2016.
[2] "Sexual Harassment at Work in the Era of #MeToo", Pew Research Center. April 4, 2018. Last accessed March 30, 2021, https://www.pewresearch.org/social-trends/2018/04/04/sexual-harassment-at-work-in-the-era-of-metoo/.

© The Author(s), under exclusive license to Springer Nature Switzerland AG 2021
S. Sanchez-Pages, *The Representation of Economics in Cinema*, https://doi.org/10.1007/978-3-030-80181-6_8

harassment has a negative impact on job training, promotions and the employment of those who suffer it.[3] Harassment has significant ethical and economic consequences: When females participate less in the workforce, and there are fewer women entrepreneurs, the economy suffers (Cuberes & Teignier, 2016).

That said, the situation of women in the labor market had changed dramatically since World War II. During the conflict, thousands of women contributed to the war effort by taking jobs in all industries. That impacted gender norms for a while, as Jonathan Demme recounted in the form of a screwball comedy in *Swing Shift* (1984). This change was met with a quite intense backlash. Only since the 1970s, it became socially acceptable again that women pursued a career. Cinema has documented these changes in the participation of women in the labor market and the many difficulties that both white-collar and industrial female workers have encountered in the process. The films about working women are often compelling because they depict courageous characters fighting against traditional gender roles and domesticity expectations. These films have also expressed the anxiety of male audiences and filmmakers toward working women. Inevitably, sex has also formed part of the representation of the role of women in the economy, either through sex workers or through the implicit exchange that working women are expected to put up with in abusive corporate environments.

Stay Home or Else

One of the first explorations of the gender issue in films about labor conflicts was *The Devil and Miss Jones*, which we already discussed in Chapter Two. The film portrays the lives of women working in a department store in a reasonably realistic, albeit comic way. They play a strong leading role in the labor action that drives the film's plot. They are feisty fighters, ready to run the establishment if given a chance. In contrast, men come across as timorous, naïve, and old-fashioned. The main male character, Joe, Mary's boyfriend, is a passionate unionist but when he is blacklisted and cannot find a job, he feels distraught because he will not be

---

[3] "Sexual Harassment and Assault at Work: Understanding the Costs", Institute for Women's Policy Research. October 15, 2018. Last accessed March 30, 2021, https://iwpr.org/iwpr-publications/briefing-paper/sexual-harassment-and-assault-at-work-understanding-the-costs/.

able to support his girlfriend. The relationship between the older couple of protagonists, Elizabeth and JP Merrick, also draws out the economic barriers to love, barriers absent in other class-based comedies of the period such as *Easy Living* (1937) or *Fifth Avenue Girl* (1939). In these films, the romance between workers and capitalists mitigated the threat the former posed to the latter. Except for *The Devil and Miss Jones*, these romances did not make wealthier characters readjust their worldview and care more about those below them (Rogin, 2002).

A decade later, *Salt of the Earth* also highlighted the gender conflict by advancing the idea that changes in the labor market are not possible without changes in housework distribution. Esperanza is the narrative voice of the film. Her strength and courage contribute to creating a sense of solidarity in the miners' community. While her husband Ramón and the other men allow themselves to be intimidated by their bosses and become easy prey to their "divide and rule" tactics, Esperanza and the other women present an organized and resilient front. "You want to go down fighting, is that it? I don't want to go down fighting. I want to win", Rosario tells her husband. The women's superior effectiveness during the strike becomes evident in a compelling sequence in which, after being identified by a strike-buster, the police arrests Esperanza and the other picket leaders, assuming that will end the protest. Once in jail, the wives and mothers start shouting and making loud noises until the sheriff releases them to stop the commotion.

But these films were the exception to the rule. Most post-war films about businesswomen or female workers depicted them as unhappy. The central tenet of these films was that there exists a fundamental trade-off between career and domestic success. This is most apparent in the case of the divorced mother played by Joan Crawford in *Mildred Pierce* (1945). Mildred goes from being a waitress to becoming a successful entrepreneur, a restaurant owner. She is ambitious and talented, but to a large extent, she just wants to provide for her two daughters and gain their love. The film blames the death of one of them and the miseducation of the other on Mildred's absence from home due to her career ambitions (Boozer, 2002). She also loses her business because she does not pay enough attention to its finance and logistics. Mildred's utter failure on all fronts serves as a cautionary tale to other women who try to find validation and success outside the home.

During the 1940s and 1950s, cinema sent an unequivocal message. Men in high-paid jobs could buy great suits, get a good haircut, and indulge in refined tastes. They formed a new royalty that relied on their wives' quiet labor, whose place was to stay at home and support their husbands. Women faced all sorts of barriers if they sought to escape their predetermined role as loyal companions and public relations. We already saw this in our survey of the corporate films of the 1950s in Chapter Four. Even in a relatively progressive film like *Patterns*, the only female characters other than wives are secretaries, either devoted to their boss or maleficent gossipers. But the film that best encapsulates this conservative view of women and work is the ironically titled *Woman's World* (1954). Directed by Jean Negulesco, its main aim was to reassure its predominantly female audience that it is possible to be happy when your husband is a corporate executive and shows up late every night, and to celebrate the crucial importance of wives in their husband's success.

The film tells the story of the efforts of the owner of the fictitious Gifford Motors, a powerful automobile company, to replace its managing director, who has died because of stress. To this end, millionaire Ernest Gifford (Clifton Webb) invites his three best salesmen and their wives to New York with all expenses paid. For four days, he will examine them and pick one. He believes that the company will only be in good hands if there is the right balance between the spouses—an excuse to show attractive married couples wearing glamorous outfits.

Lauren Bacall plays the sophisticated and intelligent wife of Fred MacMurray (Sid Burns), a savvy executive whose ambition is costing him his health and marriage. Arlene Dahl plays the explosive and greedy wife of the sincere and straightforward Jerry Talbot (Van Heflin), whom she tries to help by using her undeniable charms on Gifford. Finally, Katie (June Allyson) is the innocent, nervous wife of honest Bill Baxter (Cornel Wilde), overwhelmed by the New York skyline and the responsibility of making her husband look good. Her character functions as comic relief: she stumbles, screws up every conversation and suffers a series of humiliating accidents. Her clumsiness makes her the audience's favorite. Gifford takes the three men to visit an assembly line and the company's design studio for casual questioning and arranged a series of meetings (dinners, receptions, a cruise) to observe their wives. In the final test, Gifford invites the three couples to a weekend retreat at his mansion, where his sister will assess the three wives closely and provide her brother with all the information he needs.

Gifford and his sister evaluate the three married couples as if they were an executive team. After all, a corporation as vast and powerful as

Gifford Motors puts a great deal of responsibility on the hands of the men (always men) who run it. What if their families take up too much of their time? What if their wives are too ambitious? Or too possessive? Or too crass? The film's title is ironic because the women are presented only as wives. Often, they are not even called by name. They are trophies to be exhibited. The praise they receive is almost exclusively about their looks. They must be glamorous and sophisticated, as well as sympathetic to their husbands' ambitions. *Woman's World* wanted to convince its audience that marriage is a contract between the sexes in which women have the upper hand. As Lauren Bacall's character explains to the voluptuous Mrs. Talbot, "men work more for their children than for their wives. And you wouldn't mind because after all, they would be the children you had given him. That's why the world is not a man's world; the world is a woman's world".

In the late 1950s and the 1960s, women in industrialized countries began to enter the labor market. More and more films reflected this new social and economic reality, albeit within a contradictory framework. The narrow limits society imposed on women were denounced through protagonists who openly demanded equality, like Doris Day's character in *The Pajama Game*. Still, none of these heroines questioned their fate as wives and mothers. The new type of working woman on the screen was single or childless and juggled her career with her romantic life. For her, the job was secondary to marriage and motherhood. Her expectation, once she found love, was domesticity. In this era's films, "a woman's best choice in life is love. This will be her basic career".[4] Doris Day was indeed the key figure in this strand of films. The widowed mother and businesswoman she played in *It Happened to Jane* (1959) and the successful ad executive from *Lover Come Back* are bubbly, independent, ambitious, and optimistic characters who, despite their talent and assertiveness, would leave everything for a good man.

That said, the middle-class working women that Day portrayed during these years already hinted that female ingenuity and assertiveness are advantageous in the sclerotic and old-fashioned structures of the corporate world. *The Wheeler Dealers* illustrated this idea using the main elements of Doris Day's romantic comedies of the late 1950s and early

---

[4] Jeanine Basinger, *A Woman's View* (1993), p. 257. Hanover: Wesleyan University Press.

1960s to deliver a surprisingly caustic blow to the male-dominated finance world and the discrimination of women at work.

The female protagonist of *The Wheeler Dealers* is Molly, an assertive and emancipated securities analyst. She is one of a small group of courageous women trying to break Wall Street's glass ceiling. An industry where mediocre men thrive and where, as her roommate tells her, women "have to work twice as hard to get half as far as a man". Molly is the only woman and the best stockbroker working for the inept Bullard Bear (Jim Backus), whose brokerage firm is in the red because of the shoddy financial advice it supplies to its clients. Bear is a male chauvinist who thinks that women should not work in the stock market because they are emotionally unstable and that men should give them not even an inch because "otherwise they might turn on us like rabid dogs!". He believes that he can cut costs and ease his losses by firing Molly. To avoid any legal problems, he orders her on an impossible mission: She must sell the shares of a company that has not made any sale for decades and that produces no one knows what. Thus, *The Wheeler Dealers* offered a surprisingly feminist portrait of finance as a sector in which male colleagues and superiors relegate women to a secondary role. These are usually much less talented but support each other through the so-called old boys' networks. That is probably why the film did not enjoy much commercial success or subsequent artistic impact.

It took a quarter of a century for another female stock trader to appear in cinema. In the little-known and mildly feminist *Limit Up* (1989), Nancy Allen plays Casey, a broker in the Chicago Board of Trade who ambitions to become a trader in soybean futures. It is a harsh and male-dominated environment where she is constantly sidelined and denied any opportunity. Her very mean boss (Dean Stockwell) tells her bluntly that she will never make it. *Limit Up* is a very contradictory film. It explains well how future markets work—including the concept of a "limit up"—and the importance of finance in the real economy. The producers even rebuilt the Chicago soybean market's trading floor on a set, and some real traders appeared as extras. But the film also represents the stock market as a game of gods (literally) where talent and skill are irrelevant, and only "intuition" works. Casey succeeds in the end only because she signs a Faustian pact with an apparently evil spirit named Nike (Danitra Vance), who manipulates the market to the aspiring trader's advantage. She realizes Nike wants her to corner the world soybean market to create a famine in the Third World. Casey will have to risk her career and marriage to stand up for herself.

Working-Class Girls

The 1970s represented a turning point in women's role in the economy. The losses in household income and male employment during the decade's crises and the introduction of modern contraception and time-saving home appliances such as the washing machine or the vacuum cleaner (Fernandez, 2013) led women to enter the workforce in droves. Working women on the screen were no longer interested in catching a good husband. They became increasingly concerned about equal pay, unionization, gender norms at home, and sorority in the workplace.

Blue-collar female workers started appearing in films as breadwinners and unionization movement leaders. The first expression of this tectonic change in economic and social norms was *Norma Rae* (1978). The film chronicles workers' efforts at a fictional O.P. Henley textile mill to unionize. The plot is based on the conflict between the J.P. Stevens textile company and its factory employees in Roanoke Rapids, North Carolina. But the film also chronicles the emotional awakening of Norma Rae (Sally Field), a single mother. She lives and works with her elderly parents in the factory and risks everything in her struggle to improve the workers' conditions, which border on slavery.

Their situation is deplorable. The health of the factory's employees matters less to the company than their productivity. At the beginning of the film, Norma Rae's mother temporarily loses her hearing. The company doctor tells her not to worry because "it happens all the time". An elderly female worker explains to Norma during a meeting that "they force you to work standing up unless you have a doctor's note". Norma Rae's father dies of a heart attack, slumped over a pile of spools after asking for a break the foreman denied him.

Wages are not adequate either. Norma's father's salary did not change in the 30 years he was employed at the factory, not even to compensate for inflation. The work shifts go on forever. Norma struggles to make ends meet and barely has any time left to spend with her children and help them with their homework. Although she is outraged by the terrible working conditions and the company's indifference to its employees' welfare, Norma Rae begins the film resigned to her predicament. O.P. Henley is the largest employer in town, and there are few other options for someone with her qualifications. It is then that Reuben Warsowsky (Ron Lieberman), a union activist from New York, comes along with the idea of organizing the workers despite stiff opposition from the company and the employees themselves. Reuben and Norma become friends. He eventually convinces her that unionization is the only way forward.

Together, they persuade the other workers that it is in their power to change things. However, uniting them is not easy. They face a collective action problem for starters: unionization will only be effective if enough people support it. The incentive is to let others face the risk of retaliation by the company and wait to receive the potential benefits.

The social and cultural context further complicates matters. The factory is located in a small, religious town in the American South. Many of its citizens are violently opposed to the union because they see it as a communist outpost. Others believe it will bring nothing but trouble, that the factory will close, and they will be out of work. When Norma Rae asks the local priest for permission to hold a union meeting at the church, he refuses. She is no longer welcome there. One of the reasons behind this refusal is stifling racism. When Norma arranges the meeting at her home, her new husband (Beau Bridges) tells her worriedly, "there's a bunch of black people in there. You're going to get us in trouble". Reuben is insulted and scorned by the factory managers for being Jewish. Later, employers use racial differences to divide the workers and break up their collective action.

The other division that appears in the film is that of gender. The culture around Norma is deeply sexist. People in her community start whispering behind her back about her alleged promiscuity and lack of domesticity. Norma's husband is a good man, but he too is a product of that culture. He expects a wife to clean the house, look after the children and make him dinner. Norma's combativeness spreads to other women. In the film's best-remembered sequence, Norma raises a sign stating "Union". The first operatives to stop their machines are female. They and the black workers vote in favor of unionization at the film's climax. By the end of the film, Norma has become empowered; she has developed her latent potential. She has become an independent woman, capable of making her own decisions. She has changed in the same way the labor market and society were changing in the late 1970s.

Reality would imitate fiction a year after the premiere of *Norma Rae*. After a long dispute, workers at the Roanoke Rapids factory brought J.P. Stevens to the bargaining table. In yet another proof of cinema's power over economics, the film became instrumental in organizing a nationwide union boycott of the company. Sally Field and Crystal Lee Sutton, the woman on whom Norma Rae's character was based, supported this campaign.

Norma Rae would become a cornerstone of the cinema about blue-collar female workers. It served as a model for *Silkwood*, *Erin Brockovich*, *North Country* (2005), and *Made in Dagenham* (2010). These films are all based on actual events in which strong and determined female characters lead manual workers' struggle to improve their conditions or expose corporate malfeasances. When defying the gender conventions of their time and place, all these women pay the cost of confronting their partners, their elders, and their environments' traditionalism.

Unfortunately, J.P. Stevens kept struggling due to the economy's ups and downs in the following years. In the 1980s, the company fell prey to the wave of hostile takeovers portrayed in films such as *Wall Street* and *Other People's Money*. In 2003, the plant Roanoke Rapids closed once the competition from textiles made in India and Pakistan become irresistible. Ironically, those imported textiles were produced under the same semi-slavery conditions suffered by Norma Rae and her co-workers decades earlier. Today, the primary employer in Roanoke Rapids is Walmart, which pays even lower wages and is even more hostile to unionization.

In *Silkwood*, Meryl Streep played another courageous industrial worker who fights against her employer. She works in a nuclear plant and becomes increasingly involved with the union as she grows outraged by the appalling security measures. Some of her co-workers resent her for this, while her community reprobates her unconventional household arrangements. Like many other whistle-blowers in film, she sacrifices her love life in seek of the truth; her boyfriend Drew (Kurt Russell) does not like being sidelined by her newfound activism. The real Karen Silkwood was killed in a mysterious car crash soon before she was about to testify against her corporate bosses. Although the film does not explicitly point its finger at a culprit, it frames Silkwood's tragic end within the standard narrative of evil corporations.

Made in Dagenham is based on another real case, the strike at Ford's plant in Dagenham in 1968. The female sewing machinists walked out from the factory protesting against gender discrimination in job grading. The strike lasted for three weeks. The machinists got a pay rise but not a re-grading. However, their action decisively contributed to the 1970 Equal Pay Act.

In contrast to *Norma Rae* or *Silkwood*, *Made in Dagenham* is a much looser and glossier recount of the actual events it is based on. It is a feel-good movie in the template of *The Full Monty* or *Billy Elliott*. Its main goal was to show that individual effort can overcome economic adversity and inequalities. It uses a fictional character who serves as a surrogate for the audience. Rita O'Grady (Sally Hawkins) is a sewing machinist fed up with being patronized at work and home. She stands up, coalesces her co-workers, and persuades them to broaden their fight from job re-grading to nationwide equal pay. The women encounter male union members' resistance because they deem the machinists' struggle as subsidiary to theirs. A conflict also erupts within the household, as Rita experiences herself; husbands must reconsider the traditional gender roles and the relative importance of their careers over their wives'. The film closes with the customary passionate speech where Rita demands the union delegates to support women in their fight for equal pay.

Fairy Tales

Unionism has been just one way in which fictional working-class women have claimed equal rights in the economic sphere. There have been other routes. *Places in the Heart* (1984) tells the story of Edna (Sally Field again), a housewife who becomes a successful entrepreneur in Texas during the Great Depression. When her husband, the town's sheriff, gets killed, she is forced to run the family farm to support her children. Times have changed, so where Mildred Pierce failed miserably, Edna succeeds. She does so thanks to the decisive help of a black drifter played by Danny Glover, who teaches her the economics and science of cotton growing, including how to bargain with buyers. Their unlikely alliance shocks her community and raises all kinds of rumors. As in many other economic films, the main villains are the banks, that want to foreclosure Edna's debt, and the intermediaries, who try to take advantage of her inexperience. *Places in the Heart* suggests that the local economic powers feel threatened by Edna's financial independence and draw upon their connection with the Ku Klux Klan to deter the entry of what they perceive as a competitor on both the economic and the gender arena.

Erin Brockovich is the story of a woman struggling against social expectations that dictate that she should put her children above her work. Her ascension from unemployed working-class single mother to white-collar worker and media personality opens a rift between Erin and George

(Aaron Eckhart), her first neighbor then boyfriend. Gender roles are transposed between them as Erin becomes a businesswoman—a typically male role—while George takes care of the children and the household—a stereotypical female role. George criticizes Erin for being selfish and neglecting her family. Erin asks him to support her in her fight against P&G because people are respecting and listening to her for the first time in her life. When her job begins to take a severe toll on their relationship, George accuses Erin of being a bad mother and leaves. That her conflict with George resolves without Erin having to give up her career aspirations illustrates that the changes taking place in society and the labor market at the turn of the century were irreversible.

Joy (2015) gives a (so far) unique female spin to the stories about innovators we discussed in Chapter Five. To the best of my knowledge, all the films about creators and entrepreneurs who face the challenges of coming up with a new product and commercializing have male protagonists. *Joy* is the exception.

Directed by David O. Russell, *Joy* is not a biopic *avant la lettre*. It is inspired by Joy Mangano's life, the woman who invented the Miracle Mop. Mangano developed more than 100 patents, such as velvet-covered hangers to prevent clothes from falling off and a small steamer to smooth out wrinkles in clothes. In that respect, *Joy* markedly differs from the films about male innovators. Joy does not change an entire industry; she invents products for housewives like herself. That may not say as much about Russell's and Annie Mumolo's screenplay as it does about the abysmal innovation gender gap in our economies; female inventors file only 13% of patent applications.[5]

Two films that we have already discussed have an obvious parallel with *Joy*. The first one is *Erin Brockovich*. Joy (Jennifer Lawrence) is also a single, working-class mother, intelligent, resourceful, and willing to overcome all the obstacles she encounters. The second film is *Mildred Pierce*. Like Mildred, Joy wants to provide for her daughters and give them the financial and emotional stability she did not have when she was little, but she is also ambitious and wants to succeed. The contrast between the two films illustrates how much things had changed between 1945 and 2015.

---

[5] "Gender Profiles in Worldwide Patenting: An Analysis of Female Inventorship", UK Intellectual Property Office. October 2, 2019. Last accessed March 30, 2021, https://www.gov.uk/government/publications/gender-profiles-in-worldwide-patenting-an-analysis-of-female-inventorship-2019-edition.

Joy tells a success story. *Mildred Pierce* punishes her central character for overstepping beyond her supposed place in society.

When we meet Joy, she is a single mother of two who can barely pay her mortgage and who lives with her family, including her ex-husband (Edgar Ramirez), who stays in the basement because they remain good friends and he has nowhere else to go. Her mother (Virginia Madsen) spends her days watching soap operas in bed and brushing her hair. His father (Robert de Niro) owns a truck repair company, and Joy does the bookkeeping. When his girlfriend leaves him, he comes to live with Joy. Russell and co-writer Annie Mumolo aim to make an obvious parallel between Joy's complicated family situation and the soap operas the four generations of women in the family watch compulsively.

Her situation changes when her father's new girlfriend, an Italian millionaire played by Isabella Rossellini, agrees to invest in Joy's new mop design, a design Joy came up with, as usual in films about innovators, in a flash of genius. That is where the fairy-tale side of the film starts: Joy is a woman who liked to solve practical, day-to-day problems since she was a child, gets enough money to take her project off the ground, overcomes the doubts everyone has about her—even her own—deals with all the usual problems innovators face, and ultimately succeeds.

Because she has little to no commercial experience, Joy is especially vulnerable to scammers and charlatans. For example, she hires a company in California to manufacture the mop parts and ends up being tricked; she is told that there is already a patent for the design and that she must pay for it. Then she encounters distribution problems because supermarkets do not want to devote shelf space to her relatively expensive product ($19.95 in the early 1990s).

Joy meets Neil Walker (Bradley Cooper), an executive of the recently created television channel QVC. Walker allows her to advertise her mop in the channel, but before that, Joy must produce 50,000 units, for which she takes out a second mortgage. After the professional presenter ruins the pitch on-camera, Walker gives Joy a second chance. She demonstrates the product herself. It seems it will end in another unmitigated disaster, but Joy's charisma and spontaneity win over the audience. The Miracle Mop becomes a roaring success. In fact, in the first appearance of the real Joy Mangano on QVC, she sold 18,000 mops in just 30 minutes.

As the reader can see, there is not much of a difference between the character arc Joy goes through and that of the typical male innovator in film. Unsurprisingly, she must confront her main antagonist in the third act; in this case, a corrupt businessman who has stolen her patent. Joy's creed is no different from that of her male counterparts on the screen. She tells one of her daughters that "we have come this far thanks to hard work, patience and humility". Later, she clarifies that "you should never think that the world owes you anything because the world owes you nothing". These ideas about the value of individual effort, risk-taking, and profit motives are the basic staples of films about entrepreneurship.

Yet, *Joy* contains a key difference with respect to all films in which the innovator is a man: The importance of family in the entrepreneur's journey. In *Tucker: The Man and His Dream* or *A Flash of Genius*, the family was essential to their central characters. But even in the latter, Robert Kearns' children and wife leave him when the inventor becomes too volatile. In other films about innovators, the wife is there just to warn her man that he is not on the right track or to support him after each setback. In *Steve Jobs*, we are told that Jobs refused to acknowledge he had a daughter and only reunited with her after Apple reinstated him and the iMac met a tremendous success. The case of *The Social Network* is even starker. The innovation takes place as a reaction against an affective relationship; Zuckerberg comes up with the idea of Facebook after his girlfriend dumps him.

In contrast, Joy's success is collective. Her family often acts as a hindrance and is a constant source of worries and headaches. Her father even tells her that her initial lack of success is his fault because he gave Joy "the confidence to think she was more than an unemployed housewife". But Joy draws her strength from her family too. Her product gets off the ground because her father's new girlfriend invests in her. She meets Neil Walker through her ex-husband. When she is paralyzed with fear while advertising the Miracle Mop at QVC, her best friend Jackie (Dascha Polanco) calls the show pretending to be an anonymous caller. Recognizing her voice, Joy calms down and demonstrates her product more naturally. Her family helps her take care of her children when they are sick, or Joy is away, even bailing her out of jail. The contrast with the films about male entrepreneurs is striking. In *Joy*, entrepreneurship is not the result of individual genius alone; the support, care, and connections that Joy draws from her close-knit family are crucial.

Corporate Comedies and Femme Fatales

As women's labor market participation rates took off—from about 50% in 1970 United States to 67.5% in 1990[6]—another stereotype emerged in the popular culture of the 1980s: The "independent woman", a talented and dynamic white-collar female worker qualified for top executive jobs and hostile to the conventional gender roles. Several economic films of the decade explored the obstacles faced by these white, middle-class working women in a cultural environment that, despite all changes, still did not accept them as equals. The best-known examples of this subgenre are *Baby Boom* (1987) and *Working Girl* (1988). But the first one and most accomplished of all was *9 to 5* (1980).

Right from the opening credits—a montage of women preparing for a day's work—*9 to 5* establishes a dialogue with the new urban, working woman. Violet (Lily Tomlin), Judy (Jane Fonda), and Doralee (Dolly Parton) are three secretaries working under the shadow of the same unbearable and narcissistic boss (Dabney Coleman). These characters aimed to capture three different sources of dissatisfaction at work. Violet is looking for a promotion. She is intelligent and brilliant, much more so than her boss, yet she must fetch coffees or run errands for him. She is denied a promotion "because customers prefer a man when it comes to numbers", as his boss puts it.

On the other hand, Judy's husband has just dumped her and has eloped with his secretary. She needs a job to become financially independent. Finally, Doralee is an exuberant blonde constantly harassed by the boss, who likes to brag that she has yielded to his sexual advances. Doralee's colleagues believe him simply because of her looks. As a result, she has become an outcast. This initial lack of solidarity between female co-workers is a recurrent aspect in later films about working women.

Soon enough, the three women become friends and team up to take down their boss; first literally, then professionally. *9 to 5* offers a basic but effective metaphor for women's need to work together to get rid of a mediocre superior who enjoys a commanding position just because he is a man. It is an early cinematic example of sorority in the workplace. Another point of interest appears when the three secretaries kidnap their boss and impersonate him. They start making changes in the office (changes their boss was utterly opposed to) that lead to a 20% increase in

---

[6] OECD Stat (2019).

productivity: daycare, flexible working hours, work-sharing, and equal pay within each grade. This is another trope in films about women at work: Women run things better, a trope that can be traced back to Aristophanes' *Lysistrata*. While men favor rulebooks, authority, and hierarchy, women believe in cooperation, kindness, and humor. The reversal of fortunes at the ending of *9 to 5* makes the audience feel good because the irritating and cumbersome male regime is replaced by a simpler, more compassionate, and feminine approach to business, which turns out to be also more profitable.

Considered as a feminist film at the time of its release, the popular *Working Girl* (1988) demonstrated that the normalization of women in the labor market was still a long way off. Its protagonist, Tess McGill (Melanie Griffith), is an efficient and ambitious secretary from a working-class background who hits the "glass ceiling", that is, the set of factors that make it difficult for women to reach top positions in companies. Tess is often sexually objectified by her colleagues. Her boss Katherine (Sigourney Weaver) steals her business ideas to make things worse. To advance her career, Tess will have to cross-dress, ditch her hoop earrings and colorful clothes, and adopt the more monochrome, masculine attire of a business executive (Lee & Raesch, 2015). Still, Tess's sexuality plays a role in her rise; her body appears conveniently undressed in a couple of sequences. She even teases her immediate boss (Harrison Ford): "I have a mind for business and a body for sin". Furthermore, the central conflict in *Working Girl* is between two women: Katherine and Tess fight for the man and the career advancement they both desire. Tess prevails because she is a clever working-class girl rather than an arrogant yuppie, but her triumph is ambiguous. Tess is not even honest; she admits to being an impostor. She had to lie and pretend to get to the top.

Baby Boom (1987) represented another step back to the old gender norms. In this variation of the Scrooge arc, Diane Keaton is a successful New York executive who is taught a lesson in the virtues of motherhood and domesticity after unexpectedly "inheriting a baby". Her new life as a mother forces her to rethink her priorities: she leaves her job, her boyfriend and moves to the countryside, where she establishes a small business with the support of her new romantic partner. *Baby Boom* ultimately distrusted the career-driven woman, portraying her as insensitive and misguided.

Other films of the period, such as *Fatal Attraction* (1987), *The Temp* (1993), and *Disclosure* would not be so kind to career women. They unambiguously pathologize working women by turning them into femme fatales. These temptresses were meant to embody masculine fears toward the rise of women in the labor market and the extension of corporate logic and economic exchanges to sex and the body.

In *Fatal Attraction*, Glenn Close plays a successful professional, but single and childless. Driven by jealously and envy, she threatens Michael Douglas' character; she was to control his family in the same way she manages her office (Boozer, 2002). In *The Temp*, Lara Flynn Boyle is a hypercompetent secretary who uses sex to climb the corporate ladder. Again, she jeopardizes his boss's attempts to reunite with his ex-wife. The corporate femme fatale she embodies is as scheming and ambitious as her male colleagues; the difference is that she uses her body and looks to achieve her goals. In *Disclosure*, the same is true of Meredith (Demi Moore), another scheming executive who uses sexual manipulation to her benefit. Opposite to her is Tom (Michael Douglas again), a family man looking for a promotion using conventional means.

The film also conveys male anxieties about successful women. That becomes apparent when, early in the firm, an aged unemployed executive warns Tom: "In the old days we had fun with women. Now, one may take your job". Meredith confirms the negative stereotypes about career women. Her meteoric rise is due to her sexual dalliances and not her competency. Actually, Tom prevails in the end because his technical expertise is far superior to Meredith's. But *Disclosure* is sleazy enough to espouse the opposite view. Meredith uses seduction because in the corporate world, as portrayed in the film, everybody cuts corners and throats one way or another. As one of Tom's female subordinates puts it: "A woman has to be twice as good as a man and work twice as hard to double to get the same job and less pay". Meredith is just playing with the boys using their rules; another form of predation.

One exception to the problematic portrait of successful businesswomen in the 1980s and 1990s cinema is Kate, the young and attractive single lawyer Penelope Ann Miller played in *Other People's Money*. Kate chooses to defend her father's company from Garfield "The Liquidator". In doing so, she faces an ethical dilemma. On the one hand, she represents her father, and thus a community, in the face of corporate hostility. But at the same time, Garfield offers her the opportunity of a lucrative career, albeit one that may mean yielding to his romantic advances. Still, Kate manages to preserve her principles intact and reconcile her career with her parents and her community's loyalty.

Confused, Discriminated, and Stressed

The "cubicle films" of the late 1990s we discussed in Chapter Six had their female-cast and too often neglected predecessors in *Office Killer* (1997) and *Clockwatchers* (1997). In these films, female office workers feel the same end-of-century discomfort with their lives and jobs, depicted as alienating and soul-destroying.

Cindy Sherman's *Office Killer* had an abysmal critical reception, not without some reason. But it deserves to be vindicated and put into context. The killer in the title is Dorine (Carol Kane), who works for a publishing house. Her job is downsized, and she is forced to work from home. She rebels against her company by murdering her former colleagues. The film is deliberately grotesque, much in the spirit of Sherman's photography work, but that is just a mannerist representation of the same mood that underlies *Fight Club* or *Office Space*. Dorine uses her victims' corpses to recreate a happy office environment in her basement as a tableau vivant (sorry for the pun).

Clockwatchers is a much more straightforward film, but it is equally unknown despite it was the first film in the subgenre of alienated cubicle workers. Co-writers Jill and Karen Sprecher based their script on their experiences working as temporary secretaries. That is the job of the four protagonists, four "temps" who spend their days trying to dodge the incompetence of the executives they work for, the pettiness of their co-workers, and the long hours of boredom. Everybody in the office pretends to be working, although no one quite knows what they are working on or what they are working for.

The film begins when the shy Iris (Tony Colette) joins the company. She quickly strikes up a friendship with the group made up of Margaret (Parker Posey), a talkative and angry rebel, aspiring actress Paula (Lisa Kudrow), and Jane (Alanna Ubach), a traditional girl who is about to get married and stop working. They teach Iris the tricks of the trade: How to get through the day without being bothered too much by their bosses and how to get hold of the office supplies one colleague jealously guards. The film's title refers to their habit of looking at the clock until it strikes 5 p.m. to leave the office and have some fun.

Temporary secretaries are at the bottom of the corporate pyramid. Their direct bosses do not know their names; few people know they exist, and they are not treated with much respect. No one has spent much time inducting or teaching them how to do their job. It is understood that they will leave sooner than later. And because they will not stay for long, they have little incentive to do their job well. The exception is Margaret, who tries to impress one of the executives to become his personal secretary. But she is overtaken by Cleo (Helen FitzGerald), who enters directly as a permanent secretary because she is the niece of someone higher up.

After a series of petty thefts, the company installs security cameras. The atmosphere becomes tenser. Suspicions spread, and mistrust takes its toll on the four friends. Their friendship breaks down because the office is now an anomie; workers are not united, and it is "every man for himself". As expected, the troublemakers are picked and dismissed. The excellent cast of actresses superbly conveys this gradual deterioration process: first, the wear caused by the repetitive and purposeless work, then the cracks the robberies open in their friendship. The production design—the furniture, the objects, the unbearable and constant ambient music—underscores this environment of alienation and ultimate isolation.

Is this all there is to life? the characters of these cubicle films seem to wonder. Jane pins her hopes on her future married life; Paula on her dreams of becoming an actress. Both are attempts to find something beyond their drab and grey existence. Iris tries to resist her father, who insists that she should become a saleswoman and leave her job as a secretary. Iris dislikes both options. She just wonders what lies beyond work, what will become of her life.

Up the corporate ladder, things were not perfect either. In the late 1990s, prejudices were still pervasive in films about women's struggle to land top jobs. *The Associate* (1996) revisited the French movie of the same name from 1979, changing the gender of the protagonist to criticize male privilege in finance. Lauren (Whoopi Goldberg) opens her own brokerage when her colleague Frank (Tim Daily), a white man, is promoted after taking credit for a report she had written. After her new business fails, she has an idea: To create an imaginary partner, a white, middle-aged man. She renames the firm, and it becomes a great success. Everything goes smoothly until Lauren is forced to impersonate her made-up partner.

Both *Working Girl* and *The Associate* criticize the financial industry, described as the preserve of blatantly sexist men, very often less intelligent and hard-working than their female counterparts. While *Working Girl* has no problem highlighting Melanie Griffith's youth and beauty, *The Associate* denies sexual agency and romance to Whoopi Goldberg's character, a black woman in her forties (Lee & Raesch, 2015). Therefore, it would seem that to succeed in business in the 1990s, a woman had to give up being feminine or the opposite to display and use her sexuality.

More recent films have offered a somewhat more balanced view of high-paid women. The protagonists of romantic comedies at the turn of the millennium, such that *The Wedding Planner* (2001), *Two Weeks' Notice*, and *Sweet Home Alabama* (2002), begin their story arcs accomplished and financially independent. But they also feel that something is amiss in their lives, generally a Prince Charming who would fulfil their lives. *New in Town* may not be the best or the funniest among all of them. Still, it is the most interesting from an economic point of view because of its depiction of a very successful career woman and the difficult coexistence between career and family. It even contains a surprisingly critical subtext toward market forces, automation, and globalization.

Lucy Hill (Renée Zellweger) is a determined and ambitious executive very different from the lovable and clumsy Bridget Jones. She goes jogging every morning and has a perfectly tidy home in Miami Beach. She does not hide her conventional attractiveness (blonde, long hair, slender body), nor she is willing to give up her career for a partner. She is the only woman on the executive board of the company she works for and the only one to accept moving to New Ulm, a small, snowy town in Minnesota, to oversee the automation of the food plant there. Her goal is to move up the corporate ladder. Lucy seems to have neither a sense of humor nor scruples: she does not mind that her mission is to implement a 50% downsizing that will leave many families in New Ulm without support.

Once she arrives at the picturesque village, Lucy is in for a huge culture shock. The locals are quirky and gregarious. Their life revolves around church meetings, pubs, and agricultural contests. No one seems too keen to work. This contrast climaxes in the quarrel over female role models and the US economy that Lucy has with Ted (Harry Connick Jr.), the union liaison and local fireman who eventually becomes her romantic interest. Their dialogue is very telling:

> *Lucy*: Industrial competition in a free-market economy is what built this country.
> *Ted*: No, robber barons built this country, and they did it from the blood of working folks. Hell, you steal somebody's car, you get thrown in jail, you steal somebody's life savings, you get to be a CEO.
> *Lucy*: I'm planning on being a CEO.

As Betty Kaklamanidou points out in her study of romantic comedies (Kaklamanidou, 2013), this dialogue constitutes an unusual gender reversal: For once, it is not the man who is depicted as ambitious and career-oriented. Ted is kind, humble, and committed to his community. After her wife died, he moved to a small town to raise his daughter away from harmful external influences. In contrast, Lucy appears as a traditional alpha male who is not afraid to express her ideology and ambitions. Her devotion to her career and her eulogy for free-market capitalism describes her as someone who defends an impersonal economic system in which people are just exchangeable commodities. Lucy's lack of sensitivity and humor and her professional zeal are positive traits in the corporate world, but in New Ulm, she just seems neurotic and wrong-headed.

Lucy does not quit her job to become a suburban mother. Instead, *New in Town* suggests that heterosexual romance is compatible with a successful career. Lucy is greeted with suspicion and hostility by Stu Kopenhafer (J.K. Simmons), the gruff but honest plant foreman, and by most male workers. Despite being tricked by them on a couple of occasions, Lucy is undeterred and does not shy away from confrontation. For example, when the nearby lake freezes over, she drives down there to confront Stu for calling a covert strike. And when her company insists on automating the plant, Lucy stays with the community and creates a new product in record time—a tapioca pudding, a recipe from her secretary. The plan is very reminiscent of the one Diane Keaton hatched in the last act of *Baby Boom*, but the pudding is used here to save an entire town and not just her career.

Lucy succeeds and gets the promotion she craved. Faced with the dilemma between her budding romance with Ted and her job, she opts for the latter and returns to Miami. A parallel montage shows Lucy and Ted back to their former daily lives, somewhat sadder and more reflective than before. But the film sticks to its guns: a woman with a fulfilling professional life does not need a Prince Charming. When the pudding becomes a resounding success, her company decides to offshore the New Ulm plant to increase production and cut labor costs. In a surprising twist, Lucy comes up with an idea to save New Ulm from the effects of globalization: a group of investors buys the plant so that the workers can gradually buy it out and turn it into a self-managed cooperative. The only condition she imposes is to become its managing director.

The Intern (2015) also explored the conflict between family life and career success highly successful female entrepreneurs face. Jules Ostin

(Anne Hathaway) has founded an online clothing retailer. She is an overachiever and a multi-tasker. She rides a bike from meeting to meeting while texting, putting down fires, and intervening in almost every business aspect. Her company is tearing at the seams because of its tremendous growth. The outside investors are nudging her to hire a CEO, but she is very reluctant to give up complete control.

But her entrepreneurial drive has a price. She is always late, and her family life is suffering. Jule's husband Matt (Anders Holm) left a good marketing job to become a stay-at-home-dad and care for their daughter. The reversal in gender roles is complete, as we see when Jules picks up her daughter; she is frown upon by the non-working moms in the schoolyard. We soon learn that Matt feels emasculated and has an affair with one of the school mothers. Jules is devastated and temporarily agrees to hire a new CEO to patch her marriage. But she ultimately decides that she is not the one to blame; she should not sacrifice her ambitions to make her husband feel better.

The positive portrait of working women in recent films such as *New in Town* or *The Intern* does not mean that gender discrimination and inequalities no longer exist in the workplace; far from it. *Equity* (2016) and *The Number One* (2017) explore this burning and controversial issue in the guise of corporate thrillers. They expose the misogyny and sexism faced by women seeking high responsibility positions.

Director Meera Menon offers in *Equity* several insights into the glass ceiling problem. Naomi (Anna Gun) is an investment banker who oversees the IPO of a new and hyper-secure social network (or so it is assumed). If successful, the operation will earn Naomi a coveted promotion to director of global operations. She is a workaholic and has no husband, just an on-and-off lover (James Purefoy), a hedge fund broker at her bank. In the opening scenes, we see her speaking at a conference with other female executives to whom she describes her main motivations: Money, plain and simple. No guilt, no regrets. Her speech updates Gordon Gekko's "Greed is good" dictum in *Wall Street*.

The two female characters surrounding Naomi pose a revealing contrast with this hyper-successful female executive. Her assistant Erin (Sarah Megan Thomas) hides that she is pregnant to avoid damaging her chances of succeeding Naomi. Former schoolmate Samantha (Alysia Reiner), now turned public attorney, investigates insider trading at Naomi's bank. The male characters are just cardboard cut-outs: the vice president is just "one of the boys", the creator of the social network is a spoiled brat, and the president of Naomi's company is an arrogant loud-mouthed jerk who pits her female employees against each other.

The plot unrolls confusingly, and the financial operations work like magic tricks embellished with obscure jargon. But unlike the other films set in the financial sector that we discussed in Chapter Two, *Equity* does not trace the typical redemption arc in which the central character discovers that money does not bring happiness. Naomi indeed discovers that her personal relationships were unsound; men who feel threatened by her ambition and power sabotage her. She also finds out that success requires stabbing a few people in the back. But the moral in *Equity* is much more subtle than in other films of a similar ilk. Menon is careful not to offer a clear conclusion. She treats the events in the movie like a natural consequence of Archimedes' principle: in the corporate world, for some people to go up, other people must go down.

Sex Trades

Sex has been a constant but subtle presence in the films we have discussed in this chapter. In workplaces, sex is often transacted implicitly or explicitly. In *Working Girl*, Tess' career success is partly based on her sex appeal. The erotic thrillers of the 1990s would take this to the extreme. They shamelessly pandered to the stereotype of ambitious women climbing the corporate ladder by sleeping with their bosses. In *Equity*, female employees are encouraged to titillate their clients with the prospect of sex. Sexual harassment can also be conceptualized as a transaction where the monopsonist, the male employer with market power, pushes the female worker to accept abuse in exchange for employment or better job prospects. In the case of sex workers, the transaction is explicit. Next, we will review some films about prostitution and sexual harassment that highlight that sex is a commodity, a business, and a form of work.

Prostitution is said to be the oldest business in the world. It is undoubtedly one of the most lucrative: it contributes to about 0.4% of the UK economy.[7] It is not surprising that cinema has explored the economics of prostitution. Business comedies such as *Night Shift* (1982) and *Risky Business* (1983) presented prostitution as a legitimate business operated by middle-class entrepreneurs—two morgue clerks in the former and a

[7] Office of National Statistics (2014).

business student in the latter. It is not by chance that these films were released during the business-friendly 1980s; prostitution was considered as just any other business as long as commercial appearances concealed its sordidness (Boozer, 2002).

The representation of prostitutes and prostitution in film tends to be strongly stereotypical. It is either sordid, like in *Last Exit to Brooklyn* (1989), or excessively softened, like with Julia Roberts' character in *Pretty Woman*. Two films, however, stand out in their representation of prostitution as a form of economic exchange and production.

Chantal Akerman's masterpiece, *Jeanne Dielman, 23, quai du commerce, 1080 Brussels* (1975), recounts three days in the life of a widowed housewife (Delphine Seyrig). For 225 minutes, Jeanne methodically performs the household chores that constitute the center of her life, rarely leaving the house except to run some errands. Every moment is shot with extreme care and detail. The film's length and the ten-minute long takes underscore the minutiae of the domestic and non-remunerated female labor that Richard Gordon dubbed the "homework economy"; an economy that cinema most often renders invisible.

Jeanne boils potatoes, cleans, cooks for her son, reads and babysits the neighbor's baby. She performs these tasks relentlessly. They are never really concluded. Every afternoon, she has sex with an unidentified man. She is paid for it. Akerman refuses to treat Jeanne's sex work as a spectacle. It is a transaction portrayed as any other domestic chore. Jeanne undertakes it with the exact casual resolution she makes coffee. Homemaking and prostitution are described as two forms of reproductive labor. In her household work, Jeanne sells her labor for an indefinite period; as a prostitute, she sells her labor for a limited time (Sequeira Bras, 2019). The only other significant difference between the two activities is that Jeanne receives no economic compensation for her daily chores, not even her son's recognition, who takes them for granted. The same applies to GDP statistics, which do not include non-market household production despite it accounts for 23% of the US economy (Kanal & Kornegay, 2019).[8]

In *Working Girls* (1986), director Lizzie Borden takes a similar route. The film recounts a day in the life of Molly (Louise Smith), a prostitute in a Manhattan upscale brothel, and her co-workers. Molly is well educated and lies to her girlfriend about her job. When the film opens, we see

---

[8] Kanal, D., Kornegay, J. T. (2019). "Accounting for Household Production in the National Accounts. An Update, 1965–2017". *Survey of Current Business*, 99(6), pp. 1–9.

her waking up and preparing to go to work as if she was just one of the women getting ready for another day in the office in the opening credits of *9 to 5*.

The parallel Borden makes between "the world's oldest profession", and any other office job is deliberate. *Working Girls* portrays prostitution as just another economic exchange. It is a transaction between equals because middle-class prostitutes have some market power as the men who enter a brothel are vulnerable to blackmailing or social reprobation. Molly can choose her clients and how much she wants to involve herself. For her, prostitution is just another economic choice. It has its obvious downsides compared to formal work, but it is more remunerative than others. In an interview, Borden explained Molly's choice: "To choose to work two to three shifts a week as a prostitute and make the same money or more as working a 40- or 50-hour workweek, where the work is demeaning, exhausting, not necessarily in somebody's field of passion so that it's morally dispiriting, is a real choice".[9]

Like Akerman, Borden chose to demystify sex work, but she did it by showing it without any glamour or eroticism. The sex scenes are portrayed as an exchange of goods that follows a pre-specified ritual: the shower, the condom, the money, setting the bed. The prostitutes behave in a business-like fashion and offer their clients a drink, and some chitchat in the same way as waitresses, stewardesses, and PR women do when servicing men. Their implicit exchange is very similar.

We see the prostitutes getting bored over the day, repeating the same instructions to each new client, bantering among them, busy with minutiae like bookkeeping and lunch orders. For them, like for Jeanne Dielman, life is just a daily cycle of tedious chores. The only point of conflict is with management; their boss Lucy (Ellen McElduff), exploits them. Molly's autonomy is thus only apparent. Lucy is a compulsive shopper with the demeanor of a corporate executive. She pushes her employees to the limit asking them to take additional shifts and lies to them if necessary. Only the camaraderie between the working girls makes their day tolerable.

As mentioned earlier, sexual harassment in the workplace can be seen as another form of sexual exchange; it is highly unequal, though, as it is based on the (market) power male employers have over female employees

---

[9] "Anarcha-Filmmaker: An Interview with Lizzie Borden". (1987). Alexandra Devon and Catehrina Tammaro. *Kick it Over*, 18.

and candidates. As we mentioned earlier, sexual harassment is commonplace and pervasive and has devastating effects on those who suffer it. The societal reckoning with this problem is relatively recent. For that reason, it has been portrayed sparsely in film.

The little-known film *Business as Usual* (1987) based on a real-life case in Liverpool in 1983, was pioneering in this regard. Babs (Glenda Jackson) works at a clothes store in that city. She upholds the complaint of one of the young women in her team against the shop manager for having sexually harassed her. As a result, Babs is sacked. She turns to the union for help. Her local agrees to call a picket, which ruins the store's grand re-opening. The company responds using dirty tricks with the police's connivance. Babs' activist son and her girlfriend are arrested and subjected to abuse.

Business as Usual is an oddity in British cinema. It portrayed unions in a favorable light and was distributed by Cannon Films, famous for their action-B pictures. But it recounted a critical moment in the fight for working women's rights in Britain. It made sexual harassment in the workplace a public issue. The film also offers an interesting contrast between the increasingly activist Babs and her stay-at-home husband Kieran (John Taw), who became unemployed after failing to keep his factory open. With the traditional gender roles reversed, tensions emerge between them about whose fight is more important and, in the background, between the failing industrial sector and the rising service economy.

Cinema would not explicitly tackle sexual harassment at the workplace again until *North Country*, also based on a real case: the first successful sexual harassment class action in the United States against an employer. Charlize Theron plays Josey Aimes, a single mother of two who returns to her hometown in Northern Minnesota after getting divorced. Her parents (Sissy Spacek and Richard Jenkins) greet her with mixed emotions. Reputation is important in their small and traditional community, and their daughter's life has not been exemplary according to their values. They ask her to reconcile with her husband. But Josey is uninterested. She is determined to become financially independent and enters the job market. Josey first tries with typical women's jobs. She gets a job as a hairdresser, but it does not pay much. Thanks to an old friend (Frances McDormand), Josey considers another option: the local mine. She becomes one of the few female miners in the town. And like the rest of them, she is harassed, groped, humiliated, and assaulted by her male co-workers. Josey brings the situation to her supervisor and then all the way to the president of the company, but she is ignored, patronized, or just invited to leave.

North Country shows that the male miners' resentment toward Josey and the other women miners is partly due to competition for scarce jobs. They rationalize their attitude by saying that it is not women's place to drive trucks or haul rock. But, as Josey's father puts it very clearly, for them, Josey is taking the job away from a man "who needs it to support his family".

Another interesting aspect of *North Country* is the dynamics that Josey's decision to keep working creates in her workplace and her community. The mines are the primary source of economic activity for the town. Workers and their families have bonded and built a community around it. When Josey accuses Bobby Sharp (Jeremy Renner) of assaulting her, the community turns against her and takes her as another careerist using sex to advance her goals. She is told to "spend less time stirring up your female co-workers and in the beds of your male co-workers". Josey also suffers the hostility of her female colleagues. In that regard, *North Country* markedly differs from the stories of sorority in *Norma Rae* and *Silkwood*, other films inspired by real-life women who fought against all odds and won.

The most recent films to tackle sexual harassment were produced in the aftermath of the #MeToo and the It Stops Now movements. *Bombshell* (2019) and *The Assistant* (2019) tackle the issue from tonal and aesthetical poles.

Bombshell recounts the scandal that took down Roger Ailes (John Lithgow), the head of Fox News, after it surfaced that she had sexually harassed her female subordinates for years. Ailes used his position to engage in predatory behavior in exchange for career promotions. Director Jay Roach uses similar techniques to those of *The Big Short*: fourth wall breaks, quick editing, voice-overs, and multiple camera angles. The film blends humor and drama using three main storylines, each dealing with one of the women who come forward to expose the truth: Gretchen Carlson (Nicole Kidman), the reluctant Megyn Kelly (Charlize Theron), afraid of ruining her career, and the young and ambitious Kayla (Margot Robbie), who falls prey to Ailes' tactics. *Bombshell* is not a particularly subtle film. It wants its conclusion to be transparent: Sexual harassment in the workplace is a big problem, but the bad guys can be defeated if women team up and fight.

While *Bombshell* is told from the perspective of the victims, the point of view of *The Assistant* is that of those on the periphery of the abuse. Kitty Green's brilliant film focuses on one character down the office pyramid. Everybody else turns a blind eye to the sexual misdeeds of their superior, indirectly enabling his abuses.

Deeply influenced by *Jeanne Dielman, 23, quai du commerce, 1080 Brussels*, *The Assistant* deals with one day in the life of Jane (Julia Garner), an extremely competent assistant for a film mogul, as she churns through the menial chores that make up her daily work. She arrives before dawn and is the last to go. She cleans the odd stains on her boss' sofa, makes coffee, makes photocopies—hundreds of them—, prepares and hands drafts of scripts, washes the dishes, orders lunch, and stacks boxes of erectile dysfunction treatments. The audience only gets a few glimpses of Jane's boss, a stand-in for Harvey Weinstein. We see his silhouette and his reflection in the mirror. Like the creature in a monster film, he is never in full view. We only get to hear his frightening voice through the phone when he calls to abuse Jane for something she has done wrong verbally. She puts up with it every day because it is a big job opportunity.

Everybody in the office knows what is going on. Their boss has sex with young girls, mostly aspiring actresses, in exchange for roles or jobs. He does it in hotels and even in his office. When Jane meets one of these inexperienced girls and takes her to a luxury hotel, she grows very concerned. She warns HR about what his boss is likely to be doing with that girl. But the head of HR (Matthew Macfadyen) warns her that her career will be over if she files a report. The job market is difficult. People would die to be in her place. As the head of HR tells her, there are already 400 applicants for her position. Jane is alone and has no allies; like everybody else in the company. The two male assistants working next to her prefer to mind their own business and are happy just to survive the abuses they also receive from their boss. It is her against everybody else. Jane dreams of becoming a producer one day. She thus agrees to the implicit exchange she is being offered: she trades her silence for her job prospects in a similar way the girls her boss abuses trade sex for a career in acting. By becoming an accomplice to her boss, Jane and her colleagues perpetuate the same economic power system they are trapped in.

References

Boozer, J. (2002). *Career movies*. University of Texas Press.

Cuberes, D., & Teignier, M. (2016). Aggregate effects of gender gaps in the labor market: A quantitative estimate. *Journal of Human Capital, 10*(1), 1–32.

Fernandez, R. (2013). Cultural change as learning: The evolution of female labor force participation over a century. *The American Economic Review, 103*(1), 472–500.

Kaklamanidou, B. (2013). *Genre, gender and the effects of neoliberalism: The new millennium Hollywood rom com*. Routledge.

Kleven, H., Landais, C., & Sogaard, J. E. (2019). Children and gender inequality: Evidence from Denmark. *American Economic Journal: Applied Economics, 11*(4), 181–209.

Lee, M., & Raesch, M. (2015). Women, gender, and the financial markets in Hollywood films. In K. Silva & K. Mendes (Eds.), *Feminist Erasures*. Palgrave Macmillan.

Reuben, E., Sapienza, P., & Zingales, L. (2014). How stereotypes impair women's careers in science. *Proceedings of the National Academy of Sciences, 111*(12), 4403–4408.

Rogin, M. (2002). How the working class saved capitalism: The New Labor history and *The Devil and Miss Jones*. *The Journal of American History, 89*(1), 87–114.

Sequeira Bras, P. (2019). Time and reproductive labour in *Jeanne Dielman, 23 quai du Commerce, 1080 Bruxelles* (1975) and *Three Sisters* (2012). *Parse, 9*. https://parsejournal.com/article/time-and-reproductive-labour-in-jeanne-dielman-23-quai-du-commerce-1080-bruxelles-1975-and-three-sisters-2012/. Last accessed 30 Mar 2021.

CHAPTER 9

Crises

Economic films are experiencing a moment of splendor. Ironically, the origin of this bonanza is the financial crisis of 2008 and the subsequent Great Recession. Cinema and TV have become increasingly interested in explaining how the economy works. TV movies such as *Too Big to Fail* (2011) or *The Wizard of Lies* (2015) and dozens of documentaries like *Inside Job* (2010) attempted to craft a narrative of the financial crisis. *Margin Call* was probably the most remarkable among these for its detailed, almost microscopic portrayal of the dynamics that led to Lehman Brothers' collapse. Oliver Stone stressed in *Wall Street 2: Money Never Sleeps* that the genesis of the subprime crisis was a moral hazard problem; private financial institutions knew that they would not have to pay the full cost of the risky choices they were making. The crisis prompted another veteran, Martin Scorsese, to dust off his artillery. In *The Wolf of Wall Street*, he took advantage of the climate of social hostility against financial markets to offer yet another portrait of an addicted and self-destructive character. *Arbitrage* (2012), inspired in Bernie Madoff's case, adhered to the narrative that the world of finance is a great hustle and its gurus, naked emperors.

Before delving into these films and how cinema has represented the financial crisis of 2008, we will go back in time for a little while. The Great Recession was not the first economic crisis to appear in cinema. We

© The Author(s), under exclusive license to Springer Nature Switzerland AG 2021
S. Sanchez-Pages, *The Representation of Economics in Cinema*, https://doi.org/10.1007/978-3-030-80181-6_9

will touch first on the Great Depression of the 1930s and on the climate of economic insecurity that plagued the Western World during the oil crises of the 1970s and early 1980s.

"I'LL BE THERE TOO"

During the Great Depression, Hollywood films had an ambivalent relationship with luxury. On the one hand, it seemed unethical for characters to flaunt their wealth; plots were more often domestic and centered on working-class characters. But some upbeat comedies and musicals attempted to boost public morale by offering a lavish spectacle that humanized the upper classes. *Gold-Diggers of 1933* (1933), Mervyn LeRoy's delightful classic starring Ginger Rogers, contained spectacular musical numbers such as "We are in the money" and "Remember my forgotten man" that showed both sides of the unequal economic reality of the time. Rogers and Le Roy reunited in *Fifth Avenue Girl*, where the actress played a witty tramp taken in by a kind millionaire. In *Easy Living*, a fur coat falls from the sky over Jean Arthur's lap, taking her to hobnob with high society.

In *Modern Times*, Charlot's tribulations described the hard economic reality of the 1930s, a reality of unemployment, poverty, and social unrest. The tramp goes in and out of prison, in and out of various jobs, exposing workers' precarious life. The scene in which Charlot picks up a red flag that falls from a lorry and waves it to attract the driver's attention while a workers' demonstration gathers behind him is well-remembered. He ends up in prison, accused of subversion. Through these and other misunderstandings and misadventures, Charles Chaplin expressed the modern anxiety toward an economy over which ordinary people have no control.

When Charlot gets out of prison, he meets a tramp girl (Paulette Goddard) who steals to eat. When she is caught, Charlot takes the blame for her and returns to prison because he lived pretty well there. Their romance offers him some hope and a semblance of the life he aspires to. The couple moves into a dilapidated shack. They can only afford meagre meals, distorted imitations of middle-class comforts. When Charlot gets a job as a security guard in a department store, the couple sneaks in after-hours and creates a fantasy of comfort: they take delicious pastries in the cafeteria, a mink coat from the clothing section, and lie in a comfortable bed at the home section. The fiction they construct is a reminder that the Great Depression was a time of poverty and gross inequality.

In 1940, John Ford released two films based on best-selling novels published in 1939: Richard Lewellyn's *How Green Was My Valley* and John Steinbeck's *The Grapes of Wrath*. The former was a mournful, nostalgic ode to a bygone and better time. The latter was about the abject poverty suffered during the recent Great Depression by thousands of Americans. John Ford's adaptation of Steinbeck's bestseller would become a cinema classic, a masterful display of the director's mastery. The film is unambiguously pro-labor and pro-New Deal. For Ford, the workers' struggle was heroic, and state intervention was a positive factor during the economic upheaval of the 1930s.

The film opens with Tom Joad (Henry Fonda) returning to his family farm after spending four years in prison for killing a man in self-defense. He is unaware that the Joads no longer live there. The context of *The Grapes of Wrath* is the violent dust storms that decimated the crops of the Southern Great Plains, the so-called Dust Bowl, in the mid-1930s. Many farmers could not pay their loans, and the banks took over their land. It was then that the tractor was introduced. It became more profitable to farm with the new machinery than to employ the old owners as sharecroppers. Steinbeck and Ford located the origin of this structural change in the banks. They are represented as abstract, remote, and cruel entities, embodied by the army of bulldozers that evict farmers from their land, by tear down their shacks and destroy all their possessions. That was the fate of the Joad family too. Like thousands of Oklahoma farmers— pejoratively known then as "Okies"—they were forced off the land where they have worked and lived for generations.

Like many other displaced sharecroppers, the Joads travel to California in a rickety pickup truck, lured by pamphlets announcing that plentiful employment opportunities and good wages await them there. After an ordeal of a journey that is meant to resemble the Jewish people's exodus, the Joads arrive in the new promised land where, they believe, rivers of milk and honey flow. They find there a camp of migrants even more impoverished and desperate than them. A rancher offers them a house and a job in exchange for exploitative wages. They have little choice but to accept. Before they enter the ranch, the police have to clear a path because a hateful crowd has gathered at the sides of the road. The Joads are unaware that the ranchers are pushing local workers to accept lower wages by bringing in displaced farmers like them who are willing to accept poverty wages. This influx of hungry migrants increases the number of available workers, thus reducing the market wage and increasing the landowners' profits.

The ranch owner is a monopsonist. He has acquired enough market power to dictate the wage and the working conditions of the hundreds of pickers who offer their labor for a day's pay. The worse the starting position of these workers is, the more market power the buyer has. The result is a wage below the subsistence level. In fact, hundreds of children starved to death during the Great Depression in camps like those depicted in the film.

After meeting ex-preacher Casey (John Carradine), Tom understands this predicament, Now a union leader, casey is trying to organize a strike and unionize workers to obtain a decent minimum wage, one enough to cover the basic needs of families. Apart from ensuring a decent living, a wage floor is positive in a monopsony situation because it breaks the buyer's market power and increases the number of workers who are willing to sell their labor, thus reducing unemployment. But the ranch owner is unwilling to allow a union to form, and his men kill Casey in a skirmish. His martyrdom inspires Tom to follow in his footsteps.

The Grapes of Wrath also illustrates another very relevant economic conflict in times of crisis, the conflict between migrant and native workers. The surplus of workers deliberately created by landowners produces a drop in wages that leads Californians to resent the Okies instead of allying with them. Local workers use harassment strategies such as road blockades, provocations, camp burnings, and lynchings—with the connivance of local authorities—to drive out the newcomers. The film does not mention something that also happened during these conflicts between pickers and ranchers: The Mexican workers who joined the first strikes in the California valleys were deported to make room for the Okies.

Tom's past sins still haunt him, and he has no choice but to leave his family. He becomes the union leader of the migrant farmers. Before leaving, he makes his famous and moving "I'll be there" speech in which he explains his decision to give up his family to fight for people like them.

Ford and screenwriter Nunnally Johnson made the most significant change from the source material in the last scene. They replaced Steinbeck's bitter, apocalyptic ending with a speech where Mama Joad (Jane Darwell)—the film's real protagonist—identifies the poor as the people who move America forward.

The following three decades were a period of rapid and sustained economic growth. There were no relevant economic crises or recessions until 1973, when the OPEC countries stopped their oil exports in response to the Israeli occupation of Arab territories after the Yom Kippur War. The price of oil quintupled in a matter of weeks. There was an unprecedented global shortage, and the world order upturned. In addition to this political upheaval, the crisis also represented a formidable change in the global economy. High oil prices earned Saudi Arabia and the Gulf states millions of dollars that they could not reinvest domestically due to their limited industrialization. This money flowed back to rich countries, especially to the United States. These were the so-called petrodollars, with which the Gulf states acquired assets in the main financial centers and invested in the most important commercial banks in the United States and Europe. These petrodollars were desirable assets that could be traded under minimal regulation and were central to the plot of Alan J. Pakula's *Rollover*.

The film opens with Lee Winters (Jane Fonda), an actress married to the owner of the petrochemical corporation Winterchem, who has organized a charity gala at the natural history museum. During the event, she is informed that her husband has been murdered. She is being observed by Hub Smith (Kris Kristofferson), a rebellious and handsome businessman who already knows about the tragedy. His mentor Maxwell Emery (Hume Cronin), surprised by the empathy he finds in Smith's gaze, asks him what is wrong. "Nothing", he replies, "I was just thinking that safety is an illusion". That is precisely the central theme of *Rollover*: The economic insecurity that Americans and other industrialized countries experienced after the oil crisis, a crisis that left them weakened and vulnerable to nations beyond their control.

A couple of years earlier, *Americathon* (1979) had expressed this economic anxiety in the form of a raving satire. The film is set in the future year 1998. The United States is on the brink of bankruptcy, and its old economic rivals are eager to cash in. The dollar is worthless, and all transactions are made in gold. Everybody jogs or rides a bicycle because the country has no oil, and the United Hebrab Republic (Israel and the Arab countries somehow managed to merge) is not providing any. People live in their now useless cars. The country survives with loans from the Native Nation, but its leader has lost his patience, and it is about to foreclose the country and return it to its original owners, that is, the Native

Americans. The newly elected president has a crazy idea: to run a national telethon and raise enough money to save America.

Rollover's very serious tone deals with the same feelings of economic insecurity using the template of the financial thriller. There is great turmoil in the American economy. The Borough National bank just sold $100 million on the international foreign exchange market to cover its excess debt. The transaction has caused a dip in the value of the dollar. Emery, president of the First New York Bank known as "the lion of finance", had to bail out the Borough to prevent the dollar from collapsing. He picks Hub Smith to run the Borough and applies his business acumen to save the bank from bankruptcy and the dollar with it. Smith concludes that what the Borough needs is to grant a substantial loan to a client who is "even deeper in shit than we are" and use the commissions from the operation to stay afloat. Lee Winters' Winterchem fits the bill perfectly.

But the widow has her own plans for her company. She believes that it can be profitable if she invests in research and development. She plans to buy a small but sound Spanish petrochemical company whose profits she will later use to cover the investment costs in R&D she envisions. Predictably, the board members laugh at her proposal. They condescendingly suggest that Lee is not thinking clearly that she is still affected by her husband's murder and that, as a woman, her role in the company should be limited to public relations.

Smith and Winters join forces to achieve success in their plans. Only someone with a lot of resources can lend Winters the large sum she needs. Smith suggests that she turns to the Arabs. They agree but on the condition that Winters offers her shares of Winterchem as collateral. The issue of economic insecurity and dependence arises very clearly at this point. "I feel like a beggar begging for charity", says Winters before meeting the Arabs. "You and the rest of the world", Smith replies.

But the Arabs hold on to the money, leaving the Borough dangerously exposed. We learn that Emery and the sheikhs are partners in a cabal: the Saudis want to sell their dollar reserves and hoard gold secretly. The loan to Winterchem is part of their plan. Emery has convinced the Arabs to withdraw their money in small amounts. Otherwise, they could cause global panic and a collapse of the financial system. "You are playing with the end of the world", Emery warns Prince Khalid (Paul Hecht). "Of the world as you know it", the Prince retorts.

Smith learns about this conspiracy and confronts Emery, who retorts that he had to play along with the Arabs to prevent the collapse of the dollar and a crisis that would make the Great Depression look like "a kindergarten". The world is increasingly interconnected, and "money, capital, has a life of its own. It's a force of the nature like gravity, like the oceans, it flows where it wants to flow". Winters demands the Arabs to renegotiate the loan in exchange for her silence, making her the next target for assassination, ultimately thwarted by Smith. The next day, the Arabs withdraw all their investments causing a financial hecatomb—the economies of the world collapse like dominoes. There are revolts and riots. It is the end of capitalism, as Emery had predicted.

Cold, opaque, sophisticated, *Rollover* was a commercial flop. It is also a contradictory film. Despite its apparent anti-capitalist slant, Alan J Pakula made no secret of his fascination with the upper classes and luxury. Despite its feminist premise, the film portrays Winters as a woman incapable of doing business by herself. All in all, *Rollover* was a respectable attempt to depict the complexity of the financial system and the macroeconomy, and it was pioneering in portraying the insecurity that the free movement of capital flows would create. In the years leading up to the 2008 financial crisis, similar anxieties of dependency and vulnerability would arise from another shift in the balance of economic power: the massive accumulation of US debt in China's hands.

Understanding the Crisis

In a celebrated article in the prestigious *Journal of Economic Literature* (Lo, 2012), MIT professor Andrew Lo invoked *Rashomon* (1950) to describe the assortment of explanations for the 2007–2008 financial crisis put forward by the economics literature. In Akira Kurosawa's classic, four characters who have witnessed the alleged rape of a woman and the murder of a samurai describe the incident in contradictory ways. Although the facts presented by the four narrators seemed relatively straightforward, their interpretation was far from it. In the case of the financial crisis, Lo pointed out that even the facts remain unclear. Even its starting point was in dispute: Was it the peak of the US housing bubble in mid-2006? The liquidity crisis in the banking system of late 2007? The collapse of Lehman Brothers in September 2008?

However, one undisputed fact is that what started as a crisis in the market for complex financial instruments led to a liquidity crisis of the financial intermediaries that handled these securities or used them as collateral. In other words, the assets in which these intermediaries traded suddenly became worthless. The low interest rates, the intense financial deregulation and home-buying incentives had created a bubble of gargantuan proportions in the property sector. Mortgages of all denominations and risks were bundled and sold under the name of collateralized debt obligations (CDOs). These products were so complex that it was challenging to estimate their risk. Because they came from the traditionally sound and profitable real estate market, investors treated these financial products as virtually safe securities. The highest quality CDOs (those rated AAA) were traded as if they were Treasury bonds, as risk-free assets. When several investment banks and insurers went into technical bankruptcy, the market collapsed. Because European banks were heavily involved in the US financial market, a financial tsunami of global dimensions ensued.

Margin Call fictionalizes that exact moment when the financial sector realized there was no ground beneath its feet. Peter Sullivan (Zachary Quinto) is a brilliant young analyst right at the eye of that storm. He is a theoretical physicist by training who can see what others cannot. In a night of pure tension, he deciphers the arcane numbers and balance sheets of the company he works for—a stand-in for Lehman Brothers—and discovers that it is on the verge of insolvency. A race against the clock starts. Peter goes up, level by level, meeting his superiors, one even more detached from the market's day-to-day operations than the other, all worried about saving their skin from the impending draconian restructuring. At the top, Peter finds the decrepit and sinister John Tuld (Jeremy Irons), who asks him for a plain explanation of what is going on because "It wasn't brains that got me here". The task Peter is facing is Herculean because, as novelist Upton Sinclair once said, "it is difficult to get a man to understand something when his salary depends upon him not understanding it".

Among the many virtues of *Margin Call*, J.C. Chandor's directorial debut, one is its understanding of economic logic. Unlike *Wall Street* and *The Wolf of Wall Street*, and other films we discussed in Chapter 3, *Margin Call* does not depict the financial markets as a puppet theatre run by corrupt and nefarious demiurges. Instead, it is portrayed as a vast entity endowed with a logic of its own, a creature inscrutable even to the agents operating in it. The film is not a story of scheming or backstabbing bankers, but a disaster movie like *The Poseidon Adventure* (1972) or *The Towering Inferno* (1974). We watch the inevitable catastrophe unfolding before our eyes. The only question is who among the characters will manage to save themselves.

As the young analyst moves up through the bank's upper echelons, each new character appears as a new villain, a new final boss. Some are more sympathetic and kinder than others. Their reasons for being co-conspirators in the disaster differ: Some were motivated by political calculations, others by weakness, fear, or loyalty toward the company. But all equally believe they had no choice. They knew that if they did not contribute to this lucrative business, they would be fired. That said, none of them broke any law or conspired; none of them even committed one act that could be deemed immoral. All of them gradually, day by day, compromised their principles until the music stopped, and they all ran for a chair. Even the executive decision to sell the bank's toxic assets before the news about its insolvency break—the event that kickstarts the financial system's collapse—is an understandable choice. What else could they do? the film asks. If they did not sell first, others would. That is why *Margin Call* is not so much a portrait of individual flaws as of the weaknesses of the financial system.

This dispassionate depiction of the financial system carries an even more trenchant critique than the morality tale Oliver Stone built in *Wall Street*. If such a disaster can occur even when people are trying to do their jobs as best as they can, that means that the system's flaws are profound. The film illustrates nicely that the incentives financial agents face promote collective behaviors that lead to a disaster. In the last scene of the film, Jeremy Irons stops his leisurely lunch to list the global financial crises of the last 400 years one by one. *Margin Call*'s message is clear: Bubbles are inevitable. Financial crises will continue to happen. Picking apart a few bad apples like Gordon Gekko will not avoid it. The film's central thesis is that the financial sector suffers from a fundamental problem that only appropriate external intervention can correct.

This thesis was part of the widespread indictment against economics that followed the financial collapse of 2008. The verdict was that economists had failed to predict the crisis and even contributed to it because they had misled citizens and politicians to believe that markets worked well on their own and did not need further regulation (Coyle, 2010). The Efficient Market Hypothesis under which many financial economics models operated seemed definitive proof of this argument. This hypothesis postulates that asset prices fully and instantaneously reveal their fundamental value. This assumption allegedly blinded economists and prevented them from seeing the speculative bubble growing under their very noses. A group of distinguished British economists accepted part of the blame in a letter to the Queen of England—who a few months earlier had blamed economists for having failed to anticipate the crisis; they admitted that "many people did foresee the crisis. However, the exact form that it would take and the timing of its onset and ferocity were foreseen by nobody".[1]

Before the crisis, economists had criticized the deregulation of financial markets that had been taking place since the 1980s. Behavioral economists, aware of the psychological biases that plague human decision-making, had warned about the dangers of applying simplistic assumptions to the study of finance well before 2008. Other, more conventional economists had pointed out that many financial assets were incredibly overvalued, that their prices did not correctly reflect their risk, and that a monumental correction was looming. The film that has explored this side of the debate more even-handedly is *The Big Short*. Adam McKay's film argued that greed and herd behavior were as much to blame for the financial disaster as the models used by financial economists.

The Big Short does an outstanding job explaining the dynamics that led to the financial collapse of 2008. The film adapts the multi-award-winning non-fiction book by Michael Lewis, a sequel of sorts to his earlier *Liars' Poker* (1989), in which he chronicled his experience as a broker in an investment bank in the 1980s. *The Big Short* follows a group of eccentric investors, all on the fringes of the financial system, who foresaw the collapse of the US housing market that would eventually become the ground zero of the Great Recession. *The Big Short—The Book* was so full of data, numbers, and concepts of financial economics that its film adaptation seemed impossible. However, director Adam McKay managed to pull a perfect whip off the tablecloth trick. The result is an excellent film, halfway between the madcap comedy and the heist film, as frenetic and intense as *The Wolf of Wall Street* but substantially more compelling as an economic film.

The Big Short not only recounts what happened in the months leading to the crisis, it also explains why it happened. We are introduced to the

---

[1] "The global financial crisis—Why didn't anybody notice?", The British Academy. July 22, 2009. Last accessed March 30, 2021, https://www.thebritishacademy.ac.uk/documents/733/03-Besley.pdf.

rarefied world of high finance through a group of flamboyant and socially awkward but endearing characters. The film treats the audience with pedagogical respect. It interrupts its narrative with funny segments in which celebrities playing themselves introduce us to concepts as removed from a standard cinematic experience: short selling, collateralized put options—explained, in a nod to *The Wolf of Wall Street*, by Margot Robbie in a bubble bath—or the "hot hand fallacy". This concept, which plays a vital role in the story, is explained by one of the fathers of behavioral economics, Nobel laureate Richard Thaler, and singer Selena Gomez. The fallacy, shared by casino gamblers and investors alike, is based on the belief that past successes make future successes more likely. This is not a particularly relevant problem when confined to an individual gambler at a casino table, but it becomes a social problem when the fallacy spreads across the financial market. If an investor has a good track record trading with an asset, others may believe that that investor has a "hot hand" and discard any evidence showing that the asset is overvalued. They may invest in that asset even if they do not fully understand the complex financial product they are buying or its risks.

In 2006, everything was rosy. House prices were still rising, and people who had signed up for mortgages were paying their instalments on time. Everybody benefitted. But the banks were spending too little effort in checking whether the new homeowners they had lent money to would be able to repay. They ignored the reports that suggested that the property market was a house of cards ready to collapse as soon as house prices started to go down. Investors continued accumulating securities made up of bundles of mortgages because it seemed inconceivable to them that property prices could ever fall. And then, prices fell. Borrowers started defaulting on their mortgages. The chain reaction took the global financial system by storm.

Valuations in the property market reflected the overoptimistic beliefs of those who had bought into the hot hand fallacy while the pessimists were sitting on the sidelines. Thanks to their condition of outsiders, Michael Burry (Christian Bale) and his gang of misfits knew a market correction was coming and acted at precisely the right time. They found a way to cash in. They bought insurance against the possibility of the real estate market collapsing in a credit default swap. They paid millions in premia to keep that bet against the tide while the financial and real estate markets were still partying hard. The banks were happy to take the bet because they too were sure that house prices would continue rising.

The gamble was very risky, crazy. Each day that the crash in the real estate market did not materialize costed these extravagant investors a fortune. The dramatic tension of the film focuses precisely on this nervous waiting. It takes insider information, a great deal of confidence or total recklessness to take such a risk. But the protagonists of *The Big Short* knew they were playing it safe. Some like Michael Burry knew the market well; others, like Mark Baum (Steve Carrell), had researched rating agencies' fraudulent practices. One of the funniest and most revealing scenes of the film occurs when Baum visits a house with an unpaid mortgage. A man greets him and kindly informs him that he is not the owner of the house, only the tenant, and that the mortgage is in the name of the owner's dog.

Macroeconomics on the Screen

During its first decade (1999–2008), the euro brought economic stability to the continent. That meant that weaker European economies found it easier to borrow money and finance themselves. This, in turn, generated significant increases in their debt, either private, like in Spain and Ireland, or public, like in Greece, Portugal, and Italy. When the tsunami of the financial crisis hit Europe, these countries were the ones most hit. Their debt, private or public, was so large that each country could not manage it individually. These countries were unable to respond to their inability to continue financing themselves. They could no longer instruct their central bank to buy that toxic debt because they no longer had a central bank. They could not depreciate their currency because they no longer had their own currency.

In Ireland, the crisis's epicenter was the property sector due to a housing boom financed by foreign lenders. The country went bankrupt when it bailed out its banks. This is the story told in *The Guarantee* (2014), a modest Irish film that recounts the political and financial maneuvers that led the Irish government to guarantee the entire banking system rather than to nationalize it. As expected, the film portrays politicians as puppets of the bankers, who in turn appear like bullies. The film is effective despite its limited budget in conveying the dilemmas that governments faced during the eurocrisis; and how, in most cases, they failed to act correctly. Its numerous shortcomings also illustrate the difficulty of portraying macroeconomics on the screen. *The Guarantee* tries to explain the workings of macroprudential regulation and the banking system with news clips and on-screen quotes, but these are largely ineffective. The combination of these inserts with sequences that look like dramatized re-enactments brings *The Guarantee* closer to the docudrama than to a feature film.

Veteran French-Greek director Costa-Gavras took another avenue in *Adults in the Room* (2019). The film uses the template of thriller films to adapt the book of the same title by Yanis Varufakis in which he recounted his experience as Greek finance minister during the 2015 crisis. *Adults in the Room* was not Costa-Gavras's first attempt to make sense of the eurocrisis. In 2012, he had directed *Capital*, where he denounced the conduct of financial organizations and banks in the onset and unfolding of the 2008 financial crisis. The result was a visually attractive but rather embarrassing pamphlet devoid of interest as an economic film. *Adults in the Room* does a relatively good job explaining some macroeconomic concepts, but its shortcomings stress the difficulty of bringing macroeconomics to the screen.

Before going into the film, it is important to use just a few lines to describe the Greek debt crisis. In contrast to Ireland and Spain, the origin of Greece's debt crisis was the structural deficit of its public sector. In 2010 the Greek debt and deficit reached such high levels that the country was on the brink of bankruptcy. The European Central Bank and the European Union had to step in and rescue the Greek economy. A spiral of budget cuts and austerity followed. Taxes were raised, salaries and pensions were cut, and public companies were privatized. Between 2010 and 2014, Greece's GDP fell by a staggering 25%. Of course, tax revenues fell too because economic activity was contracting, making it even more difficult for the government to pay its debts. In January 2015, the left-wing party Syriza came into office, and Yanis Varoufakins became Greece's finance minister. The new government looked for a solution to the crisis and aimed to end austerity. The gambit failed. Most EU countries pushed the Greek government to adopt new austerity measures. The European Central Bank cut off loans to the Greek banks. The exit of Greece from the euro system seemed imminent. In the end, Prime Minister Alexis Tsipras folded. The budget cuts and the austerity measures continued. Greece did not recover from the crisis until 2017, and it is estimated that it will finish paying off its debt by 2060.

The source material for *Adults in the Room* lent itself to an adaptation as a suspenseful political thriller. In his book, Varoufakis is supposed to have revealed his confidential conversations with European leaders during the Greek crisis. But the actual result is that the ex-finance minister is the unambiguous hero of *Adults in the Room*. He always knows what will happen and always has a witty and correct answer to everything. His figure contrasts with that of the European bureaucrats, mediocre economists who envy Varoufakis' charisma and talent. European leaders are not treated much better. They are cruel, cowards or liars interested only in saving their own skin by siding with the bully, Germany's Finance Minister Wolfgang Schauble, caricatured like Dr. Strangelove, the half-Nazi mad scientist Peter Sellers in *Dr. Strangelove or: How I Learned to Stop Worrying and Love the Bomb* (1964).

Both the real and the fictional Schauble had no qualms repeating the stereotypes about the profligate South and the thrifty North. It is also true that the film exposes the not-so-secret measures of the troika against Greece, which Jean-Claude Junker, president of the European Commission, acknowledged years later was "unsympathetic". But *Adults in the Room* presents a one-dimensional narrative where Varoufakis is the undisputed hero and Tspiras a wimp surrounded by a cabinet full of leftist intransigents and traitors willing to accept everything that EU's impositions.

The film makes constant references to the Greek people's plight and their suffering, but that suffering is barely visible. Like in *The Guarantee*, *Adults in the Room* takes place in offices and meeting rooms. In part, this is deliberate. Costa-Gavras uses the repetition of meetings and interior sets to create a Kafkaesque portrayal of European bureaucracy. The film also tries to explain the macroeconomics of the Greek crisis to the audience. In a scene, Varoufakis explains the so-called "diabolical cycle" between sovereign debt and the banking system to the team, helping him design his famous plan B: Greece's exit from the euro. There are other scenes in which the characters explain to each other the state of Greece's national accounts using PowerPoint presentations.

At the end of *Adults in the Room*, Costa-Gavras abandons realism and opts for the allegory to portray the Greek crisis's final act. It is effective because the coldness and formality of *realpolitik* are suddenly interrupted by a literal dance of ministers and politicians inside institutional spaces. It is a good solution to overcome the fundamental difficulty of narrating macroeconomic crises in film. Perhaps a more radical approach in the style of *The Big Short* would have been more successful.

Post-Crisis Landscapes

For most of *The Big Short*, Adam McKay and co-writer Charles Randolph (who would write *Bombshell* a few years later) lead the audience to root for Burry, Baum and their companions. The audience wants them to prove themselves right, teach a lesson to the irresponsible financial institutions and become millionaires. Before concluding, the film reflects on its whirling and dazzling images by reminding both the characters and the audience about the intimate connection between the financial economy and the real economy.

In the last scene of *The Big Short*, Brad Pitt's character scolds two young brokers celebrating that they just pocketed $100 million from the financial meltdown. "A 1% rise in unemployment leads to 40,000 deaths", he tells them. It is a sobering reminder about that millions of people who are about to lose their job, default on their mortgages and lose their homes.

The Company Men (2010) takes the point of view of three male executives who have dedicated their lives entirely to their company, a shipping corporation called GTX. When banks falter and the stock market crashes, GTX laid them off together with three thousand employees. The first one is Bobby Walker (Ben Affleck), a sales executive with 12 years of service. Walker lives in a luxurious house in the suburbs with his attractive wife; he likes to wear expensive suits and drives a sports car. The second one is his immediate boss, Gene McClary (Tommy Lee Jones), who is outraged by the job cuts GTX is about to make to increase its share price. But McClary does not want to lose his privilege and prefers to keep quiet; after all, he has a spendthrift wife to support. The third man is Phil Woodward (Chris Cooper). He has been working for GTX for three decades and has worked his way up the corporate ladder. He is approaching 60; unemployment will mean the end of his professional life.

The Company Men uses these three men who were at the top of the job market to expose the devastating consequences of unemployment. Their egos, libidos, and self-image as breadwinners and men of status disintegrate. Walker and Woodward apply futilely to hundreds of jobs and conduct countless job interviews, while McClary, who eventually separates from his wife, spends his days moping at his mistress' house. At first, Walker is convinced that the situation is temporary and will get his job back in a few days. Like the protagonists of *The Last Laugh* (1924) and *Time Out*, he cannot admit to his family that he lost his job. His wife, who comes from a working-class background, is much more realistic and goes back to work as a nurse. Piece by piece, his old life is dismantled: the country club, the Porsche, his son's Xbox, and finally, his house. In the end, he must return, humiliated, to his parents. There, he will wallow in self-deprecation and anger. "I'm a 37-year-old loser who can't provide for his family", he says. Desperate, Walker asks his brother-in-law, a small-time builder, for a job. And so he ends up building the houses he used to buy. *The Company Men* thus reiterates the film narrative we discussed in Chapter 3, which deems the production of tangible commodities as the only moral type of work.

Woodward's situation is even more desperate. Expenses and bills pile up. As he feared, his chances of re-entering the job market are remote. He dyes his grey hair and edits his CV to make himself look younger, but to no avail. His family keeps demanding that he provides for their old lifestyle. Embarrassed, his wife orders him not to come home until after six o'clock so that the neighbors believe that he still has a job. Woodward sums up his situation tragically: "My life is over, and nobody noticed".

Another point of interest of *The Company Men* is its representation of corporate practices in a changing economy. GTX is a traditional company. Its goal is to maximize shareholders' value, so it cuts labor costs to get out of the red. When at a press conference a journalist asks McClary what the company plans are, his answer is: "wait for things to get better". No one has a better idea. None of the three protagonists offers an alternative plan to save the corporation. They are managers like those in Dilbert's comic strips: they know very little about the market and use the company meetings to boast about their golf prowess.

After a corporation takes control of GTX, McClary and Walker vow to resurrect the company. They take a walk in the old shipyard, now rusted and crumbling. They long for the old days when 6000 men earned "an honest wage" there when the company built something you could "see, feel and touch". McClary starts looking for new investors while Walker assembles a group of former employees. And herein lies a fundamental flaw of *The Company Men* as an economic film: the company's downfall was not due to an evil CEO and his unethical practices but to a lack of sales. Reopening the shipyard will not solve that problem. The misfortune of GTX was not due to a cyclical downturn. It was due to structural change. As economist Joseph Stiglitz argues, globalization and a considerable increase in industrial productivity have caused this change.[2] Globalization has led to a decline in developed countries' weight in the world economy. The second phenomenon meant fewer workers were now needed to meet the global demand for goods, thus reducing the demand for workers in manufacturing. The accounting acrobatics and the downsizing implemented by the apparently heartless CEOs at GTX's were not the cause of the company's decline but an attempt to address the structural nature of its problems.

The Company Men was pioneering in depicting the human toll of the financial crisis of 2008, but it focused on relatively well-off characters. Post-crisis cinema, especially the one produced in Southern European countries, has also explored the devastating consequences of the crisis on ordinary people. A handful of films such as *Warrior* (2011), *Beautiful Youth* (2014), *The Measure of a Man* and *Saint George* (2016) probed audiences about how much abuse is someone willing to tolerate to put food on their table. *Food and Shelter* (2015) and *The Florida Project* (2017) explored the lives of the new poor, who live under the economic statistics radar. *Five Square Meters* (2011), *99 Homes* and *Hell or High Water* (2016) approached, from very different angles, the housing problem that arose when hundreds of thousands of families were evicted from their homes, leading to a mass displacement of people within the borders of developed countries.

The deregulation of the mortgage market during the 1980s had let the proverbial genie out of the bottle. Mortgages became assets that banks, and investors traded in packages called collateralized debt obligations (CDOs). Real estate seemed a safe bet. US house prices rose for 132 consecutive months between 1995 and 2005. In that same period, there was a significant increase in these CDOs' riskiness. During this housing boom, banks exerted an abysmal, often non-existent oversight over mortgage lending because they were more interested in pocketing fees and selling these assets to other financial institutions. The slowdown in the housing market that started in early 2007, and the collapse of Lehman Brothers brought on a recession that led hundreds of thousands of people to default on their mortgage payments. Default rates rose exponentially,

---

[2] "The Post-Crisis Crises", Project Syndicate. January 7, 2013. Last accessed March 30, 2021, https://www.project-syndicate.org/commentary/global-warming--inequality--and-structural-change-by-joseph-e--stiglitz.

and a wave of evictions ensued. In September 2010 alone, 120,000 American homes were foreclosed.[3] Six million homeowners were evicted over a few years, leading to a displacement crisis unprecedented since the Great Depression. Banks were processing so many evictions that they found themselves unable to foreclose. They hired independent agents to handle the removals for a commission or purchase the now-vacant homes and then trade them.

Although *99 Homes* went largely unnoticed, it offers a formidable albeit distressing portrait of that devastated economic landscape. In this ecosystem, the weakest serve as food for those who, like the scavenger fish living at the bottom of the sea, just wait for it to fall in their mouth.

Dennis Nash (Andrew Garfield) is a single father and a construction worker. He is summarily evicted from his home and his family by Rick Carver (Michael Shannon), a nasty real estate broker who has found in foreclosures his particular gold mine. Like the Joads in *The Grapes of Wrath*, Dennis and his family find themselves homeless, their belongings piled on the pavement. Still dazed, they find refuge in a seedy motel. They are convinced they can get back on their feet in a matter of days. But it is 2010, and there are no construction jobs around. After reclaiming the tools one of his helpers stole from him, Dennis starts working for Carver. He has no choice. Dennis takes on increasingly repulsive assignments: cleaning foreclosed houses, removing air conditioners and appliances, finding owners who violate the most trivial regulations to hasten their eviction and, finally, evicting entire families.

Director Amir Naderi and his co-writer Ramin Bahrani do not hide that they have written a morality tale along the lines of *Wall Street*. Dennis is a young man who signs, out of ambition and hunger, a Faustian bargain with a Mephistophelian but attractive character who becomes his surrogate father. The pact throws him into a moral abyss from which he ultimately manages to escape by performing a costly act of penance. But whereas Oliver Stone used this plot template to portray the world of big finance, *99 Homes* shows an unglamorous albeit relevant reality. In one heartbreaking scene after another, Dennis evicts hard-working people without warning, older people with nowhere to go or immigrant families where only children speak English and understand what is going on.

---

[3] "United States Residential Foreclosure Crisis: 10 Years Later", CoreLogic Insights. 17 March, 2017. Last accessed March 30, 2021, https://www.corelogic.com/research/foreclosure-report/national-foreclosure-report-10-year.pdf.

These eviction scenes are tense and suffocating. Naderi uses a documentary style, aggressive editing, and a pulsating soundtrack to orchestrate almost unbearable crescendos.

99 Homes finds its own Gordon Gekko in Rick Carver (Michael Shannon), a jackal who executes his routine coldly and relentlessly. Like Gekko, Carver is a magnetic villain. He is also a self-made man. His father was a construction worker who had to retire due to an accident. Carver worked his way up from his working-class origins taking advantage of every opportunity he found along the way. He is drawn to Dennis because he sees in him the same ambition he felt as a young man. But Carver is also a product of his circumstances. As he tells Dennis, "the American dream doesn't come to those who wait". Carver was just another real estate agent who became an opportunist when a failing economy and a regulation plagued with loopholes gave him every incentive to do so. "America doesn't bail out losers. America was built by rescuing winners", he concludes.

Carver adopts Nash as his protégé, coaches him on eviction protocols, and lets him in on the dirty secrets of his success and personal life. Here, *99 Homes* approaches the gangster film genre: Dennis's initiation is not unlike Ray Liotta's in *Goodfellas*. Like a kingpin, Carver warns Dennis that "when you work for me, you're mine", underscoring the idea that criminals are often represented in cinema as a grotesquely distorted reflection of businessmen (Ribstein, 2012). Dennis betrays his own principles because he convinces himself that Carver offers him the means to reclaim the family home. Dennis will have to lose everything, including the ability to look himself in the mirror, before finding a glimpse of redemption.

REFERENCES

Coyle, D. (2010). *The soulful science: What economists really do and why it matters*. Princeton University Press.
Lo, A. W. (2012). Reading about the financial crisis: A twenty-one-book review. *Journal of Economic Literature, 50*(1), 151–178.
Ribstein, L. E. (2012). Wall Street and vine: Hollywood's view of business. *Managerial and Decision Economics, 33*, 211–248.

CHAPTER 10

Conclusion: Post-Scarcity and Utopia

In one of the last scenes of *Nomadland* (2020), Fern (Frances McDormand) returns to the now-empty town of Empire, Nevada, where she spent most of her life. Like all employees at the US Gypsum plant there, she was evicted from company housing when the factory shut down. Empire ceased to exist. Its ZIP code discontinued. Fern drives through empty streets; all houses are uninhabited and derelict. She walks into her old home, now vacant. Only a few objects remain of the life she shared with her late husband. The barren winter landscape adds a post-apocalyptic quality to the images. Indeed, the plant's closing was the end of the world for the people of Empire; of the world as they knew it.

The landscape of Empire is not dissimilar to those of post-apocalyptic films like *Time of the Wolf* (2003) or *The Road* (2009). Traditionally, apocalyptic texts were essentially utopian (De Cristofaro, 2019). The material world may end after the apocalypse in *The Book of Revelations*, but it does so to give way to a new and better world, the New Jerusalem. However, the end of days is radical and irreversible in these and other recent post-apocalyptic films. They offer no hope for a better future.

Undoubtedly, the recent surge in dystopian fiction results from the economic insecurity and the climate crisis that we are already experiencing. The current coronavirus pandemic has also contributed to the feeling that humanity is at the end of the road. The financial collapse of 2008 upturned the livelihoods of millions of people who found

© The Author(s), under exclusive license to Springer Nature
Switzerland AG 2021
S. Sanchez-Pages, *The Representation of Economics in Cinema*,
https://doi.org/10.1007/978-3-030-80181-6_10

themselves unemployed and without a home. War and extreme weather spawned a massive refugee wave, which later brewed political unrest in host countries. The COVID-19 crisis decimated the service industry and destroyed millions of jobs; lockdown measures, while necessary, exacerbated pre-existing inequalities in health and educational outcomes. In this context, it seems impossible to remain hopeful.

Cinema influences the way we imagine the future. Dystopian and post-apocalyptic fictions may contribute to spread the belief that there will be no further progress for humans and that the world cannot be a better place. It is now very hard to imagine a better future. We even feel childish and naïve when we try, to the extent that "utopian" has become a derogatory term. The risk of this mindset is that the apocalypse can become a self-fulfilling prophecy.

However, it is not a given that the future will be worse. Cinema offers us seeds of hope if we look closely enough. Several films have depicted better futures, better economic systems, and fairer societies. There are not many of these, though. One preconception is that utopia means "the end of history" and, hence, nothing happens in well-functioning communities. For instance, the policewoman Sandra Bullock plays in *Demolition Man* (1993) asks her colleague, "Don't you ever want something to happen?" because she is bored by the lack of relevant crimes in the seemingly utopian Los Angeles of 2032. But there can be conflict in utopia, as will see next. The films that we will be discussing in these last few pages explore different utopian horizons and discuss the economic and social implications of these alternatives.

The Better Future Is in the Past

A common trope in post-apocalyptic films like *Doomsday* (2008) or the *Mad Max* franchise is the return to the past. The future is neo-medieval or a new Stone Age. There is a similar strand in utopian fiction. One of the first examples was Frank Capra's *Lost Horizon* (1937). Based on a John Hilton's novel, the film tells the story of a group of Westerners whose plane crashes in the Himalayas. They find there the legendary Shangri-La, an idyllic valley where people live happily and cannot get old. *Lost Horizon* thus delved into the "lost civilization" tradition to describe a utopia that evocates a more straightforward and happier existence away from the conflict and turmoil of modern life. The inhabitants of Shangri-La are satisfied and content because they live in harmony with the natural world and its rhythms. Another version of this utopian horizon are the Native American communities as portrayed in revisionist films such as The New World (2005) and *Dances with Wolves* (1990) (Fitting, 1993).

More recently, James Cameron's *Avatar* (2009) took this idea to the future by contrasting a dying and polluted Earth with the planet Pandora. In the twenty-second century, humans are colonizing other planets searching for resources. Pandora is an exuberant and paradisiacal world, a new garden of Eden. The indigenous Navi live in a utopian society, connected to nature and every other creature in the planet. They worship goddess Eywa, who keeps Pandora's ecosystem in equilibrium.

In contrast, humans live separate from the natural world. Their culture is hyper-technological, aggressive, and dystopian. Their quest for the precious mineral called "unobtanium", abundant in Pandora, is led by a big corporation and conducted with military help. *Avatar* thus makes clear that money and profit-seeking corporations have ruined the Earth and are about to do the same with Pandora.

In *Avatar*, James Cameron thus adheres to a narrative that equates technology and material progress with moral decadence. The Navi are peaceful and morally superior because they are hunter-gatherers who live in harmony with nature. They just take from it what they need. They may not have developed technologies, but their world's forests conform a vast network even more complex, we are told, than the human brain. All creatures in Pandora are interconnected through this giant network. Although beautiful and inspiring, *Avatar*'s anti-progressive narrative offers no real possibility for a better future. The film warns us about the dangers of abusing the natural environment. But a return to a primitive society like the one of the Navi is not necessarily a desirable alternative nor opens a space for change.

Techno-Utopias

In the other extreme of the utopian imaginations, we find techno-utopias—societies where advanced technologies have brought order and progress. Robotization, gene modification, and advances in medicine have eliminated most suffering and hunger and have produced astonishingly high living standards. In some sense, techno-utopias are a secularization of the utopian apocalypse of Christian eschatology. The comforting end of history is not brought about by God but by science (De Cristofaro, 2019).

One of the first techno-utopian films produced was *Things to Come* (1936), based on a novel by H.G. Wells. The film narrates three stages in humankind's future. After a war has ravaged the world, a group of scientists raised from the ashes of civilization to create and lead a technocratic World State. There is no more poverty and illnesses. Nature has been conquered. Humans are now rational and pacific creatures because they have learned the lesson from their troubled history. They are about to reach outer space.

The concepts and futuristic look of *Things to Come* derive from the era's technological utopianism and Frank Lloyd Wright's modernist architecture. However, the film offers almost no detail about the economics of this utopian society. This is a recurrent problem with techno-utopias in cinema. We are not told much either about the ambiguous utopian future Sylvester Stallone's character wakes up in *Demolition Man*: an aseptic and technocratic paradise created by Dr. Cocteau (Nigel Hawthorne), CEO of Cocteau Industries. Cocteau is a successful revolutionary technocrat who somehow rose to power during the social turmoil of the late 1990s. The world is a corporate monopoly. All restaurants are Pizza Hut. Cash no longer exists, and all transactions are done digitally via a credit chip in the back of one's hand. Violence is a thing of the past. There has not been a murder in over 15 years, and the worst crime that afflicts the city is occasional graffiti. Other techno-utopias with a dystopian streak suffer from a similar lack of detail. In *Gattaca* (1997), *The Giver* (2014), or *The Host* (2015), the future looks slick and bright but how their economies work remains obscure. In the ideal world created by the alien invaders in *The Host*, people just walk in gigantic storages, pick the goods they need, and walk out without paying anything.

Tomorrowland (2015) continued the tradition of *Things to Come* and Ayn Rand's *Atlas Shrugged* (1957)—adapted for the screen as a trilogy of films in the 2010s—in depicting a utopia resulting from a cabal of scientists and entrepreneurs. Tomorrowland is a parallel dimension created at the end of the nineteenth century by great thinkers and scientists so they could be "free from politics and bureaucracy, distractions, greed - a secret place where they could build whatever they were crazy enough to imagine".

As in most techno-utopias, the film does not attempt to describe the economics of Tomorrowland or the working and living conditions of its inhabitants. The science seems focused only on gadgetry, as seen in the classic World Fairs: rocket travel, humanoid robots, jet packs, electronic newspapers, and monorail. It is a near-magical realm that set itself on a course of total isolation from humanity. *Tomorrowland* may inspire awe but does not detail any alternative for a better future.

The most successful techno-utopian film to describe how an alternative economic system can work is *Black Panther* (2018). It generated quite a buzz among economists and political scientists for its depiction of a fully working utopian society.[1]

Wakanda is based on a natural resource of great power, the fictional vibranium. The country has wisely used the metal to enhance technology and spread its benefits across society. Wakandians have developed advanced technologies such as hover jets, advanced healthcare, and a public transit system based on magnetic levitation.

One key element is that Wakanda hides from the rest of the world through an invisible barrier. All other nations believe Wakanda is just another rural and developing African nation without much to offer. Thanks to its self-isolation Wakanda has been able to fence off colonial powers. The country functions as one of the counterfactuals economists use very often in their analyses. How would resource-rich African countries have fared if they had never been conquered or suffered slave trade?

The economic model of Wakanda is thus highly unusual. It does not trade its natural resources and is an autarky. Interestingly, a central conflict in the film is a struggle to redefine the economic system of Wakanda and its economic policies. The main antagonist of King T'Challa (Chadwick Boseman) is Erik Killmonger (Michael B. Jordan). He believes that it is morally wrong to keep vibranium in Wakanda and that the metal should be used to liberate people of African descent from all over the world living under oppressive conditions. Nakia (Lupita N'yongo), King T'Challa's love interest, has similar ideas. She believes that Wakanda should use the resource to assist foreign nations and share its technology with the rest of the world.

Most remarkably, Wakanda has been able to dodge the natural resource curse we discussed in Chapter 1. It is a prosperous and peaceful country. The benevolent Wakandian monarchy has stimulated the private economy and its institutions. It has invested the revenues from vibranium into

---

[1] See Subrick (2018) among others.

creating the industrial and scientific capacity to apply the metal to new technologies. The key to the Wakandian success is a solid attachment to its traditions. The utopian society that vibranium has created is stable because its citizens respect their ancient rituals and traditional forms of government. The bonds of tribe, family, and custom remain strong. Black Panther thus suggests that technological utopias are viable if social capital is high.

Collective Utopias

Worker cooperatives, communes, and kibbutzs are real-life examples of another type of utopian project. The members of these small communities work together to benefit the collective, sharing resources and responsibilities and taking care of each other. These arrangements aim at creating spaces where collective action and communal spirit can flourish.

It might seem surprising, but one of the first films to articulate the possibility of a collective better future came from Roger Corman, the king of horror and sci-fi B-movies. The social criticism in some of his films from the late 1960s and early 1970s is not very well-known. His *Gas-s-s-s! Or: It Became Necessary to Destroy the World in Order to Save It* (1970) starts as a post-apocalyptic film: a military accident releases a gas that kills everybody over 25. The young must now create a new society. The film follows a group of them who sets out on a trip looking for a "groovy old pueblo in Mexico" where a utopian community has been established. On their way, they encounter some of the new socio-political orders that have arisen in the aftermath of the cataclysm. In one town, the local football team has found a violent and fascist regime. In a golf course, they meet a community of Hell's Angels who talk like professional politicians. When the gang finally reaches the pueblo, they find a rural anarchist society. It is democratic, peaceful and runs as an eco-friendly barter economy. There are no gender or ethnic cleavages. However, science and technology are seen as helpful. When the violent football team wants to rob them of their supplies, the community does not resort to violence. In a town meeting, they decide to dialogue with the footballers and eventually convince them to join their community. The film ends with a big party. The new order may not be perfect but constitutes a promising first step on the road to utopia.

Animated films starred by social insects have portrayed another kind of collective utopias. These are societies with a very strict division of labor and where everybody joins forces toward a common goal. Work is a fundamental part of the nature of these insects. Everybody has a role to play in society, even if they feel insignificant.

Antz (1998) focuses on an ant colony where everybody goes dutifully about their assignment from birth, never questioning why some ants are workers and some warriors. The ant named Z has a mind of his own, though. He is an individualist. "Am I supposed to do everything for the colony?" Z asks his psychiatrist. "And what about my needs?" The anthill is full of motivational messages like "Conquer idleness". Work is idolized, and even dancing is regimented. Otherwise, it is a prosperous society where all needs are met. The only threat to the anthill is General Mandible, who has invented reports about an impending termite invasion to seize power.

Z escapes the anthill together with Princess Bala searching for Insectopia, where food is supposed to be plentiful and there is no need to work. It is a post-scarcity utopia (actually, it is a dump). When they get there, Mandible kidnaps Bala, and Z realizes that Insectopia is not a real alternative. He cannot just save himself. He has to go back to the anthill and protect it from Mandible's plan to flood it so the warrior caste can prevail. Z will have to unite all ants and work together with them, something he had rebuffed in the past. When the ants thwart the threat, the colony's collective utopia is restored. Z is now happy thanks to his personal transformation: "I finally feel like I found my place, and you know what? It's right back where I started. But the difference is, this time I chose it".

Bee Movie (2007) had a similar premise. Barry, voiced by Jerry Seinfeld, who also wrote the script, is a recently graduated bee who is about to join the workforce. He finds the prospect of working in the same job his entire life not particularly enticing. He challenges the status quo and sets himself to fly as a "Pollen Jock", the caste of bees who collect pollen from outside the hive, despite not having the physical qualities or training to do so.

By his own admission, Jerry Seinfeld found inspiration for the utopian hive in the film in the mid-century corporate films we discussed in Chapter Four. Workers in those films still believed in society, the government and their corporation. Similarly, all bees are happy and thoroughly enjoy their time at work. The hive is represented as a branch of Honex Industries, but there is no management or bosses around, suggesting that it is a cooperative. The factory looks like an amusement park with rides and slides. There is full employment in the hive and an apparently unlimited honey supply, an effective metaphor for money (Sidhu, 2013). Unlike in *Antz* and *A Bug's Life*, bees choose their job in the hive, and the political system is a democratically elected monarchy. In contrast, the bees humans exploit in honey farms live a grey existence drugged, in identical office-like cubicles.

These collective utopias highlight the centrality of work in (economic) life. Work gives purpose and meaning to their characters' lives. When Barry successfully sues humans and honey extraction stops, bees no longer need to work. They have already all the honey they need. They no longer perform the tasks which gave their lives meaning and structure before, leaving them feeling bored and depressed. In these films, abundance and idleness are a curse rather than a blessing.

Post-Scarcity Economics

Collective utopias, especially those in animated films, are not devoid of problems; they often contain threatening dystopian elements. *Monsters, Inc.* (2001) pioneered this dual structure. The city of Monstropolis is presented as a seemingly utopian society. It is a perfected version of our own. Everything is order and happiness. Workers at the energy plant where the main characters work are very collegial. The work environment is friendly and pleasant. There is an informal competition for the title of best worker, but, unlike in *Glengarry Glen Ross*, there are no monetary consequences associated with it. As the action unfolds, the protagonists discover that this utopia hides a sinister side. The energy that the world of monsters uses to function is obtained by unnecessarily exploiting children's fear—a subtle comment on child labor in third world countries being used to produce the commodities we enjoy in the West.

Thneedville, the city where the protagonist of *The Lorax* (2012) lives, is vibrant and colorful, but that colorfulness comes from countless plastic products. There is no living thing other than its human inhabitants. All these goods have polluted the air, and the city is bounded away from a wasteland by massive and (almost) impenetrable walls. The villain is a monopolist who commercializes clean air in bottles. In *The Lego Movie* (2014), the conformist, bustling, and seemingly paradisiacal Lego City is actually a corporate dystopia under the yoke of the tyrannical President who eradicates all dissent most expeditiously. In *Zootopia* (2016), the apparent peaceful coexistence between the preys and predators that inhabit the beautiful and futuristic city of Zootopia hides a reality of mistrust and discrimination between species, which is meant to represent the racial problems within our societies.

But the firm that best encapsulates the duality between dystopia and utopia is *WALL-E* (2008). This Pixar film also offers a first peek at the organization and consequences of a post-scarcity economy.

WALL-E is set in a distant future in which a monopolistic megacorporation called Buy N Large destroyed the planet. Due to pollution, garbage, and waste, the Earth became inhabitable and was evacuated. Buy N Large built five starship cruisers to transport all humans into space while trying to clean the planet. These cruisers are completely automatized and offer passengers a resort-like experience where every need is taken care of; there is no work, and passengers lead an existence of relaxation and leisure.

Before departing, the Global CEO of Buy N Large told the autopilot to "take control of everything". That seems to have included the economics of the ship. Because the cruises are generational ships, they have dispensed with money, although it appears that the central computer had kept running accounts for each passenger. This would suggest that the starship operates under a basic income scheme, and everybody receives a monthly stipend they can then choose how to spend. The two elements which define collective utopias, labor and sharing of resources, are absent. No one works, and everybody has unlimited leisure because robots do everything. Access to all products, services, and entertainment is free and unlimited, a fortunate consequence of the global monopoly Buy N Large had over all commodities pre-departure. This removes the need to manage resources communally. In sum, *WALL-E* imagines a post-scarcity economy.

However, this post-scarcity society contains bothersome aspects. Humans continue as wholly divorced from nature as when they roamed the Earth. They languish in a stupor of fully automated luxury. They have become big obese babies, floating around on hovering chaise-lounges, drinking sodas, and watching screens. They never communicate verbally, only via their devices, and leave child-rearing to robots, who undertake all reproductive labor. This is a common trope in films imagining utopias. The seemingly utopian societies in *Demolition Man* and *WALL-E* suffer from an "End of History Syndrome", which portrays them as static, dull, and devoid of any creativity. In contrast, the post-apocalypse seems a much more exciting place.

The utopia in *WALL-E* is not complete until technology and purpose combine. The ships' return to Earth ushers a new golden age where humans set themselves to re-conquer the planet and make it fertile again. It is no longer a pre-industrial stage plagued with backbreaking labor, scarcity, and poverty. Robots and AIs will take care of the most repetitive, difficult, and dangerous tasks. Humans will spend their day working to improve the world, but they will do it free from suffering, factory labor or office work.

The fiction that has best explored the consequences of a post-scarcity economy is *Star Trek*. The franchise spans 13 films and over 800 TV episodes that imagine a future where humanity has thrived within the United Federation of Planets and explores the universe using faster-than-light vessels.

The TV series *Star Trek: The Next Generation* (1987–1994) was set in the twenty-fourth century. It spawned four feature films. There is no physical work in this world, and the production of all necessities is fully automated. Robots take care of all manual and repetitive tasks. There are machines called replicators that can produce any object out of thin air and for free. The replicators are available to all, so unlike in *Elysium* or *In Time*, abundance and wealth are evenly distributed. Money has become obsolete because nobody has to pay for anything when everything is plentiful. Material needs no longer exist. Human labor is almost non-existent.

But unlike in utopian fictions suffering from The End of History Syndrome, the post-scarcity economy of *Star Trek* is a vibrant and exciting society. As Saadia (2016) has argued, the franchise can be seen as an exploration of "what happens to motivations and psyche and the set conditions of post-scarcity" due to accelerated technology-driven economic growth.

Because there is no scarcity, there are no longer any budgeting or spending choices in everyday life. Lionel Robbins's definition of economics as the "relationship between ends and scarce means which have alternative uses" no longer applies. Consumption and wealth accumulation no longer signal status because everything is available to all. Profit-maximization is entirely irrelevant, and there are no markets. As Captain Picard (Patrick Stewart) states in *Star Trek: First Contact* (1996), "the economics of the future is somewhat different. You see, money doesn't exist in the twenty-frouth century [...]. The acquisition of wealth is no longer the driving force in our lives. We work to better ourselves and the rest of humanity".

Liberated from the need to work, humans have shifted their economic activities to knowledge-intensive goods and services. Artistic and personal endeavors are also highly valued, like the Bordeaux wine Captain Picard's family still grows despite it being replicable. People can devote their time and energy to science and art because they are free from economic needs. Because there is no poverty, every talented individual can contribute to society. Competition is no longer about wealth or economic status but about reputation and honor. People invest and innovate in expectation of glory and social recognition, not material rewards. The only meaningful choice for Federation citizens is how to allocate their talent and time between self-improvement and bettering of the world. Work is no longer a burden but part of the social contract; it bonds Federation citizens together and gives them purpose. Egalitarianism is an essential part of the Federation's ethos. When in *Star Trek: Insurrection* (1998) Admiral Dougherty is offered a rejuvenating technology for his personal enjoyment, he declines because he prefers to wait until it is available to all Federation citizens.

In that film, Captain Piccard and his crew encounter an even more utopian society than the Federation. A seemingly rural community that, however, knows faster-than-light travel but is not using it. Intrigued by this, Piccard probes local leader Sojef (Daniel Hugh Kelly) about it, who responds, "our technological abilities are not apparent because we have chosen not to employ them in our daily lives. We believe that when you create a machine to do the work of a man, you take something away from the man". Picard feels tempted to stay because he longs for a simpler life where human labor still exists and is valued. But he chooses to leave because, as a model Federation citizen, he feels drawn to creativity and exploration, which require liberation from scarcity.

The society depicted in the *Star Trek* franchise has rendered obsolete most traditional economic concepts. Because humans can now manipulate matter easily, they no longer need to worry about scarcity. They have outgrown money and finance. *Star Trek* suggests that the need for economics and the idea of an "economy" might be just another phase in human history, a blip in our civilization's technological trajectory that, at some point perhaps, we will leave behind.

The End?

Using documentary-style and non-professional actors mainly, *Nomadland* investigates the lives of the thousands of Americans who now live in their vehicles. The film is based on a non-fiction book by Jessica Bruder. It documented the predicament of thousands of senior citizens who, after the 2008 financial collapse, had little choice but to change their way of life. They traded their homes for a van and went back to basics. Older people like Fern, who have lost their families, their communities, and their homes, have realized that they cannot afford to grow old. They have found a new life on the road, on the fringes of the economy. They live cheaply and frugally. Climate change-induced natural disasters have only intensified this phenomenon. These new nomads have the feeling that they are abandoning an economic and political system that is dying.

In some sense, these nomads are the pioneers; they are ahead of us. *Nomadland* pushes us to think that we are next. What will we do about it? We must start thinking very seriously about how we want to organize the economy and our society as we go through increasingly catastrophic and extreme environmental conditions. The Great Recession and the coronavirus pandemic have already pushed millions of people along that path; they have lost everything or almost everything they had. They need a future.

It is a bleak road. But what these nomads have found out there is a modern-day utopia. It is a small community of equals who enjoy each other's company and freely roam the country away from the demands of an economy that is not offering much in return. These new dispossessed do not hoard toilet paper, food, or guns. They are not survivalists, just regular people. Little by little, in their daily lives, they are answering the most fundamental question of our time: how to live better in the future.

The road in *Nomadland* becomes a very apt metaphor. The Uruguayan journalist and writer Eduardo Galeano once wrote, "Utopia lies at the horizon. When I draw nearer by two steps, it retreats two steps. If I proceed ten steps forward, it swiftly slips ten steps ahead. No matter how far I go, I can never reach it. What, then, is the purpose of utopia? It is to cause us to advance". Roger Corman had put forward a similar idea in *Gas-s-s-s!* On their road trip in search of a better society, the protagonists visit "The Oracle", searching for a definite answer. But the oracle offers them the opposite: "There is no answer, but keep looking".

References

De Cristofaro, D. (2019). *The contemporary post-apocalyptic novel*. Bloomsbury.
Fitting, P. (1993). What is utopian film? An introductory taxonomy. *Utopian Studies*, 4(2), 1–17.
Saadia, M. (2016). *Trekonomics*. Pipertext Publishing.
Sidhu, N. (2013). *Fantasy at work: Representations of labour and economy in children's animated films* (School of Labour Studies working paper 2013-1). McMaster University.
Subrick, R. J. (2018). The political economy of Black Panther's Wakanda. In B. O'roark & R. Salkowitz (Eds.), *Superheroes and economics*. Routledge.

Film Index

A
A Beautiful Mind, 6
A Boy and His Dog, 12
A Bug's Life, 21, 99, 208
A Christmas Carol, 38, 39, 41
A Corner in Wheat, 2
Adults in the Room, 193, 194
A Flash of Genius, 115, 116, 165
A Good Year, 41
Alamo Bay, 147
American Beauty, 4, 122
American Madness, 61, 62, 64, 65
Americathon, 185
The Angry Silence, 136
Antz, 207, 208
The Apartment, 80, 82, 84
Apocalypto, 20
A Quite Place, 10
A Raisin in the Sun, 67
Arbitrage, 181
Ares, 20
The Assistant, 178, 179
The Associate, 170
August, 14, 104, 105, 116

Avatar, 203
The Aviator, 55, 102, 103, 115
A View to a Kill, 31
The Axe, 124

B
Baby Boom, 166, 167, 172
The Bad Sleep Well, 71
The Bank, 49, 61
The Banker, 66–68
Beautiful Youth, 197
Bee Movie, 207
Bend the River, 24
The Big Country, 23
The Big Operator, 136
The Big Short, 3, 6, 33, 46, 178, 190, 192, 194, 195
Billy Elliott, 136, 162
The Birth of a Nation, 3
Black Fury, 131
Black Panther, 205, 206
Blood Diamond, 3, 26–28, 45
Blue Collar, 136
Boiler Room, 53, 57–59, 83

216   FILM INDEX

Bombshell, 178, 179, 195
The Book of Eli, 12
Brassed Off, 136
Bread and Roses, 148, 150
Bringing Out the Dead, 55
Business as Usual, 177

C
Capital, 193
Cargo, 20
Cash McCall, 37, 42
Casino, 56
Charlie and the Chocolate Factory, 5, 145
Chicago Confidential, 136
The China Syndrome, 82, 89
Chisum, 23
Citizen Kane, 43
Civil Action, 90, 91, 94
Clockwatchers, 169
The Company Men, 8, 195–197
Comrades, 127
The Constant Gardener, 71
The Contestant, 32
Corporate, 72, 124
Cosmopolis, 17
The Counterfeiters, 32
Country, 61, 161
The Crash, 62
Crypto, 61
The Current War, 116

D
Daens, 128
The Damned United, 112
Dances with Wolves, 203
The Dark Knight Rises, 17
Dark Waters, 3, 90, 93–95
Dawn of the Planet of the Apes, 17
Day of the Dead, 10
The Debt, 45, 61

Demolition Man, 202, 204, 209
Desk Set, 139, 143, 144
The Devil and Miss Jones, 43, 132, 154, 155
Dirty Pretty Things, 149, 150
Disclosure, 84, 167, 168
Divergent, 15
Doomsday, 202
Draft Day, 112
Drag me to Hell, 45
Dr. Strangelove, 194

E
Easy Living, 155, 182
El Dorado, 23
El Norte, 147, 148
Elysium, 17, 18, 20, 210
Equity, 173, 174
Erin Brockovich, 46, 90, 91, 161–163
Exam, 124
Executive Suite, 7, 72, 73, 76, 77, 79, 86

F
The Family Man, 45
The Far Country, 24
Fast Food Nation, 149, 150
Fatal Attraction, 167, 168
Fifth Avenue Girl, 155, 182
Fight Club, 122, 169
The Firm, 87
Five, 7, 10, 163
Five Square Meters, 197
The Florida Project, 197
Food and Shelter, 197
The Founder, 117, 118
The Fountainhead, 98, 99, 101, 103
Freedom for Us, 140
Full Monty, 136, 162

G

The Garment Jungle, 134
Gas-s-s-s!, 206, 212
Gattaca, 204
Germinal, 7, 128
Gilda, 87
The Giver, 204
Glengarry Glen Ross, 58, 82, 84, 208
The Godfather, 58, 87
Gold-Diggers of 1933, 182
Goldfinger, 5, 30–33
Goodfellas, 55, 56, 199
The Grapes of Wrath, 61, 130, 183, 184, 198
The Guarantee, 192, 194

H

Hamlet Goes Business, 71
Head Office, 85, 86, 123
Heartbeat Detector, 124
Heaven's Gate, 23
Hell's Angels, 102
Hell or High Water, 197
High Flying Bird, 113, 114
High-Rise, 18
Horrible Bosses, 124
The Host, 204
How Green Was My Valley, 131, 183
How to Succeed in Business Without Really Trying, 78, 80–82, 84, 86, 123, 135
The Hudsucker Proxy, 73, 85, 86
The Hummingbird Project, 60, 61
The Hunger Games, 15

I

I'm All Right, Jack, 136
In Dubious Battle, 129–131
The Informant!, 86–88
In Good Company, 41, 132
Inside Detroit, 136

The Insider, 71, 87, 94
The Intern, 172, 173
The International, 61
The Internship, 132
In Time, 16, 20, 210
It Happened to Jane, 157
It's a Wonderful Life!, 45, 61, 64, 65, 86

J

Jeanne Dielman, 23, quai du commerce, 1080 Brussels, 175, 179
Jerry Maguire, 112
Joy, 7, 163, 165
Jupiter Ascending, 16

K

Kinky Boots, 142

L

L'Argent, 33, 49
La Sortie de l'Usine Lumière à Lyon, 2
Last Exit to Brooklyn, 175
The Last Laugh, 195
La Terra Trema, 129
The Laundromat, 30, 33, 46, 47, 60
The Lego Movie, 208
Limitless, 49
Limit Up, 158
Live and Let Die, 31
Local Hero, 91
Lonely Are the Brave, 23
The Lorax, 208
Lord of War, 45
Lost Horizon, 202
Lover Come Back, 50, 157
Loving, 68

M

Made in Dagenham, 161, 162
Mad Max 2, 10, 13
Mad Max Beyond Thunderdome, 10
Mad Max: Fury Road, 13, 19
The Magnificent Seven, 22
The Man in the Grey Flannel Suit, 72, 76, 77, 123
The Man in the White Suit, 108–110, 113
Man Without a Star, 23, 24
Margin Call, 7, 56, 61, 181, 188, 189
Matewan, 128, 129
The Maze Runner, 15
The Measure of a Man, 124, 197
Meet John Doe, 72, 86
Metropolis, 99, 140
Michael Clayton, 7, 71, 87, 94
Mildred Pierce, 155, 163
Modern Times, 7, 139, 140, 182
The Molly Maguires, 129
Moneyball, 112–114
Money Monster, 45, 46
Monsters, Inc., 208
Mr. Deeds Goes to Town, 72, 86
Mr. Smith Goes to Washington, 101
The Muppet Christmas Carol, 39

N

The Navigators, 137, 138
Never Steal Anything Small, 136
New in Town, 143, 171–173
Newsies, 130
The New World, 203
Night Shift, 174
9 to 5, 7, 166, 176
99 Homes, 8, 197–199
Nomadland, 201, 212
Norma Rae, 7, 128, 148, 159–162, 178

North Country, 177, 178
The Number One, 173

O

Ocean's Eleven, 53
Office Killer, 169
Office Space, 122, 124, 126, 169
The Omega Man, 10
On the Waterfront, 7, 136, 141
Open Range, 23
The Organizer, 128
Other People's Money, 33, 36–38, 161, 168
Owning Mahowny, 53

P

Pain and Gain, 56
The Pajama Game, 134–136, 157
The Pale Rider, 23
Patterns, 72, 74–76, 156
The Pelican Brief, 90, 94
Pi, 6, 49
Places in the Heart, 162
The Platform, 18, 19, 23
Portland Exposé, 136
The Poseidon Adventure, 188
The Power and the Prize, 72, 77
Pretty Woman, 41–43, 59, 175
Pride, 136
The Promised Land, 91, 93
The Promotion, 124
The Proud Valley, 131
The Purge, 20

Q

Quantum of Solace, 31
Quest for Fire, 20

R

Raining Stones, 136

Rapa Nui, 25
Rashomon, 187
Retribution, 45
Riffraff, 131
Risky Business, 174
The River, 61
The Road, 10, 201
Robocop, 71
Rogue Trader, 7, 49, 53–55, 59
Rollover, 33, 185–187

S
Sabrina, 41
Safe, 93
Saint George, 197
Salt of the Earth, 131–133, 136, 155
Saving the Tiger, 82
Scarface, 58
Scrooge, 38, 39, 43
Scrooged, 39
The Secret of My Success, 33
Self/less, 16
Selma, 68
Seven Samurai, 22
Shane, 23
The Shawshank Redemption, 30
Silkwood, 89, 161, 162, 178
Singin' in the Rain, 134
Snowpiercer, 19, 20
The Social Network, 7, 60, 105, 107, 117, 165
The Solid Gold Cadillac, 37, 78, 79
Sorry to Bother You, 82, 121, 126
Sorry We Missed You, 126, 127
Spotswood, 43, 44, 142
The Stagecoach, 72
Star Trek, 8, 210, 211
Steve Jobs, 107, 108, 116, 117, 165
The Sting, 53, 88
Strike, 128
Sweet Home Alabama, 171

Swing Shift, 154

T
Take This Job and Shove It, 143
Taxi Driver, 55
The Temp, 167, 168
The Thinning, 16
Things to Come, 204
Time of the Wolf, 201
Time Out, 124, 195
The Toast of New York, 49
Tokyo Sonata, 124
Tombstone, 23
Tomorrowland, 204, 205
Total Recall, 18, 71
The Towering Inferno, 189
Trading Places, 7, 51–54
Trainspotting, 55
Tucker: The Man and His Dream, 100–103, 165
28 Days Later, 11
Two Days, One Night, 126, 127
Two Weeks' Notice, 41, 171

U
Up in the Air, 124, 126
Upside Down, 18

V
The Van, 136

W
WALL-E, 209, 210
Wall Street, 17, 33–38, 55, 56, 58, 73, 104, 105, 161, 173, 188, 189, 198, 199
Wall Street 2: Money Never Sleeps, 38, 181
Warrior, 197

Waterworld, 10, 13, 25
The Wedding Planner, 171
The Wheeler Dealers, 33, 50, 157, 158
The Whistle at Eaton Falls, 139, 141, 142
The Wolf of Wall Street, 4, 53, 55–57, 59, 181, 188, 190, 191
Woman's World, 74, 156, 157
Working Girl, 166, 167, 170, 174
Working Girls, 175, 176

Y
You've Got Mail, 110

Z
Zootopia, 208